THE THINGS OUR FATHERS SAW

THE UNTOLD STORIES OF THE WORLD WAR II GENERATION FROM HOMETOWN, USA

VOLUME V:
D-DAY AND BEYOND

Matthew A. Rozell

WOODCHUCK HOLLOW PRESS

Hartford · New York

Information at matthewrozellbooks.com.

Maps by Susan Winchell.

Front Cover: "Into the Jaws of Death - U.S. Troops wading through water and Nazi gunfire" (WWII: Europe: France) Franklin D. Roosevelt Library, Public Domain Photographs, National Archives Number 195515, Unrestricted.

Back Cover: General Dwight D. Eisenhower addresses American paratroopers prior to D-Day. Unknown photographer, United States Army. National Archives, public domain.

Any additional photographs and descriptions sourced at Wikimedia Commons within terms of use, unless otherwise noted.

Publisher's Cataloging-in-Publication Data

Names: Rozell, Matthew A., 1961- author.
Title: D-Day and beyond : the things our fathers saw : the untold stories of the World War II generation, volume V / Matthew A. Rozell.
Description: Hartford, NY : Matthew A. Rozell, 2019. | Series: The things our fathers saw, vol. 5. | Also available in audiobook format.
Identifiers: LCCN 2019914755 | ISBN 978-1-948155-10-6 (hardcover) | ISBN 978-0-9964800-8-6 (paperback) | ISBN 978-1-948155-11-3 (ebook)
Subjects: LCSH: World War, 1939-1945--Campaigns--France--Normandy. | World War, 1939-1945--Campaigns--France--Normandy--Personal narratives, American. | World War, 1939-1945--Personal narratives, American. | Veterans--United States--Biography. | Military history, Modern--20th century. | BISAC: HISTORY / Military / World War II. | HISTORY / Military / Veterans. | BIOGRAPHY & AUTOBIOGRAPHY / Military.
Classification: LCC D755.6 R69 2010 (print) | LCC D755.6 (ebook) | DDC 940.54/8173--dc23.

matthewrozellbooks.com

Created in the United States of America

~To the memory of
The World War II Generation~

'They will be sore tried, by night and by day, without rest—until the victory is won. The darkness will be rent by noise and flame.
Men's souls will be shaken with the violences of war.'

— PRESIDENT FRANKLIN D. ROOSEVELT, ADDRESS TO THE NATION, JUNE 6, 1944

THE THINGS OUR FATHERS SAW V:

D-DAY AND BEYOND

THE STORYTELLERS (IN ORDER OF APPEARANCE):

JAMES A. CALASCIONE
PAUL F. HILLMAN
FREDERIC G. SHEPPARD
ELLSWORTH J. JONES
MEYER SHEFF
HARRY ROSENTHAL
JOHN O. WEBSTER
JAMES E. KNIGHT
WILLIAM GAST, JR.
ANTHONY F.J. LEONE
JOSEPH S. DOMINELLI
JACOB N. CUTLER
FREDERICK G. HARRIS
FRANK W. TOWERS
WILLIAM C. BUTZ
JOHN H. 'JACK' VIER

THE THINGS OUR FATHERS SAW V:

D-DAY AND BEYOND

TABLE OF CONTENTS

AUTHOR'S NOTE 11

THE GREAT CRUSADE 23

THE GYRO MAN 27

ELECTRICAL SCHOOL 31

THE GYRO MACHINE 32

TWO MEN GONE 34

SALERNO 36

'NORMANDY WAS A HORROR' 39

MEETING ERNIE PYLE 41

'I'LL TEAR THAT SHIP APART' 42

THE MASTER MECHANIC 49

'SOLDIERS ARE NOT REPAIR PEOPLE' 53

WATERPROOFING SCHOOL 56

Wheeling and Dealing 58

The Concentration Camp Boy 62

THE DRIVER 67

Guard Duty 72

The Pathfinder 73

The Disaster 74

Normandy 75

AIRBORNE 83

THE PARATROOPER 85

The Jump 88

Wounded at Carentan 91

Hospitals 93

'He Shouldn't Have Been There' 94

THE GLIDER PILOT 97

Overseas 100

The Last Mission 103

Prisoner of War 105

Liberation 108

THE 'GREAT WALL OF HITLER' 115

THE CRYPTOGRAPHER 119

CROSSING THE ATLANTIC 122

OMAHA BEACH 125

THE FLAGSHIP 126

THE COMBAT ENGINEER 129

THE 20TH COMBAT ENGINEERS 132

H-HOUR 136

THE TANKERS 138

THE DEMOLITION MAN 141

DEMOLITION TRAINING 146

LOADING UP FOR THE 'REAL MCCOY' 150

STARTING IN 153

THE BELGIAN GATES 156

THE VISION 157

OMAHA BEACH 158

THE TANKER 159

THE MEDICS 160

THE FIRST NIGHT 162

THE SECOND NIGHT 165

'THIS WAS A SUICIDE MISSION' 167

THE TANKER 171

THE LANDING 176

'THROWING MARBLES AT A CAR' 177

THE COAST GUARDSMAN 179

'THE SHADOW' 184

THE 'BLAST FURNACE' 185

THE 'SUICIDE NAVY' 187

THE INFANTRYMAN 193

'MOVE, MOVE, MOVE!' 196

'BODIES FLOATING IN THE OCEAN' 197

THE MILITARY POLICEMAN 199

THE LANDING 201

THE 'VENGEANCE' ROCKETS 204

THE NAVY SIGNALMAN 207

'A Unique Situation' 209
Hundreds of Bodies 210
The Mulberry Harbors 210
The Great Storm 214
The End of the War 215

FIGHTING INLAND 221

HEDGEROW COUNTRY 223

COBRA/MORTAIN 233

Showdown at Mortain 235

ASSAULT ON BREST 241

Prisoners 243
'Keep You There Until You Get Killed' 244
'Got No Job Here For You' 249

THE ARMORED SERGEANT 255

The Foxhole 259

OVERSEAS 260

BREST 264

THE 'SUNDAY SCHOOL PICNIC' 266

SILVER STAR 268

THE HÜRTGEN FOREST 273

THE BATTLE OF SCHMIDT 274

'PEOPLE CANNOT MAKE THE SAME MISTAKES AGAIN' 276

THE FORWARD OBSERVER 277

TOUGH GUYS 278

CONVOY 282

BRITISH COMMANDOS 284

LANDING IN NORMANDY 288

GERMAN TANKS 289

THE HEDGEROWS 293

THE HÜRTGEN FOREST 297

FLASHBACKS AND NIGHTMARES 303

THE COMMON BOND 306

THE BATTLE OF THE BULGE 311

THE MILITARY POLICEMAN 313

The Bulge Breaks 313

Into Germany 314

Buchenwald 315

The Russians 316

THE ARMORED SERGEANT 321

Battle of the Bulge 321

Wounded 324

Buchenwald 327

The Hardest Part 329

'When the Shooting Stops' 330

'You Don't Owe Me a Thing' 331

THE HIGH PRICE TAG 335

ABOUT THIS BOOK/ 348

ACKNOWLEDGEMENTS 348

NOTES 351

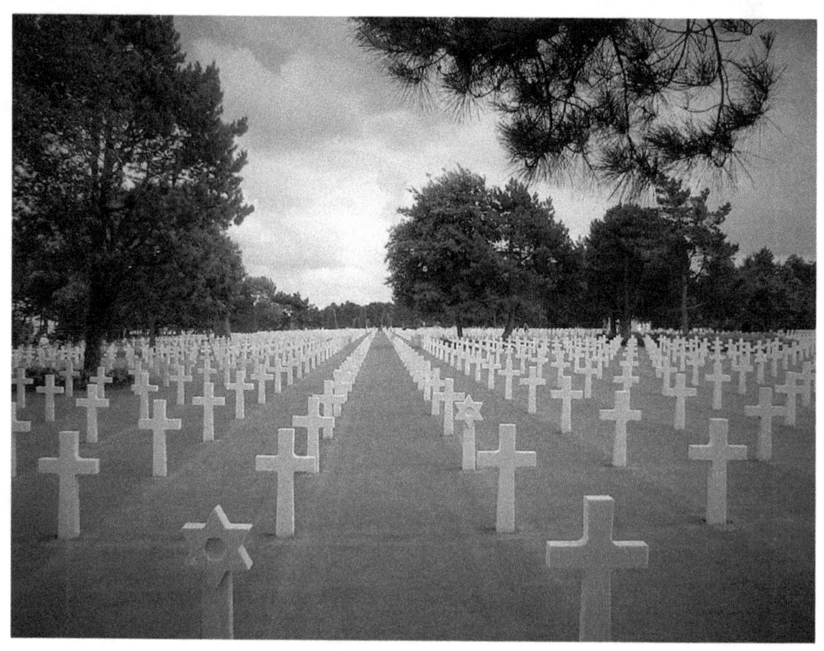

Normandy American Cemetery.
Credit: Bjarki Sigursveinsson, Public Domain

Author's Note

"We know we don't have much time left, so I tell my story so people know it was because of that generation, because of those guys in this cemetery. All these generals with all this brass, that don't mean nothing. These guys in the cemetery, they are the heroes."

-99-year-old Steve Melnikoff, World War II veteran, standing at the Normandy American Cemetery, June 6, 2019.[1]

Two days after the beginning of the greatest land-air-sea invasion in the history of the world, the first American dead were laid to rest in makeshift cemetery just off the beach, now the front yards of some vacation homes. The bluffs overlooking the western sectors of Omaha Beach would later become the American Cemetery at Colleville-sur-Mer. Today, nearly 9400 Americans lay at rest on over 170 acres of sanctified ground meticulously maintained by the American Battle Monuments Commission, watched over by the 22-foot-tall bronze statue, 'Spirit of American Youth Rising from the Waves.' Thirty-eight sets of brothers lie here, and on the Walls of the Missing, over 1500 names are inscribed. And shortly before the first men killed were buried, President Roosevelt informed the nation of the long-anticipated invasion by beginning a prayer broadcast over the radio to the families back home:

---

[1] *Steve Melnikoff, World War II veteran- D-Day at 75: Nations honor aging veterans, fallen comrades.* Associated Press, June 6, 2019.

Almighty God: Our sons, pride of our nation, this day have set upon a mighty endeavor, a struggle to preserve our Republic, our religion, and our civilization, and to set free a suffering humanity.

Lead them straight and true; give strength to their arms, stoutness to their hearts, steadfastness in their faith.

They will need Thy blessings. Their road will be long and hard. For the enemy is strong. He may hurl back our forces. Success may not come with rushing speed, but we shall return again and again; and we know that by Thy grace, and by the righteousness of our cause, our sons will triumph.

They will be sore tried, by night and by day, without rest—until the victory is won. The darkness will be rent by noise and flame. Men's souls will be shaken with the violences of war.

For these men are lately drawn from the ways of peace. They fight not for the lust of conquest. They fight to end conquest. They fight to liberate. They fight to let justice arise, and tolerance and goodwill among all Thy people. They yearn but for the end of battle, for their return to the haven of home.

Some will never return. Embrace these, Father, and receive them, Thy heroic servants, into Thy kingdom.[2]

On June 6, 2019, surviving D-Day veterans gathered, many probably for the last time, to honor the fallen from the nations

---

[2] *this day have set upon a mighty endeavor*- "Let Our Hearts Be Stout," https://www.fdrlibrary.org/d-day

engaged in storming 'Fortress Europe' and liberating the continent on the 75th anniversary of D-Day.[3]

Today, the ocean laps at the lateral thirty-five-mile advance of sand littered with relics of a different time, the hulking remnants of the tide of battle. The surf rolls in and kisses the beach as the last participants mix on the hallowed bluff above with the politicians who have gathered from all over the world.

Thirty-five years ago, I watched as the American president honored the fallen, and the living, at the cemetery for the fortieth anniversary. Just out of college, something stirred inside me. Something was awoken.

Those thirty-five years have passed. I began by writing letters to the newspaper. I began to interview D-Day veterans and others. I began to collect stories—not relics, prizes, or artifacts. I really had little interest in captured Nazi flags or samurai swords.

I wanted to talk to the men who were there.

The fiftieth anniversary came next with great pomp and more reflection. It graced the covers of the major newsweeklies. 'Saving Private Ryan' would soon stir the consciousness of a new generation, and the reflections of the old. And I learned so much more of the war beyond the beachhead. That there were so many beachheads.

The sixtieth anniversary came around. Students on their annual trips to France would bring me back their photographs and the

---

[3]*the nations engaged in storming 'Fortress Europe'*-Besides the United States, Great Britain and Canada, soldiers and seamen from several other Allied countries played a role in the landings and subsequent battle for France—'Australia, Belgium, Czechoslovakia, Denmark, France, Greece, the Netherlands, New Zealand, Norway and Poland.' Source: The D-Day Story, www.theddaystory.com, Portsmouth, England.

requisite grains of white sand from Omaha Beach. Teenagers had their emotions a bit tempered, I think. I would go on to introduce them to so many who were there, when they themselves were teenagers.

*

Some time has passed since I sat with the veterans I interviewed, but my memory of the smiles, the laughs, the emotion and the tears have not faded, though the day is approaching when no one with firsthand memory of World War II (and then, even people like you and me who may have heard these stories directly) will be alive. According to the National World War II Museum, citing statistics published at the end of every fiscal year by the U.S. Department of Veterans Affairs, fewer than half a million of the 16 million Americans who served in World War II are still alive, with nearly 350 passing each day in 2018.[4] Most veterans have gone the way of the World War I and Civil War generation without ever having told the tale outside of their own brothers and sisters who experienced it with them. So, thank you for your interest in this book series; it's the culmination of a mission that for me, as a history teacher and oral historian, turns out to have been lifelong. In reading it, you will have done something important—you will have remembered a person who may be now long dead, a veteran who may have lived out his or her final days wondering if it was all worth it. You will witness with me the extraordinary achievements of the participants and survivors of the most catastrophic period in the annals of history, which brought out the best—and the worst—of mankind. And these people were our everyday neighbors, our teachers and coaches, shopkeepers and carpenters, millworkers and mechanics,

---

[4] *nearly 350 passing each day in 2018*-Source: 'WWII Veteran Statistics, The Passing of the WWII Generation.' National World War II Museum, www.nationalww2museum.org/war/wwii-veteran-statistics.

nurses and stenographers, lawyers and loggers, draftsmen and doctors, people from every walk of life, high school dropouts and college graduates. They were the World War II generation, and there was a time after the war when we just simply took them for granted.

I happened to come of age, as a young history teacher in training, those thirty-five years ago, nodding silently at the black-and-white television screen in my college bedroom, the American president asking a question that I would go on to ask, over and over again:

"Why? Why did you do it? What impelled you to put aside the instinct for self-preservation and risk your lives to take these cliffs? What inspired all the men of the armies that met here?

*

We stand on a lonely, windswept point on the northern shore of France. The air is soft, but 40 years ago at this moment, the air was dense with smoke and the cries of men, and the air was filled with the crack of rifle fire and the roar of cannon. At dawn, on the morning of the 6th of June, 1944, 225 Rangers jumped off the British landing craft and ran to the bottom of these cliffs. Their mission was one of the most difficult and daring of the invasion: to climb these sheer and desolate cliffs and take out the enemy guns. The Allies had been told that some of the mightiest of these guns were here and they would be trained on the beaches to stop the Allied advance.

The Rangers looked up and saw the enemy soldiers [at] the edge of the cliffs shooting down at them with machineguns and throwing grenades. And the American Rangers began to climb. They shot rope ladders over the face of these cliffs and began to pull themselves up. When one Ranger fell, another would take his place. When one rope was cut, a Ranger would grab another and begin his climb again. They climbed, shot back, and held their footing. Soon, one by one, the Rangers pulled themselves over the top, and in seizing the firm land at the top of these cliffs, they began to seize back the continent of Europe. Two hundred and twenty-five came here. After two days of fighting, only 90 could still bear arms...

These are the boys of Pointe du Hoc. These are the men who took the cliffs. These are the champions who helped free a continent. These are the heroes who helped end a war...

We look at you, and somehow, we know the answer. It was faith and belief; it was loyalty and love."[5]

And as you will read, it was more.

So back to this book, Volume 5. When I began 'The Things Our Fathers Saw' series, I began in the Pacific Theater and worked my way through the stories of that arena of the war, from Pearl Harbor to Tokyo Bay. Most of the veterans hailed from an area where I grew up and taught surrounding Glens Falls, New York, a small city that *Look Magazine* renamed 'Hometown, USA' in 1944 and devoted six wartime issues to, illustrating patriotic life on the home front.[6] That book was well received, and a nationwide readership clamored for more veterans' stories in the vein I wrote in. The second and third volumes highlighted the men who fought in the skies over Europe, and the fourth tackled the war in North Africa and Italy, a

---

[5] *We stand on a lonely, windswept point*-President Ronald Reagan, June 6, 1984, Omaha Beach, Normandy, France. http://www.historyplace.com/speeches/reagan-d-day.htm

[6] *Most of the veterans hailed from an area surrounding Glens Falls, New York, that Look Magazine renamed 'Hometown, USA'*-In keeping with the hometown theme, the series title remains the same for this book. Some of the veterans have a direct connection to 'Hometown, USA,' and others a more circuitous one, but most hailed from New York hometowns bound together by the simple hope that the boys would return. Many did, and many did not.

campaign so brutal that news of it was downplayed at home. In this book I set out to have our veterans guide you through their experiences on 'D-Day and Beyond.'

*

A final tribute, and thought, if I may, before you go on. On the 65th anniversary of the June 6, 1944 landings, 87-year-old Marion 'Buster' Simmonds returned with nine other Battle of Normandy veterans matched with American college students in a trip financed by the Greatest Generation Foundation. Buster, a former combat medic with the 30th Infantry Division and friend, was paired with a student named Ben Doss. Twenty-year-old Ben remarked, 'When I'm standing on the beaches of Normandy, I just want to remember that men died here, men with families and men with dreams.' Ben, who was nearly the same age that Buster was on D-Day, continued, 'It's something that I've been thinking about a lot lately. If people my age today were put in the same situation...'

Finishing Ben's thought, Buster raised a finger, and slowly leveled it at Ben. 'If you were placed in the same situation that we were then, you and your comrades would rise to the occasion. *You're an American!*[7]

Buster delivered that statement with confidence, not a trace of doubt in his mind, or a need for hope in his heart. Ten years later

---

[7] *You're an American!*-You can actually watch this moving encounter in an ABC News clip from June 5, 2009. Buster called me on the telephone. He was excited to tell me how his dentist helped to arrange for funding and put him in touch with the Greatest Generation Foundation, pairing college kids from Missouri's College of the Ozarks to travel over for the 65th anniversary of D-Day. ABC World News was interested. He asked me to help ABC News get the liberation photo you see in the broadcast; meeting the survivors of this train near the end of his life really picked him up and gave him a new-found appreciation for what his generation had done. The clip can be viewed on my YouTube channel at http://bit.ly/BusterSimmons.

on the 75th anniversary, I recall Buster's smile, the Southern drawl and the twinkle in his eye when he ribbed his comrades. I remember the way he greeted my ten-year-old son at the reunions we attended with the 30th Infantry Division Veterans of World War II Association, rubbing his head and letting him draw the raffle names from the big tub at the annual final banquets where he served as the colorful fundraising auctioneer. Buster also served as the chaplain, and opened each reunion by reading the names of those fellow soldiers who had passed away in the past year, with president Frank Towers tolling the bell for each man who had gone forth; my son and I, and the Holocaust survivors I helped to reunite with the men of the 30th, were privileged to witness this moving ceremony several times.

His health fading, Buster passed away in 2013. Later, I was told that he died alone. I know he was very lonely after his wife passed, and this was followed by the death of his son Sandy, a Vietnam vet who would accompany Buster to the reunions. With ranks thinning, the 30th Infantry Division Veterans of World War II (which had met annually since 1946, sometimes taking over more than one downtown city hotel) folded its reunion tent in April 2015 in Nashville, Tennessee, on the 70th anniversary of the 1945 Nazi death train liberation. And I think Buster, who had lost his brother Bill in the air over Europe, died wondering if they would be forgotten. In working through the narratives in this book, remember to pause with me for a moment, maybe after you finish a section, to think about what they did, for us and generations not even born yet, those 75-plus years ago. Here are the stories that a special generation of Americans told us for the future when we took the time to be still, and to listen. Did they wonder, at the end, was it all worthwhile?

Matthew Rozell, June 6, 2019
Washington County, NY

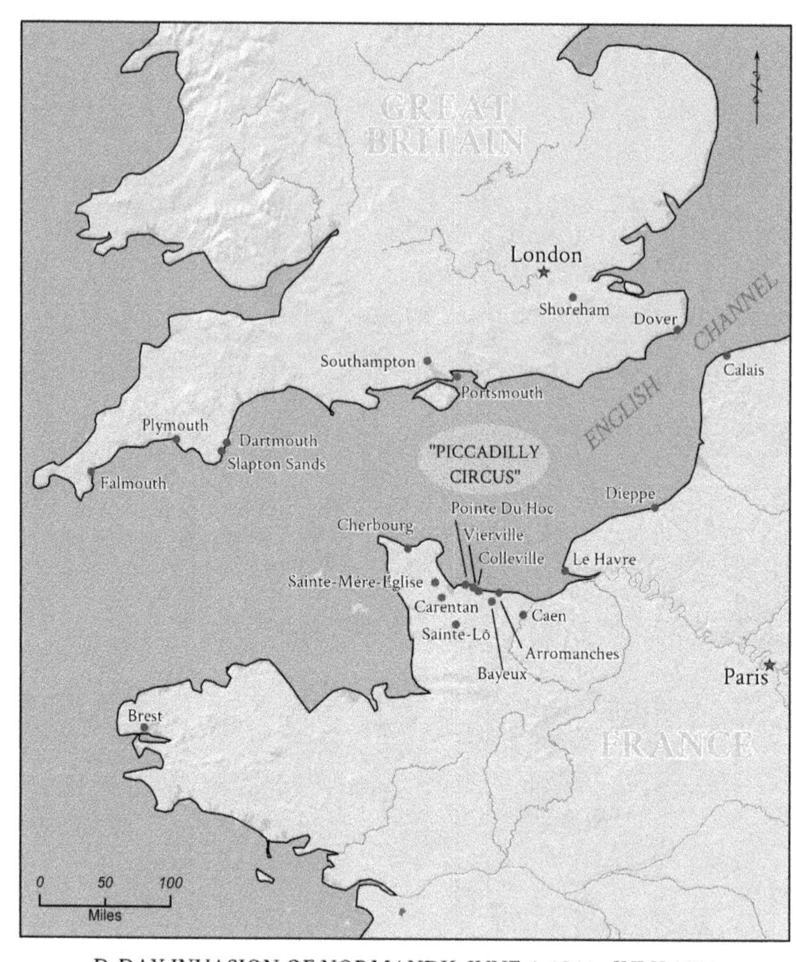

D-DAY INVASION OF NORMANDY, JUNE 6, 1944 - JULY 1944

The Invasion of Normandy. Map by Susan Winchell.

PART ONE

D-DAY IN CONTEXT

"Our landings in the Cherbourg-Havre area have failed to gain a satisfactory foothold and I have withdrawn the troops. My decision to attack at this time and place was based upon the best information available. The troops, the air and the Navy did all that bravery and devotion to duty could do. If any blame or fault attaches to the attempt it is mine alone."

—Press release drafted on the eve of the invasion, June 5, 1944, by Gen. Dwight D. Eisenhower for a statement to deliver in the event that the D-Day invasion failed.[8]

---

[8] *"'D-Day' was an Army designation used by military planners to indicate the start date for specific field operations. In this case, the 'D' in D-Day doesn't actually stand for anything—it's merely an alliterative placeholder used to designate a particular day on the calendar. 'H-Hour' referred to the time on D-Day when the action would begin; the codenames would also prevent actual mission dates from falling into enemy hands, and just helped when the start date for an attack was still undecided. Military planners also used a system of pluses and minuses [D+1] to designate any day or time occurring before or after D-Day or H-Hour.'"* Source: *Why is it called D-Day?* History.com., www.history.com/news/why-was-it-called-d-day.

Gen. Dwight D. Eisenhower speaks with men of Company E of the 502nd Parachute Infantry Regiment, 101st Airborne Division in England on the evening of June 5, 1944, as they prepare for the Battle of Normandy.

Credit: U.S. Army photograph, Public Domain.

CHAPTER ONE

The Great Crusade

SUPREME HEADQUARTERS
ALLIED EXPEDITIONARY FORCE

Soldiers, Sailors, and Airmen of the Allied Expeditionary Force!

You are about to embark upon the Great Crusade, toward which we have striven these many months. The eyes of the world are upon you. The hope and prayers of liberty-loving people everywhere march with you. In company with our brave Allies and brothers-in-arms on other Fronts, you will bring about the destruction of the German war machine, the elimination of Nazi tyranny over the oppressed peoples of Europe, and security for ourselves in a free world.

Your task will not be an easy one. Your enemy is well trained, well equipped and battle-hardened. He will fight savagely.

But this is the year 1944! Much has happened since the Nazi triumphs of 1940-41. The United Nations have inflicted upon the Germans great defeats, in open battle, man-to-man. Our air offensive has seriously reduced their strength in the air and their capacity to wage war on the ground. Our Home Fronts have given us an overwhelming superiority in weapons and munitions of war, and placed at our disposal great reserves of trained fighting men. The tide has turned! The free men of the world are marching together to Victory!

I have full confidence in your courage, devotion to duty and skill in battle. We will accept nothing less than full Victory!

Good luck! And let us beseech the blessing of Almighty God upon this great and noble undertaking.

—General Dwight D. Eisenhower's Order of the Day (1944)

On Sunday, June 4, 1944, battle weary soldiers of the United States Fifth Army under General Mark Clark shuffled along Rome's cobblestones, the first Allied soldiers to enter the first Axis capital to fall. Five months after landing in Italy, the Allies had sustained over 100,000 casualties slogging it out 'up the bloody boot' to now walk over flowers tossed to them in the Eternal City, which was hastily abandoned by retreating German forces only hours before. The prize was more symbolic than significantly strategic, more an honor the general was determined to snatch for himself after nearly five years of world war. Flashbulbs popped and Clark and the fall of Rome did indeed dominate the newspaper headlines—for all of about 24 hours. Eight hundred miles to the northwest, a greater drama was about to unfold.

The multi-year top-secret planning for the 'Operation Overlord' and the liberation of German-occupied France and Europe was coming to fruition in a rapid full-scale frenzy of last-minute preparations. By the spring of 1944, a million-plus men and supporting matériel from the United States had settled in Britain, so much that a wit remarked that if not for the barrage of balloons tethered to the ground, the island would have sunk.[1] The previous year and a half of waging war on the German Luftwaffe by Allied airpower had been largely successful, and now, part of the grand strategy depended on a steady supply of replacement bodies for those killed or wounded in the Normandy landings, the largest combined land-sea-air assault in the history of the world. By midnight on June 6, 175,000 men would be landed on the beaches or dropped behind German lines, with over 6000 ships in the cross-channel armada and thousands of aircraft taking to the nighttime skies to provide invasion cover and deliver men, vehicles, and heavy weapons near strategic crossroads and towns. By the time the first inland towns fell, massive artificial harbors built in England had been towed across the English Channel and more than 100,000 vehicles and multi-ton support supplies were landed. All of this required meticulous, down-to-the-minute planning and coordination, yet the flexibility to flow with the forces of nature and the factors of the unknown.

By early June 1944, the Axis empire in Europe and the Pacific had already experienced its imperial multicontinental apex but was by no means finished. After the fall of Rome that June, another year of fighting in Italy alone raised the Allied killed, missing, or wounded list to 320,000 names. By war's end, Germany had raised 315 infantry divisions, a monumental achievement when compared to the United States' sixty-six Army infantry divisions, with one quarter of those, along with six Marine Corps divisions, committed to the Pacific. And few persons today realize that on the eve of World War II, the United States lagged behind Bulgaria as the 18th placeholder for the largest army in the world.[2] Incredibly, by that spring of 1944, 11,000 men were being inducted into the armed forces every day; yet of the men who landed in Normandy in those coming weeks, less than fifteen percent had seen combat before.[3]

That summer of 1944 in the Central Pacific brought joint Army-Navy thrusts to within air striking distance of the imperial Japanese homeland with attacks on the Marianas at Guam, Saipan and

Tinian, but the horrific battles for the reconquest of the Philippines, Iwo Jima, and Okinawa, as well as the planning for the bloodletting in the event of the invasion of Japan itself, all lay in the immediate future. It is hard for Americans today to grasp the fact that the United States, and Great Britain, were essentially fighting two full-blown wars at the same time; we also tend to view our history as if the way things turned out was somehow preordained, as if it was a foregone conclusion that Americans and their allies were destined to win the war from the outset. The Allied invasion of Normandy stands as an epic testament to the planning, innovation and execution of the ordinary men and women who made it happen—the soldiers, sailors, airmen, medics, doctors and nurses whose stories capture the spirit of the time, the triumphs and the tragedies of the greatest drama of our age. Eisenhower began the 'Great Crusade' with his 'Order of the Day'; privately, he penned his press release at the same time, and quietly slipped it into his wallet:

The troops, the air, and the Navy did all that bravery and devotion to duty could do. If any blame or fault attaches to the attempt, it is mine alone.

CHAPTER TWO

The Gyro Man

Like many World War II Navy veterans, James Calascione seemed to move everywhere during the course of the war. His narrative begins as a boy in the 1920s and moves through the height of the Great Depression, setting the stage for the larger context of the war as the D-Day Normandy landings began to come into focus by military planners. His combat experience begins with war for North Africa and Sicily and Italy, paralleling the United States' entry into the European conflict. Mr. Calascione was in the thick of it in many campaigns throughout World War II, an appropriate person to begin our 'D-Day and Beyond' journey.

A soft-spoken man, Mr. Calascione relates his story from the heart, bringing to life once more the things our fathers saw that they could never forget, and perhaps needed to share to ease a silent burden for time, carried by so many for so many years.

*

"I always got calls, 'Sparky, I need a hand,' especially out on the outer deck. They'd bring the landing craft up to the main deck, leveled with the main deck. With the canvas stretchers, they'd pass the wounded in over the gunnel of the boat. We'd take the stretcher, lay it on the deck. We'd have to transfer those men that were on the canvas stretchers, that were bleeding on the stretchers. I helped many of the wounded men. Up to very recently, I dreamt of it, I always dreamt of it. A lot of my friends tell me, 'Jim, look,

that was the war. Forget about it. You don't want to remember things like that."

'I can't forget it. It's indubitably marked up here in my brain. Do you know how many boys I helped there?'

James A. Calascione

I was born in Brooklyn, New York, back in 1916—December 6, 1916. South Brooklyn, we used to call that neighborhood Red Hook; now they call it Cobble Hill. They changed the name of it, but it was mostly Italian and Irish. The Irish were a few blocks up from us, but we more or less intermingled. A lot of brotherliness there, very close people, very close. I grew up and went through PS 29. When I got out of there, I went to the Brooklyn Technical High School for electrical engineering. I was there two terms, and we had five different annexes other than the main building. We had to change periods and go from one building to the other.

In about this time of the year, it's very cold. We weren't allowed to carry our overcoats with us. We had to keep them locked up in the locker, but I used to wear a sweater, probably two sweaters, so that I could make my trip three, four, five blocks away to the other annex. But I caught a dose of rheumatic fever from it. I woke up one morning, I was stiff in bed—so stiff I couldn't get out of bed for nine weeks. After nine weeks, I started to move around a little bit, but I couldn't walk. Then I had a friend of mine who used to come over every day, pick me up, take me out, and put me in the sun, so I could sun myself. He's dead now. He was a little overweight; at the age of 12, he was 291 pounds, but he was a model of a boy. Well, I continued with my education. I got to the point where I couldn't hack it anymore. The seventh term, I got out.

*

I started to look for work in the electrical business. I wasn't too lucky. In those days, in 1929, '28, '29, it was bad, very bad. The stock crash came, and everything dropped out. I kept getting little odd jobs here. Electrical work, I couldn't get electrical work, no way, no how. In those days, the electrical union would only take on a member if his father was in the union. It was a father and son deal. That's the only thing I hold against local trade in the electrical union.

So, I started working my way up. A friend of mine said to me, 'I know you wasn't too interested in it. Why don't you try for the police force?' It's an idea. So, I tried. I went to Delehanty [High School], went through the course there, took the exam, got a pretty high mark, but it wasn't good enough. In the meantime, Europe starts rumbling. I had been working in a department store, in Brooklyn; I was in protection there.

They asked me if I would do any undercover work for them. I said, 'Well, if it pays, I'll take a crack at it.' So, they took me up into the personnel office, and there was the personnel manager there. A man from the protection department interviewed me, and he said, 'Look, this is no baby job. This is a tough job.'

He said, 'We're losing over $3000 a month in one department alone, stolen dresses. We want to get these guys, and we want to hang them. Do you think you could do it?'

I said, 'I think so.'

He says, 'What are you good at?'

I said, 'I'm good at painting.'

'Very good, very good. It's just what I want, somebody that can work at night.'

I said, 'Okay, I'll take it.' I said, 'I'll come to the bottom of it.' So, I did. I worked at it for eight weeks. Six of them went to jail. The next thing I know, I got a call from the draft. I was Navy-minded. I wouldn't make a good soldier. If I was going to die, I was going to die clean. I talked to my father and my mother.

I said, 'Look.' I said, 'I'm going to go into the service. I'm going to pick what I want.'

My father said, 'Well, why not?'

I said, 'Well, maybe you don't like the idea that I go back in the Navy like Uncle Frankie.' I had an uncle who had been in about 22 years so far.

So he says, 'Look. You do what you want. You want the Navy, go.' So, I went down to the recruiting station to enlist.

'What can I do for you?'

I said, 'I want to enlist.'

'How come?'

I said, 'I just got this call from selective services. I don't want to go in the Army. I want to go in the Navy.'

'Oh, that's good.' He says, 'All right, come on, sit down here. Let's talk this thing over.'

Then he asked me a question. He says, 'Do you have anybody in your family that is in the Navy?'

I said, 'Yes, I have an uncle in the Navy right now. He's been in the Navy over 22 years, I think.'

He said, 'Oh. What's his name?'

'His name is Frankie Majorana.'

'That son of a b—!'

I says, 'What do you mean?'

He said, 'We used to play baseball together out on the west coast in San Diego!'

I said, 'Well, he's not in San Diego now.'

He says, 'Where is he?'

I says, 'He's in Chifoo [Zhifu], China. He's been there for 10 years.'

'What is he doing there?'

I said, 'He's a chief optical machinist. He takes care of gunsights.'

'That son of a gun! He always went for the easy jobs. Good, good.' He says, 'Look. I'm going to give you a tip, you're in the Navy, you're not going in the Army. If they offer you any school when you get up to Newport, Rhode Island,' he says, 'take it. At any time in the Navy that they offer you schooling, take it because it's to your advantage.'

I said, 'Okay, I'll take it.' So, I went to Newport, Rhode Island. I went up there on October 23. I was supposed to leave there on December the 13th, but Pearl Harbor came, and I was talking to the commander up there in Newport, Rhode Island.

Sunday afternoon, I got a call to come down to the OD's office. He says, 'I'm going to give you a belt and a stick; I'm sending you in to pull anybody back that's [on leave] in Providence. They got to come back to the ship.' He says, 'Just in case you don't know, we're at war. Pearl Harbor was just attacked this morning.'

I said, 'Oh my God. Are we going to get to leave next week?'

He says, 'Don't count on it. Better make hay while you're here, because I don't know where you're going to be going. Anyway, go out with this crew here. Here's your night stick and your belt.'

We went down. I had my leggings on. There were four busloads that we brought back that night. Guys were all hollering and screaming, 'What do you mean? This is my liberty! What are you guys telling me?'

I said, 'Look, don't worry about it. You're going to be all right. Just get on the bus and go.' A lot of them were three sheets to the wind already.

Electrical School

The next week, I got transferred to St. Louis, Missouri. I spent three months there in electrical school. I used to fall asleep in the class. It was all old stuff to me. I would go to the back of the class and fall asleep. This one teacher wanted to put me on report. I had a chief of the company there. He was a chief water tender in the Navy; he had put in 32 years. He spoke to the math teacher.

He says, 'What's the idea? Why are you putting him on report?'

Teacher says, 'He sleeps in the class.'

He said, 'Let me talk to him.' He talks to me. He says, 'Jim, what are you sleeping in the class for?'

I said, 'This is all old stuff to me. This is all kids' stuff!'

'What do you mean it's kids' stuff?'

I said, 'I was through Brooklyn Tech, got a good electrical education.'

'What are you doing here?'

I says, 'It's where I was assigned, so I took it.'

He said, 'I've got an idea. A couple of guys in your class are not doing too good. Would you want to tutor them?'

I says, 'Anytime. Sure. Why not?' So, he gave me eight fellas. I didn't go on report. He gave me eight boys that were falling behind in their math and I took them on. Out of the eight, seven made it. The other one couldn't make it, he just didn't have it.

The Gyro Machine

Mr. Calascione's Navy gyro school training was probably to master the operation of the gyro compass, 'a form of gyroscope used widely on ships employing an electrically powered, fast-spinning gyroscope wheel and frictional forces among other factors utilizing the basic physical laws, influences of gravity and the Earth's rotation to find the true north, an indispensable instrument in almost all merchant ships or naval vessels for its ability to detect the direction of true north and not the magnetic north.'[4] *It was a very fine technical instrument, and it took a special kind of person to master its operation.*

From there, they sent me to gyro school, 15 minutes away from my home in Brooklyn at the Brooklyn Navy Yard. I was supposed to be there for thirteen weeks, but after nine weeks, I says, 'No, no way. There's no way; I'm going to get out a little sooner here.'

From there, they sent me down to Portsmouth, Virginia. I went there, and I'm waiting for my ship, the *Charles Carroll.* It wasn't coming. What am I going to do now? I kept asking and asking, and finally, they came to me and they said, '*Carroll* is in. It's in Portsmouth. You go out tomorrow.' Okay, good. I went aboard.

Soon as I got aboard, a guy looked at me. He says, 'Sparky. Captain wants to see you.' The captain don't even know me. He says, 'You're third class electrician?'

I said yes.

He says, 'You're the guy he wants to see.'

I says, 'Okay. Let's go. Where's the captain?'

He says, 'I'll take you there.' He took me up to the captain's office, his stateroom really. Right away, I get in, I salute him.

'Come over here. I've got to talk to you. Calm down.'

He says, 'This is something man to man. I want to have a little confab with you. You just came out of gyro school, didn't you?'

I says, 'Yes, sir.'

'You had pretty good marks there, too, didn't you?'

'Yes, sir.'

He says, 'I've got a key for you to the gyro room. This key is yours. You don't give this key to nobody, absolutely nobody. You are the only one that will ever be allowed in that room.'

I said, 'That's all right with me, I wouldn't let anybody else touch my gyro.'

'That's what I want to hear.' He says, 'I think you and I are going to get along very good together.'

I said, 'I get along with everybody, sir.'

'Very good, Sparky. Here's the key. This key takes this ship all over the world. We're going to do a lot of traveling. That gyro must be tip-top at all times.'

I says, 'It will be, sir.'

'Okay. Go on about your business. When I need you, I'll call you.'

'Thank you very much, sir.'

I got up, I saluted him. He saluted me back.

He says, 'Welcome aboard. You're one of my boys now.'

So, I left. That was Captain Bismeyer. He was onboard with me close to two years, and he was taken off; he sat on the Pearl Harbor Investigation Board, that's the only reason why they took him off the ship. The day he left, we all cried. He was a really good man, very good captain.

Then we started the North African invasion. We didn't lose any men there. We lost a lot of boats. Out of 36 landing craft from the *Charles Carroll,* we got about 30 of them back. The rest of them were all broached up on the beach.

So, we made our way back to the States. When we got back, they started putting radar on the ship. They wanted help with the electrical circuits. I said okay; I had a nice little electrical shop. I also took care of all the sound power telephones. They put an automatic telephone system in. So, they needed a room to put the jeeps in that was in control balance. They put that in the back of my electrical shop.

Two Men Gone

We went along. Next thing you know, we're told, 'Well, the *Charles Carroll* is going to leave in a week.'

'Okay. Where are we going?'

'I don't know yet.' So, about four or five days before, the navigator calls me up. He says, 'Sparky. I got to talk to you. You've got to make sure that we get all the settings in the gyro before we leave, but what I'm going to tell you is top secret.'

'It's all right with me.' I says, 'I'm Sicilian. I got a deep stomach. Whatever comes in, doesn't come out.'

'Very good.'

So, he gave me the routing that we were going to go through the Panama Canal, we're going to deliver some troops down in New Zealand. So, on the way into the Panama Canal, they had the anti-submarine gates there, and they opened the gates for us. When they opened the gates, one of the bombs was attached to the cable, a two-inch steel cable called criss-cross with the shackles holding the netting together, and as we were just about getting into the gate, there was a blast right under the fantail. Wham! When they opened those gates, one of the charges that was attached to the gate [went off]. We lost two men. They were sitting on the fantail, they were mess cooks, sunning themselves. When the bomb went off, they went over the fantail out into the water. They tried to back the ship down, but they couldn't back it down. The two men were gone—never found them. The ship had to be towed through the Panama Canal—it had the distinction of being the first ship ever to be towed through the Panama Canal—they towed us through onto the Pacific side, put us in dry dock; there was none on the east coast.

We stayed there for two months waiting for a piece of a shaft. The last section to the shaft going out to the propeller, and a new rudder that had to come down from northern Virginia. So, we waited there for it. While we were there, we'd go ashore back and forth, back and forth. They took us out of dry dock. They put us over on the side. Finally, the parts came, and we had to go back up to northern Virginia for final repairs, to get ready for something else. We got ready.

Little did I know, we were starting to get ready for the Sicilian invasion. We picked up 45th Division, and we were on our way out. A lot of pictures were taken of the ship, the planes. In fact, I've got a picture home with men all lined up on the ship on our way out to Sicily. We made the Sicilian invasion. That was a breeze. The Sicilian invasion, we walked in, put our troops in. It was one of the easiest invasions we had.

Salerno

We went back to North Africa, and we picked up troops there. The troops, everybody was hollering and screaming, 'Where the hell are we going? What are we going to do? What are we going to do? Sparky, you know where we're going to go.'

I said, 'I don't know about anything.' So, I got a call from [the navigator]. He told me where we were going to go, he said, 'Please don't let it out.'

'Don't worry about it, Lieutenant. I won't let it out.'

We were going to Salerno. Salerno, Italy, was a bad deal, very bad deal. There was a meeting in the wardroom, a briefing before the landing. There was a major general onboard. He said, 'This is going to be a surprise attack.'

The commodore, he was kind of tough. He said, 'Absolutely not. This is not going to be a surprise attack.'

'Why not?'

He said, 'Because last night, we picked up some boys that were in there.'

'Well, what about it?'

'Don't send your boys in there unless you shell the beach.'

'Oh, no. This got to be a surprise attack.'

'If it's going to be a surprise attack, it's going to be a surprise on you.' He said, 'Those Germans have 88s lined up along the beach and up into the hills. They're going to take shots at those landing crafts going in. They're going to knock them right off.' And that's what happened.

We had a bad time there. We were there for the first day, and we took on wounded; wounded were coming on like mad— [it was like it had been] converted into a hospital ship. When we were at a transport area like that, the boats wouldn't come back empty. They'd come back with the wounded. I was floating on the ship. I had access to any part of the ship that anybody could go. Enlisted men were not allowed in 'officers' country'; I was [the exception] because my gyro was right in the middle of 'officers' country.' I could go anywhere on the boat. I always got calls, 'Sparky, I need a hand', especially out on the outer deck, 'Sparky, I need a hand.' They'd bring the landing craft up to the main deck, leveled with the main deck. With the canvas stretchers, they'd pass the wounded in over the gunnel of the boat. We'd take the stretcher, lay it on the deck. We'd have to transfer those men that were on the canvas stretchers, that were bleeding on the stretchers. The blood was all over the canvas. You had to put your arms under, pick them up, lift them up. They'd pull the stretcher out and would lay the men down in there. What would happen, the blood would cake. They'd start ripping their clothes off. You got that dried blood caked on your clothes, just pulling it. [*Shakes head, gets emotional, continues with shaky voice*] That was a feeling... I helped many a man...

I can't forget it. It's indubitably marked up here in my brain. Do you know how many boys I helped there? One night during one of the bombing attacks in Salerno, we were getting ready to put these stretchers over the side because the Germans were bombing the hell out of us. Finally, the captain says, 'We're not staying here. We're getting the hell out of here.' He said, 'Cut the anchors away.' One anchor was cut away. One anchor, they were able to get up. The other anchor ... 'Don't wait. Let's get the hell out of here.' We got the hell out of there.

The wounded that had come aboard already were all in stretchers. They put them out in the passageway. They had one boy right next to my gyro room. I'm standing ... During action, I had to stay in the gyro room constantly in case the ship would get hit. The gyro would start rocking, and I had to tend to it right away. I had my door to the gyro room open. Right in the passageway, there was a young lad there. All I could hear him say is, 'Ma.' He'd take a breath, and it'd be a whistle. 'Ma.' [*cries softly*] Oh, God.

I was looking down at him lying on the deck. He looked up at me. 'Ma.' Then I realized what was happening. When he was going, 'Ma,' he was taking a breath, and his lungs were filling up with air, and it was leaking out the back. He had a little hole in the top of his lung up here, but it came out and it ripped a couple of his ribs off, and knocked a couple of his vertebrae out of line. He had a hole in his back about that big [*gestures with hands*]. They couldn't do nothing for him. All they did was, they padded him up with absorbent cotton and bandaged him up. They said, 'Just wait for him to die.'

I found that out later; one of the pharmacists may have told me about it. His name was Rodriguez. He came from the Bronx; he died the day after. When I was there with him, I knelt by him. I held his hand. He felt I held his hand; [he gripped my] hand tight, very tight. I knew he was still alive. Those things, you can't forget. You don't forget. I thank God that I was able to help some of those boys. Whenever there was an operation going on in the sick bay, not only the sick bay, the state rooms had to be turned into operating rooms, doctors all over operating, taking arms off.

One day, I'm called into a state room in Salerno there. They were amputating a boy's arm, his right arm. I happen to be passing by. 'Sparky, get in here. Give us a hand. Come on, hurry up.'

I went in. 'What's the matter?'

'Hold this man down.' They had him on the operating table. They were going to take his arm off, but the ether ran out. They had to send one of the pharmacists down to get more ether down there in the storeroom. This guy started going wild on the table. They go, 'You got to hold him down. He's going to hurt himself more than what he is!'

I said, 'I got to cross his legs,' holding his legs down so he wouldn't kick.

Finally, the man came up and gave him more ether. It put him out. He says, 'All right, Sparky, come on. Okay. Stand by here. Don't leave in case anything happens. Please stand by with us.'

'Okay, I'll stand by with you.' So, they took the arm off. The pharmacist mate is holding the arm as the doctor is cutting it off. He turns around. He hands it to me. Like a jerk, I grab it. The doctor says, 'Put that over there. Come back here, Sparky.' So, I put that arm over in one of the bunks that was in the state room. I put it on one of the bunks and I came back.

He says, 'He's starting to move again. Hold his legs down.' Okay. I held his legs down. Then he started to calm down a little bit. They gave him more ether; [now] they had him out completely. 'All right, Sparky, thanks a lot. Thanks a lot, Sparky.'

That was Salerno.

'Normandy Was a Horror'

On June 5, 1944, the USS Charles Carroll *left England headed for Omaha Beach, landing troops of the 29th Division under enemy fire, and plied the waters landing additional troops and equipment and evacuating casualties.*

From there, we went to Normandy, Omaha Beach, Blue Beach. Normandy was a horror for me. I had made chief in three years from an apprentice seaman, so I wasn't [normally] allowed off the ship, but I had to come down with some batteries. I didn't have any more men on board. I was chief at the time, chief electrician's mate.

I had to go in with a couple of batteries, 90-amp power batteries, 225-volt amp. Oh, God. The boats are around the beach, but the batteries are dead. Okay. So, I grab six batteries and I go in with one of the boats. I left one of my boys ready. We were at anchor. I figured the ships aren't going to go anywhere, I'll be back. I got permission from the captain to go. He said, 'Yes, go.' So, I went. I took care of three boats on the beach, two batteries in each of the boats. The men got them off. On the way back, I'm looking out into the water, and I see this hand come up out of the water.

'Hey, hold it, coxswain!'

'What's the matter? What's the matter, chief?'

'We just passed a wounded man! Get around there. Come on, let's get him!'

'Are you sure?'

I says, 'Look, I'm sure; I know what I'm talking about! I saw the man waving his hand! He's got a life jacket on and all, but he's waving his hand—he's alive! Bring the boat around!'

Sure enough, we picked him up, got him into the boat, and brought him back to the ship. He was pretty well shot up, machine-gunned right through the midsection. He was bleeding in the water, [bleeding in the] boat. We got him into the boat, but he died the day after.

*

From there, we went to Southern France. Southern France was a little bit of a horror. We were on our way into Southern France, and there's the *USS Richelieu,* the biggest battleship that France had. It was coming off the beach, and it was intercepted by the destroyers, it was taken.

The Germans did a rotten thing; they massacred the people there. On the ship with our glasses, we could see a horrible sight.

There was a barn right at the edge of the beach, and they had captured a lady that was involved with the underground. They killed her, and they hung her up on this barn door with her hands outstretched and her legs outstretched. She was cut from the privates all the way up to her neck. All her guts were all hanging out. It was a horrible sight, seeing that woman with her guts hanging out. I can't forget these things.

From there, we came back to the States. Thank God, thank God, we got through [the European part of the war] all right! We went into the yard; we were supposed to be there for 60 days. Twenty-eight days and, 'You're on your way, boys. You got to leave right away. Within three days, you're going to be out of here.' Okay. Within three days, we'll be out of here.

I set the gyro and all. We went through the Panama Canal. This time, we got through all right, no bombs blasting. We went to Hawaii, and from Hawaii, we went to a little island just away from the Solomon Islands and we picked up some Marines there. We went island hopping, we picked up more Marines on other islands. Next thing you know, we're on our way to Okinawa. We made the Okinawa invasion.

Meeting Ernie Pyle

We had what they called the Fifth Marines. That was a bad invasion. Bad in the sense that the Japs would come in, these kamikazes, and we lost a few ships there. Thank God *Carroll* made it all right. Then we came back to the States, to San Francisco. On our way back, we picked up a man on a little island there, Ie Shima. He was onboard with us; he had gone into Okinawa. We brought him in there. His name was Ernie Pyle.

When we left, he said, 'Sorry, I'm not going back with you fellas.' He used to spend a lot of time with the enlisted men, in the chief's quarters; he was always writing. 'Let me have your name and address to get in touch with your parents, your family.' We were about two or three days out of Okinawa, and we find out that he was sniped, he was killed. That caused a heartache onboard because he was so close to us, he was close to everybody on that ship. He was always with the men. What a wonderful man he was, a wonderful man.

We picked up troops. They were all PWs, American military prisoners who had turned bad under fire. We had to take them to the Philippine Islands and went to Samoa and dropped them off. On that trip, all the chiefs were given .45s to keep in their lockers at night, lock them up, make sure that none of those guys got a gun. So, I had mine. I used to keep mine in the bunk above me between the spring and the mattress. We had to be careful of the PWs. We had .30 caliber machine guns all around the upper deck in case they tried to attack us. Those guns were manned 24 hours a day.

'I'll Tear that Ship Apart'

So, we came back to the States. They wanted to take me back out again; it was the month of October 1945. I had gotten a letter from home that my father wasn't doing too well. He had a heart condition. When we got back to Seattle, Washington, I said, 'I'm going to leave the ship.'

The captain says, 'Oh, you can't leave the ship.'

'What do you mean I can't leave the ship? I got 48 points here. They're letting them out for less than 40.'

'Oh, you have the points, but I can't let you go. I don't have a gyro man.'

'That's tough, get one.'

'No, no. You got to get one.'

'I got to get one?'

'Yeah, you gotta get your own relief.'

'Where am I going to get a relief? You can call up and get a man if you want.'

'I can't. I can't do that. I'm going to hold you.'

'Oh, you're not going to hold me.'

'Why not?'

'No, I'm going to get off the ship because my father isn't doing too well, and I want to get back home. If something happens to him, I want to be there.'

'I can't help you, chief,' he says. 'I'm sorry. I can't help you.'

I said, 'Well, I'll go see the commander of western seafronts here.'

He said, 'I don't know what good it's going to do you.'

I says, 'I want to see the captain of western seafronts here. Maybe I could get a relief from him.'

'Okay, go ahead.'

There was another chief that I was very close with called Sink; he came from Brooklyn also. He was chief machinist and now took care of the evaporators. I says, 'Sink, I'm going to see.' They wouldn't let him go either. 'I'm going to go to the western seafront here. You want to go with me?'

'Yeah, sure, Jim. Come on, let's go. I got to get back home. My mother isn't doing too well.'

'Okay, let's go.'

So, we went there, and there's a first-class yeoman there.

'Yes, chief, what can I do for you?'

I said, 'I'd like to see the commander of western seafront tier, please.'

'What is this about?'

'Well, I'd like to get off the *Charles Carroll*, but they won't release us.'

He said, 'Let me have your name, serial number, and you, too, chief.' He took it all down. He says, 'Have a seat here a moment.' I said okay.

There was a big door, a beautiful mansion it was; it was about 18 feet high. He opens the door and walks in. All of a sudden, I hear, 'Get those two guys in here.'

I recognize the voice. I says, 'Carl, you recognize that voice?' He said no.

I said, 'But I do.'

He says, 'Who is it?'

I said, 'I want to make you a bet right here and now, that it's Captain Bismeyer.'

'You're kidding me.'

Door swings all the way open. Now he's coming out from behind this big desk.

'Sparky, here you are! Hey, Sink, how you doing?' He remembered us. 'Come on in. Come on in! Have a drink with me! What can I do for you boys?'

I said, 'Captain, we want to get off the *Carroll.* It's not that we don't like it,' I said, 'but my father isn't doing too well.' I told him the whole story. I says, 'He's got trouble with his mother.'

He says, 'What do you mean they won't let you off?'

I says, 'I'm the gyro man. They can't get a replacement.'

'Yeoman, get in here.' The yeoman comes in.

Captain Bismeyer said, 'I want you to write two letters. I'll dictate it to you. But different names. On one, you put Chief Calascione. The other one, you put Chief Sink.' He dictated the letter to him. It was a letter to the commanding officer of the *Charles Carroll.* Each one of us had one. He says, 'I want you to go back as soon as possible and get this [delivered].'

The ship was going to leave the following morning at 9 o'clock, something like that. He says, 'I want you to deliver it to that captain.'

He said, 'If the captain is not aboard, then to the lieutenant commander in charge. I'll take care of that captain. But there's something else involved.'

I said, 'What is it?'

He said, 'Tomorrow morning at 7:30, I'll be on the dock.' He said, 'I'll come there with my limo, and I'll have a pickup truck following me. You two guys better be out at the foot of that gangway when I get there, because if you're not there, I'm going aboard and I'm going to raise hell on the *Charles Carroll.* I never did that before, and I'll do it now. You guys are getting off that ship. You have done enough. I don't want to hear any more about it.'

I said, 'Captain, that's kind of rough.'

'Don't worry, Sparky. I'll be there. It'll be all right. I'll be there.'

The next morning 25 after 7, he pulls up. I had my trunk. Carl had his trunk and sea bag right up on top there. Out comes a big Buick Limited. The limo was a seven-passenger car. He said, 'I'm glad you boys are down here, because I was going to go up there on a rampage. I was going to tear that ship apart; I put it together. I was going to tear it apart. I'm glad you guys are here.' He said, 'Come on. We'll go to the receiving station.'

He dropped us off at the receiving station. He kissed me. He said, 'Good luck to your ship.' He did the same thing with Carl. He praised him, kissed him. 'God bless you both. You guys went through hell on earth. Now, you know what hell looks like. Have a happy life.'

'You too, Captain.' I saluted him. That's the last I saw him. Then I found out he passed away.

*

I got out November 11 of 1945. For one year, I had been writing to my wife, making plans. I knew what I wanted. I wanted a home, get a nice little job in the electrical field, and get married, settle down. I didn't want no more protection work, no more anything like that because I had learned how to kill with my bare hands. Somebody would come to me and would try to throw a fist at me, he was gone. I'd grab him by the throat and by the nuts, and I'd pull him apart. That's the way I was taught. I didn't want to go into protection. My father asked me, 'Why don't you try for the police force? You know they're taking on cops like mad.'

I says, 'Pop, I don't want no part of protection anymore. I'm an electrician by trade, and I'm going to stay with it.'

He says, 'Son, you do what you want. This is your life.'

I said, 'Okay, it's my life.' I said, 'I want to get married, raise a family, work like a human being, not like an animal. Having to go out and hit people, I don't want that no more. I'm through with that. No more.' So, we made plans, and we got married. I got married in 1947. But I couldn't get a job in the electrical business.

The local trade said, 'No, no. If your father was in, okay.'

I said, 'So what?' I says, 'My father was a barber. What does that got to do with me?' I said, 'I'm an electrician by trade. If I was a barber, and I say I'll just come to you for a barber's job, it'd be a different story. But I'm an electrician by trade. I was chief electrician in the Navy. I can take motors and generators apart. My electrical equipment never suffered when I was onboard. I was a gyro technician onboard. It's a very fine instrument. It's even finer than a wristwatch.'

'Sorry.'

Finally, one day, I went down to local again. One guy got me in the hall. He says, 'You know, I see you here coming around every day. Maybe I can do something for you. What do you want?'

I said, 'I want a card, so I can get work in the electrical trade.'

He says, 'You know, I could work something out. But it'll cost you $1000.'

I said, '$1000 for what?'

He says, 'For a temporary card.'

I said, 'What good is that going to do me?'

He says, 'Well, you go in on a job.' But then he says, 'But if a union man comes and bumps you, you tear the card up. That's the end of it.'

I said, 'I gotta give you $1000 for that? I'm going to be on the job for two hours, and some guy bumps me, and I'm out $1000. What do you think? I was in the Navy to make money? I didn't make no money in the Navy.' I says, 'I want to work like a human being in my trade.'

'That's the only deal I can give you. That's it.'

'Forget it, shove it.' And I walked out.

So, I went to work doing a little bit of everything, peddling. I bought a truck, peddled for a while. I knew fruit and vegetables; I was pretty good at it. Ann and I were traipsing around, and I got a couple of offers. Go with this guy, go with that guy. No, I don't want to go nowhere, I just took what I got. I started to work in the machine business. I could take a machine apart and put it together in nothing flat.

What can I add? I thank the good Lord that I'm still here, still living, enjoying my family, my wife, my children, my grandchildren. I'm just glad to be here.

Mr. Calascione died on December 21, 2011, at the age of 95.

CHAPTER THREE

The Master Mechanic

I interviewed Paul Hillman with one of my students on a quiet evening at his home on Lake George, New York, just before Thanksgiving in 2003. I had called him up and we had gone out to breakfast earlier in the week at a local eatery where everyone knew him. One of my oldest interviewees and closing in on his first century of life, he related stories of growing up on a small farm, delivering milk by horse and wagon, and going on with his brothers to revolutionize the shipping industry. That same ambition and problem-solving intuition led the United States Army to tap him as an officer, although he had no military training, right out of civilian life at the age of 38; the Army was serious about this coming invasion and needed the best men.

'I ran a waterproofing school down in Wales for all the vehicles that were going into France, driving off the ships and going into the water, some of them pretty deep... I can always remember General Patton, getting a call from headquarters to report to the general. I had to make sure his division were all schooled in waterproofing to go in. He sent his men down there to the school so they knew how to do it, because you'd be surprised that without waterproofing, the most stupid little thing will stop your engine, shorting any exposed electricals right out, and that'd be it, you'd be a sitting duck.'

Paul F. Hillman

I was born December the fifth, 1904, in the town of Easton, Washington County. I will be ninety-nine soon. But see, I've got two birthdays. Down in the family there [on the farm], the family one is December second; and the town one is December fifth. I don't remember which one is correct, [*laughs*] but anyway one's in the family history and the other is the town; no telephones to speak of then, you know, in 1904—someone would have to get to the town hall to put it in. That's where the difference is, you know. There were seven in our family and one sister. They are all gone now; I was next to the last. I had one younger brother, but he's gone too. They're all gone but me.

There were seven in our family and my parents ran the family farm. It's been in our family since 1800, down in Easton. It's my mother's family farm. See, I'm working on the whole genealogy right now. We're getting that all brought up to date and I know a lot [more about my ancestors now]. A lot of them didn't have any money; the only thing they had was ambition.

*

I got into the war different than anybody else. I was at my [trucking business office], Fort Edward Express, and I got a call one day from the Mack Truck company in Albany and they were having trouble in Pine Camp near Watertown with the equipment in winter of 1942. Well, they had a lot of troops up there, and they had trouble with engines freezing up and oh, big problems, because these are greenhorns who don't know anything about cold weather and they had thirty below zero weather up there, you know. They had Arkansas troops, came from down in the south, and they'd never been in cold weather at all; [their colonel] had been stationed in Cuba well before the time before Castro got in. He was trying to tell them what to do; well, he didn't know anything about cold weather. Never been in cold weather, you know.

Mr. Hillman explained how he was sought out for his logistical and technical knowledge, which began as a teenager on the farm, to help solve seemingly intractable truck problems for the Army. In 1917, the brothers launched their enterprise at the family farm, Brotherhood Farms in Easton, first using a team of Belgian horses for power, and then acquiring a 1920 stake body truck to haul milk in cans from farm to market.

Our trucking company today hauls gasoline, fuel oil, propane, et cetera. I started in the milk business in 1932, my brother Frank and me. We revolutionized the hauling of milk in these United States.

A dairy company was set up and they started a new plant in Fort Edward, [to bring the farmers' milk to market in New York City, 200 miles to the south]. We had been hauling the milk before. We had a 1920 truck right out in the garage on the farm. We would haul one hundred and fifty cans, going twenty miles per hour. That was fast, faster than the horses, you know, but anyway we knew a little about the hauling, so my brother Frank went up and met [the plant supervisors] and they said if you can help us buy the milk [from the individual farms], you can haul it to New York. Now this is a crazy idea, you know, because it's never been done. Everything was all on trains back in '32.

We knew the farmers. My father had sold a lot of them the equipment from around Washington County and the farmers knew him. Well, he said it was all right. The farmers would trust us, you know to sell their milk, because they had so much milk and no money, you know. What are you going to do? So, my brother and I were taking milk away from some of the big competitors like Hood and all farms down [who had worked with Borden's Milk]. Borden's had it sewn up around the railroads, you see, all in day railcars, that was the way it had always went with them. We brought it in cans [to the dairy company] with horses and wagons first, then they had to tell the Mack trucks to haul it on. My brother Frank went up and told them we'd help them. Well, anyway, we had a good idea because we had hauled milk before you know, with horses, wagons, and this truck.

So anyways we started a trucking business with the milk hauling operation. We gradually picked up over seven hundred cans of milk and we got four trucks ourselves to pick up the milk and bring it in. You'd have to be at the farmer's house at seven o'clock. You've got to get it by ten o'clock and be on the road [to satisfy the] New York City Board of Health. We brought it from the farm, right into the milk plant, weighed it, tested it, and cooled it, and [transferred it to] a tank and a truck to take it to New York City. You see, nothing like this had ever been done before. Crazy idea, you know. We got a company to build a two-hundred-can tank for us. See, nobody's got any money, everybody's on credit you know, this is the Depression time. You have to work, so we got it on credit. Everybody wants to sell, hoping to God you're going to make some money for them. So anyway, my brother Frank went with the first load, two hundred cans to Yonkers. Now this was revolutionizing the business, it was upsetting all the other milk companies in New York because they had it sewed right up, you know. It did so well we had to buy another tank, we got another truck, [and so on]. So the other companies see what's going on, then they want us to haul milk for them and then competitors got in, they were haulers like we were, and they started hauling milk down to New York and that's the way these things start, you know. And remember, this was before big highways, all the regular, old-fashioned roads you know, 35 miles per hour. Forty was going wide open, you know. [*Laughs*]

Then we got a call from the General Oil Company, who wanted us to also put a tank on and haul some gasoline for them. It was like a snowball. We had an idea; don't blame us if we've got the ambition to work. But we revolutionized the hauling of milk in these United States.

'Soldiers are Not Repair People'

Well, [getting back to World War II], the Mack Truck Company had a man from the War Department. I don't know what section, but they're having a pile of trouble at Pine Camp, with all their engines frozen up. They came up, talked to us about it, and so I said, 'I'll take some time and go up there and help them out for a couple of weeks.' Well, that couple of weeks lasted quite a while, but anyway I went up and introduced myself to General Henry Baird and I was there before the letter from the War Department got in. I worked for the War Department for oh, about two or three months, and then General Baird said to me, 'I want you to go with us [overseas], sign right here.' [*Laughs*] One day I'm a civilian walking around; the next day, I had captain bars on, right off the bat. I was an officer then and don't you think there were a lot of envious people? And I can't do a right-face; I never had any military training at all—I learned from being there, you know.

*

We got the problem straightened out and it cost the government a lot of money for this colonel who was ordnance officer, but he didn't even know what it was all about, never been in any cold weather. I have to get people in direct from General Motors. The soldiers are not repair people; they are maintenance people! Had a GM man come out here, I called him on the phone and talked to him, told him, 'You better get here to see all this trouble.' Well he came here, I showed him around. He can't believe what he's seeing, because this is a lot of money, a lot of money, and the base has hardly any trucks that can run! General Motors had to come in with I think 150 men, they had a good crowd, came right in and they had to rebuild all these engines. And I can always remember well this ordnance officer, he was a pretty good ordnance officer, but he didn't know anything about what he was doing in this situation. He had these engines taken out and I can always remember showing this top man from General Motors this whole bin full of [destroyed and damaged] engines—I won't repeat what he said; the pistons were all spoiled, you know. [*Laughs*]

It cost the government a lot of money, just because one guy didn't know his business. Now how many times do you suppose that's happened with other people [in the Army?]

*

Now I worked for the general, the chief of staff in G-4, and they'd put me in G-4 office in charge of maintenance and repairs on vehicles and all of that. I was 38 at the time.

I was with the Fourth Armored Division the whole time. We had like 13 or 14 in our division, after I'd got in there and got the government to send people in, and they did it with other divisions. We went down on Tennessee Maneuvers, helping the government bring in individuals to help educate these soldiers on maintenance of vehicles. Guys who had retired, you know, they'd come out and help them up in this North Country [weather] and I guess other parts of the country, too. They were mechanics and maintenance people who knew all about the equipment because these soldiers didn't know anything about equipment.

Then we were shipped to Camp Bowie, Texas, our whole division, and I'm doing the same job down there, then they changed the organization all around and they put me under the ordnance officer of the maintenance battalion, of course he wasn't [qualified], I had worked with him before. Well, he got mad because I had better relations with the generals, General MacArthur and General Whitney, you know. [*Laughs*] He was kind of envious of that, you know, you can see why.

Now, in Texas we were getting ready to go overseas, but before that, this character put me in as company commander, took me out of G-4 and put me in as company commander—remember, I can't even do right-face, I've never had any military training! The company commander is supposed to get up and order these 230 men around, get them lined up, march them out to 800 men in the battalion.

Well I never did a bit of that, what am I going to do? So after a while, they got my Dutch up, and I says, 'I'll fool them,' and I took two good training sergeants and we went a ways from the camp down in Texas where nobody could see us, [and they taught me] over four days. Everybody bets, you know; they were all betting whether Hillman would make it or not. Oh, they had a great time in the whole battalion, 800 men in a battalion, everybody knew everybody, because you live right together. Well, I never heard who made out on the bet; they wouldn't tell me, you know, but I knew they were doing it. I had good relations with all the soldiers you know, and a lot of the officers look down on the soldiers, and so anyway I went out and marched them right up you know. Even if I hadn't used the right commands, they still would have done it because I got along good with the boys, and after I did it for a week it was old habit. Then one day they took me out of command of the company, and I wasn't doing a darn thing [wrong]. I had been married 18 days when they took me out of command of the company, and I was wondering where they were going to send me—to another training company? Well, it wasn't that at all. I had to go up to see the chief of staff to report to him, and he handed me a sheet of paper and he said I'm going with 330 men. This is early 1943; I had five days' time to head on the train to New York City and England, just like that you know, 'Top Secret' on the paper they give you. Nobody could say anything; no sir, couldn't tell [my new wife] a damn thing. Top secret means top secret. We were going to do something, I don't remember what it was, but anyway when I got this notice I said, 'I've got to cancel, I can't do it.' I never dared ask her how worried she was, you know. But I was on the 5 o'clock train with all these men headed for New York City, then we went from New York City to England. And I'll tell you it was some different place than what we've been used to. Oh, big change, big change! It was all blacked out, and let me tell you, when you had a blackout, you had blackout. You weren't running no lights like we've got lights here, wouldn't have a light in here, you'd have to have special curtains for your windows so the light wouldn't show out. There were airplanes going over dropping bombs down if they see a light, they know it's down further—that's what happened all over England; their blackout was blackout.

Waterproofing School

As the spring of 1944 unfolded, every vehicle destined for the beaches of Normandy required 'waterproofing to a depth of fifty-four inches with a gooey compound of grease, lime, and asbestos fibers.'[9]

I was in the Cheltenham, this is about 14 miles from the coast. Traveled all around there because I was in, had a lot of men with me and we were getting everything organized there, gearing up for the invasion.

---

[9] *waterproofing to a depth of fifty-four inches*- Atkinson, Rick. *The Guns at Last Light: The War in Western Europe, 1944-1945*. New York: Henry Holt & Co., 2013. 27. Atkinson continued: 'A single Sherman tank took three hundred man-hours to waterproof, occupying the five-man crew for a week.'

Our division moved troops in at night, I'll say that. So, I had to meet them and take them to where they were going to live, and then after a while everybody got over here, got in their place, then we had maneuvers and everything else. I still stayed on the G-4 section, I didn't have any troops under me, and I was doing inspections, looking at old equipment.

Captain Hillman received special commendation in England at the beginning of the invasion for superior work in the waterproofing of vehicles of the headquarters of the Third United States Army.

I ran a waterproofing school down in Wales for all the vehicles that were going into France, driving off the ships and going into the water, some of them pretty deep, until they made a big ramp early. You would be sitting in the jeep with the water coming right up on you, so you'd better have it running so we greased all your electrical stuff, that's the main thing. We had the whole division have their vehicles waterproofed [for the invasion], and everybody had to know how to do it. So I ran that waterproofing school and I can always remember General Patton, me getting a call from headquarters to report to the general. Then I get the notice, I have to get men to come with me to waterproof and make sure his division or his headquarters, 600 men, were all schooled in waterproofing to go in. He sent his men down there to the school so they knew how to do it, and we were just checking them over making sure they were doing it right, because you'd be surprised that without waterproofing, the most stupid little thing will stop your engine, shorting any exposed electricals right out, and that'd be it, you'd be a sitting duck.

[I was in charge of that] for everything going into Europe. I used to have these boys come down, they'd head [another] school once they all got taught at [my] school. A certain number would come down and I'd take them and see if they could run through my test; I'd drive [through seawater] right up their stomach, have them do it again and check them and you know, people are so anxious to want to pass and get through that they don't listen to what you're telling them. Two and a half [ton trucks] weren't too bad but you take a jeep, that's the one that was hard. Just everything was [in] water right up to your stomach.

Wheeling and Dealing

I was traveling all over on the maintenance deal and I wanted to get something for myself. I thought I'd stop into this English plant so I go in, see the fellow there that I met, and I wanted to get something while he went to go have tea. I was sitting in the chair there and I'm looking around and I see a great big aircraft engine. He came out and I said, 'What are you doing with an aircraft engine there?'

He says, 'All plants around here got them lying there,' and I said, 'Why do they do that?' They didn't want to put them all in one place because they'll bomb the plant, you'll lose one engine, wouldn't lose them all.

I said, 'What are you going to do with it?' and he says, 'I might get rid of it.'

So I said, 'You want to get rid of it?'

He says, 'Sure.'

I said, 'I'll be up tomorrow with a couple soldiers with me and we'll look it over. If it's good, we'll take it.'

'Oh,' he says, 'that'd be great.' No paperwork. So we do just that and we load it up in our pickup, took it down to our maintenance battalion and we got that engine and I says to the guy, 'Other plants around here?'

'Oh yes,' and he named some plants and I said, 'How about writing the names down?' So he does. So I get a pickup and a soldier, and we go to these plants and ask them if they have engines, and they all want to get rid of them, and we take them. We ended up with thirteen engines and we went into the invasion [force], went into Europe right after the infantry went through first, you know. We're about 13, 14 days in. Had to drive through the water and then you've got to take off, we were about five miles in. Well, there was an old engine by the side of the road and one of those new ones [we brought]. I took their wrecker, because these engines were big heavy things, and picked it up, brought it over, and put it in the tank. Put it together and the boys took off, going with their outfit. The big trouble with the ordnance in the service, again, was a lot of guys get to ordnance and they don't know anything about equipment. It was easy for me because that was my business, you know.

And I was doing that all the way through Europe. Then, after everybody got in Europe, I was on supply. Tanks and jeeps and big guns and all of that, not rifles or pistols or anything, but automotive equipment. My job for the ordnance was to have a bank of maybe 60 or 70 men to go back to a depot to get the equipment and bring it back to ordnance. Then the line companies would come down and pick their equipment up, and you have to know what you were doing, you don't want to get them lost. You got to have fuel in them and everything. Sometimes they came from 100 miles, maybe 110 miles away.

Well in Europe that's what I did, take care of them, get the supplies, because I knew the equipment. Why, the railroad trains, they used to bring equipment into Metz, France, big dump. I pulled in there one day and there was a train full of new tanks made in Schenectady, New York, where they built these tanks, put them together, Ford engines and everything. But they had a lot of trouble with them; somebody over here should have been shot because they weren't doing a good inspection, and I found it cost a lot of money because most people weren't any good on engines. And I can brag about this; I know the first new ones we got off right off the train, came right in from the ships, and they put them on the trains and it could drive right off—anyway, the ones we backed off the train, we had three of them come off, boy those engines sound good, and the fourth one didn't come off [sounding] good.

I said to the soldiers, 'Well, I guess we've got a job. You've got a bad spark plug.'

Well, they bet me a bottle of cognac, kept telling me it's all right.

I said, 'I'll bet you this bottle of cognac that it isn't.'

Well they could taste the cognac, you know. I could tell whether my ear was good because I worked on Chevrolets and Ford engines and I could tell in the old days if something was missing or not. Most people couldn't do that. So anyway, boy, they could taste the cognac. Oh, they pulled out a big metal plate, this was a lot of work, you know, about 3 ½ feet squared, maybe 5 square feet. Had to take it off you know, it's heavy on the back end with the tank shells. They get in there, so we got the plate off and we start in on the left side on the V8 Ford and they tug a plug and the next one and boy, they get four of them pulled, all good, they can taste the cognac. Then they go down the other side, pulled three out of four plugs, which are fine, and now they are sure they are going to have it and they touch that fourth silver tip and up she comes, and I said, 'Boys, I guess I'm going to have to drink all that cognac myself.' It was bad. [*Laughs*] But they got so they wouldn't question me, I know what I'm doing; well, the people on the engines, they didn't know a damn thing about engines. How could they know, they never worked on them if they ran well! With my ear, I could tell right away if that spark plug was missing, or loose in the tank. Quite a few tanks we saved; one had four spark plugs missing or loose in the tank! Brand-new tanks! Somebody in the factory right here in Schenectady where they were made, they didn't check those. Either it was sabotage intentionally—and that's what I told the ordnance colonel, maybe it was sabotage—or they didn't have anybody that knew a damn thing about them. So when the war is going on, I'm keeping [the army] supplied with tanks and jeeps and two and a half ton [trucks and half-tracks] and all that, right across Europe. You had to be living on your own, you know.

Mr. Hillman received a citation for fixing a supply problem situation regarding the relief of Bastogne during the Battle of the Bulge.

Well, they had to have the equipment in order to win the battle. That's why I was [charged with] bringing the equipment in, in from Third Army to our division, to give her tanks or jeeps or whatever it is. See, I had to keep them supplied; as soon as they lose them, I had to go out and get them. My last big order was for 62 pieces of equipment, brand-new because they lost them totally, you see. We had been getting into Germany, and getting into Germany you're losing [touch with the supply chain]. Boy, I was busy all the while picking up the equipment; had a driver with me, I had to take a truck and to take men because I was picking up 62 pieces and I had 6 men with me. They came from the boat, to the railroad, right into Metz, which was a supply depot for all kinds of ordnance for the Army.

And all the divisions come in there to get it, the same as I was doing you see. I know, it cost me, oh seven or eight bottles of cognac to get a big wrecker away from somebody else. [*Laughs*] First you've got to deal with all these ordnance officers in there and sergeants and everything, and you don't go in and try to throw your weight around. If you do, forget it. You'd be at the end of the line. So it didn't cost me anything but I need some cognac. I'd send the guys to where I could get it, 'liberated cognac,' you know. [*Laughs*] I knew how to wheel and deal.

Mr. Hillman received the Bronze Star medal for meritorious service and exemplary devotion to duty while on the continent; 'During this period Captain Hillman personally convoyed the majority of the replacement vehicles from the supporting depots to the rapidly advancing Division. When available personnel for driving the replacement vehicles became critical, Captain Hillman personally drove vehicles from the depots to the fighting troops.'

*

The Concentration Camp Boy

When the war ended, I was way over into Austria. I had a Mercedes Benz touring car that was 'liberated' and I had the gas, and a couple other guys and myself we drove right around Austria. Oh, nice country, nice homes, you know.

I was in Munich three or four times. I can tell you a good story. In Luxembourg, my office was right next to where the German Gestapo had their office, oh, nice office, so we took it right over. Well, right next door to it was a mother and she had three or four sons. She could speak English, a little English. Anyway, she had a son who said something against the Gestapo and they put him in a concentration camp. I took his number down and wrote the name of the concentration [camp]. No name, just a number, and I said, 'If I get near that kid I'm going to retake him, I'm going to get up to see him.' Well, this was across the Rhine River quite a ways over, middle of Germany now, 25,000 people in that camp. When we got over there, our ordnance battalion had headquarters right near there, [in Munich].

So, I went up to the concentration camp to see what happened, the prisoners had to stay there—the first ones the Army let them go free, and boy, if that didn't cause a lot of trouble. These people are hungry. Where are they going to get anything to eat? Nothing to feed them. They were stealing, going in and doing everything to get something to eat. So, after that first time, they had about, I don't know, four or five thousand guys let loose, you see. Of course, these concentration camps had twenty, thirty thousand people in them. These were big affairs. No little bit of a thing. They were big and [now we've] got to hold the people in there, so you can control them. They've got to have food; they've got to have water. They've got to have a doctor, the whole thing, you know.

Well, I went up to the gate there and I had them call over for this number, this kid. I didn't know his name, just the number. Finally, this young guy came down and I had a letter to show him. Oh, he smiled and brightened right up! He'd never seen me before, but that was his mother's handwriting. I told him I was going to get him home. So, I got across to him and I took him down to our camp and our battalion.

He was just about sixteen or seventeen years of age, I was going to feed him up, you know. George Potter, our battalion doctor, says, 'What you want to do, you want to kill that kid? Just give him the same as he's been having.' That's what I had to do, I found out. When people get out of concentration camps they go out and steal or eat too much or something and they die. You can't do that, you see. So I just gave him enough for him to have something to eat. Now I've got him, but how am I going to get him from the middle of Germany over to where he lived outside of Luxembourg? So, I finally told my sarge I had to go to Paris. We're turning things in now. The war was all over and we got word that the Germans all gave up. Anyway, then you've got to take care of the people in the towns and everything. It's a big operation, no little deal. So anyway, I had a sergeant; I had to take some stuff to turn back into the service [headquarters] back to Paris. They had a reception area where [they accounted for government property turned back in], how many watches you turned in, binoculars and all this stuff; being in ordnance we get that stuff to turn back into headquarters]. So I take this kid with me, they gave me extra gas and we take four or five cars. [Him getting home on his own] wouldn't have been cheap.

I took the kid home and went on to Paris for me to deliver this stuff. Well, about fifteen or seventeen years afterwards, our division had a tour of the battlefields of Europe where we landed during the end of the war. We stopped in Luxembourg and I went into the house. The mother was still there and wasn't she so happy to see me! This boy was there, too. Well, I'll tell you I stayed there the rest of the night. [*Laughs*] Too much food, too much drink.

*

I was all over Germany after the war. [When the battalion left suddenly for the war], I remember it was a Friday and my wife came to the apartment and said, 'Oh, I've got a good supper to fix for you tonight.'

I said, 'That's great, I'll enjoy it.' Lying like the dickens you know, I couldn't tell her what I was doing and left my Chrysler and everything I owned, but she didn't realize what I was doing. I didn't come home that Friday night, but being in the service she didn't think anything about that, though I was on the train headed for New York with all these soldiers. She had a good dinner cooked for me at home [and I had said], 'Oh yes, [I'll be there for dinner]'; I just didn't tell her what year. [*Laughs*]

The Army wanted to know if I wanted to sign up again. I didn't want to sign up. I wanted to go home.

After the war, Mr. Hillman continued to innovate, even to the point of corralling politicians and New York State Governor Nelson Rockefeller to get a major north-south interstate highway built—I-87, the Adirondack Northway—which created an economic boom for the towns between the state capital at Albany and Montreal, Canada; it all happened because of a rural farmboy's ambition. His company's highly specialized transportation services even delivered the nation's Christmas tree to Washington, DC during the Johnson and Nixon administrations. He died at the age of 103, five years after this interview took place.

CHAPTER FOUR

The Driver

Frederic Sheppard served in the 321st Glider Field Artillery Battalion and the 506th Parachute Infantry Regiment of the 101st Airborne Division in Europe during World War II. He participated in the D-Day invasion and several others; in this account, he speaks of coming of age as the war began, and of a terrible disaster that befell young American troops on the eve of the Normandy invasion, in England.

Frederic G. Sheppard

I was born on June the 8th, 1924, in Yonkers, New York. I finished grammar school, and I went to high school, two different schools. The second one was a military school in Washington, D.C., military and business, called Theodore Roosevelt Business School. I got back up north again and continued my high school education; I got as far as November of my senior year, and I got drafted out of school. I couldn't finish my last year of school, which my father got very upset about.

On December 7, 1941, I was in a movie theater in Poughkeepsie, New York. A friend of mine and I double dated, and we had a couple girls with us, we went to the movies. I don't know the name of the movie, but [a news flash began scrolling] across the bottom of the screen, 'The Japanese bombed Pearl Harbor!' So, we just looked at it; it didn't hit us right away. And all of a sudden, in fact in the whole theater, all of a sudden, we heard everyone gasp at once at the news.

*

I was with the artillery and I was put in basic training, and then I was classified as I think 1B, limited service. I had just finished a bout with pneumonia and I was down to 120 pounds, and I went up and got my physical, and they said, 'Okay, you passed, but you're going to be limited service.' But in twelve weeks, I went from 120 to 172 pounds. The army life agreed with me. My dad told me when I left that morning, he says, 'I'll give you some advice.' He says, 'If they can dish it out, you can take it, but don't be a smart aleck about it.' And that's the attitude I took when I went in. I tried to excel at everything in basic training; at the bayonet course, I almost had to pay for two gun stocks—I broke the gun stocks on the bayonet! A group of us got called to the train station and we were going to ship out, but we didn't know where, and there were about eight of us left there standing. They didn't call our name off, and to make it a long story short, I wound up in the 106th Infantry Division, being so enthusiastic about training. [*Laughs*] But we stayed there, about eight of us, and the 106th shipped out [without us], who knows where. It wound up that they got annihilated in the Battle of the Bulge, the 106th and the 28th. And there we are, we're standing there again, and we wound up at Fort Meade, Maryland. And we took these unusual courses in lectures and nomenclature on equipment. We spent three days in tanks, and we spent half a day on this plastic explosive. I think it was called C-3 or C-4, which I never saw again the rest of the war. And we went through a weapons carrier, we did some grenade tossing and you know, but then we got shipped to Nyack, New York, for the port of embarkation to Europe.

We're on the North Atlantic for ten days, and nine days of it was stormy. It was a British cruise ship converted to a troop ship, the *Capetown Castle,* which later burned to the waterline. We had British rations, and we complained about [everything] and one of the British sailors said, 'Don't complain, Yank, as long as this storm lasts, we won't get torpedoed!' I guess it was too rough for the subs to surface or the torpedoes to hit their target.

[We were in a convoy], I was shipped out at night; the first morning we were on the southern flank of the convoy on the outside—we didn't care too much for that—and the next morning when we woke up, we were in the center of the convoy! We had baby aircraft carriers, we had I guess destroyers and whatever, troopships, and merchant ships. The following day, we were in a bad spot, we were on the tail end. That's where the Germans picked them off; they worked from the tail end up, and if your ship gets crippled somehow, the subs go after it like a shark after a wounded fish. But we got over there without incident, and we landed in I believe Liverpool, and we went to a 'repple depple' [replacement depot], about 100,000 guys in the place. They all came in on a boat and they gotta be assigned.

Well, what we wound up doing every single day, this is now October, we did the coal detail or we did garbage detail. We unloaded trucks, loaded trucks, and we couldn't wait to get out of there, and I mean we were filthy. Garbage and coal, we were filthy rotten dirty at the end of the day, and everybody wanted to get out of that place. So, they had the bulletin board, we watched the bulletin board for our names to come up, see, and they wouldn't come up. But there was a notice on there that they're forming a new division over in England, and it was going to be, you're going behind the enemy lines. They called it something; it wasn't covert operations or anything like that, but a new division, we decided, hey, we'll sign up and our chances of promotion will be good. So, about six of us went down and we listened to this guy. I think he was a captain, telling us about this division. You get jump boots, you get flight pay, you get this, you get that, and you would go in behind the lines, secure an area. So, I said to a fella, I forget his name, I said, 'What do you think?'

And he says, 'Anything to get out of this place.'

I said, 'Okay, let's go.'

So we signed up, and they told us up there it's going to be an airborne division. And we said, paratroops? They said yeah. Down at Fort Bragg, we used to watch these guys at the 101st jump out of the planes, and when they said they'd make it an extra $50 a month, well, we liked that. So, we're going to go to the paratroops. Now, this captain never denied it, see.

So about two days later, we're lined up in our 6x6 truck in England, and we're going down the country roads, and we lined up at this farm. It's called Whatcom Farm. We come out of the truck and there's this thing there with no motor on it. It's got wings and everything. I said, 'What the hell is that?' This guy says, 'Uh-oh, it's a glider.' Of course, the only gliders I know are down in Elmira. So, we got up, we lined up. Boy, we didn't like this idea at all, but we stuck it out.

And they sent me to a gun battery, I think it was A Battery, and we had four guns. Anyway, all you did was dig, fill sandbags, and then dump them out, fill the hole in after you pull the artillery piece out. I said, it's not for me. So, I went to the orderly room, and talked to the corporal down there who was the orderly or the captain's secretary, and I said, 'I gotta get out of the gun section.'

I said, 'Look, I got a military license to drive up to a 6x6, pulling trailers, pulling guns.'

And he says, 'I'll see what I can do.'

A few days later, they were looking for a driver on a Saturday. I had been to town with the guys, and it's a two-mile walk and two miles back. I mean, you're drilling all day long, you're tired. If you want to go out and have a beer, shoot darts, you had to walk. So, I didn't go out too much.

So, they needed a driver, and I just walked out of the company orderly room, and when I heard they said they needed a driver; all their drivers are out on pass or something. This was a Saturday, and I just went back in and I said, 'I got a military license.'

I said, 'Where we gotta go?'

He says, 'Put on your ODs, report to the motor pool. What's your name?'

I told him. I ran back, put my dress uniform on, and I went down to the motor pool, gave me a dispatch. I had to take two officers to London in a jeep, and that started; I was assigned to the motor pool. And I got to see Stonehenge, I'm sure you heard of that, and I got to see that. It was dusk when we got there. Took a captain there one day.

My captain, he was a prince, I says, 'Captain, where are we going?'

He says, 'We're going to Stonehenge.'

'Oh,' I says, 'where's that?'

He says, 'Show you when we get there.'

So, we hustled right along, we got there about dusk. I got a couple pictures, and I look at this thing. I said, 'Who did this?'

He says, 'Nobody knows.'

I says, 'You're kidding.'

So anyway, I had a good career. They always knew that I was around if they needed a driver for a truck or an officer had to go someplace, I was there. The only other driver that was around would be the colonel's driver, and of course the colonel, you don't take the colonel's driver.

Guard Duty

One exciting thing, I had to pull guard duty one night. One night, so it was a 24-hour period, and they put me up on a hill overlooking a battalion area, and they say, 'Now you go down along the fence, this wire fence, and then you cut across where the wooden fence is. Always keep the fence on your right. Then you come back up the hill again.'

And this is all on top of the hill, and then you come around the thorn tree, there's a thorn tree, right. It was like an apple orchard; they had that thorn tree there, so he leaves me. And I made maybe two trips, and I used the thorn tree as a stop and go, take a break, sit down, whatever, careful where you sit because some of the branches come down, and you sit on them, and boy you really get stabbed. [*Laughs*]

So, I stood up and I heard this plane, very faintly, I heard the plane. It wasn't laboring. It wasn't racing or anything like that, and it was like way up, I could just about hear it. All of a sudden, I hear a 'psst, bang!' It was a flare. That plane dropped a flare, and I guess it was timed so it'd light up so many feet above the ground. Well, I want to tell you, mister, I was scared! I'm all by myself up there, see, so I put one in the chamber, a live round in the chamber, and I froze and then I slowly slid back and I went right back into the thorns of the thorn tree, and I didn't care. All I wanted to do was get the hell out of that field of view as it burned. I don't know if you've ever been there in a flare, but the flare's coming down and shadows are moving, a branch, a tree, or a post. Everything is moving all around me. I don't know if it was the enemy or what that parachuted in, and I got through it all right, and that was about the most interesting, the first really scary thing I'd been in was that flare, because we were told the Germans will parachute in at night, but fortunately we weren't on the coastline; they had the Home Guard taking care of the coastline.

The Pathfinder

Then we got alerted for Normandy and I had a friend of mine who had wanted to be in a parachute infantry regiment, but he wound up in the artillery, see. And he and I became real good friends, and he finally signed up to be a pathfinder for Normandy. Now a pathfinder goes in like 24 hours before the invasion starts, and then the jumpers go in. In Normandy, the jumpers went in about 12 hours ahead of time roughly, and a pathfinder goes in [ahead of them] and he sets up a transmitter, and he sets up a beacon. Now he's got communications, and of course it's turned down very low. Oh, he had to go to school and learn Morse code. I remember he told me that. He disappeared for a while.

Well anyway, never heard anything about him after that. Never heard a thing, but after Normandy we got back in July, I guess, we got back to England, back to Whatcom Farm. Captain Williams [was the one who] told me about Anthony. He didn't want to be called Tony; he'd rather be called Scag. His name was Scagliari or something like that. Well anyway, Scag had a teammate, you know a two-man team, and his teammate landed okay at night as a pathfinder, but Scag went through the roof of a barn and both his legs were broken. This was the story that came back to us, and his partner had to leave him, and nobody knows whatever happened to him. He was with the 502nd—we called it the Deuce—and we don't know if he got killed or captured or what.

On April 28, 1944, a secret naval exercise code-named TIGER commenced to practice the landings of Normandy at Utah Beach.

The Disaster

So we were getting ready for Normandy, like gee whiz, we were down the southern coast, but before that happened, you may know it, you may not know it, but there was a real disaster—we lost 700 men before Normandy even started. There was a place called Slapton Sands, S-L-A-P-T-O-N, Slapton Sands, where the coastline resembled Normandy, the Utah Beach areas, we found out much later. And they were going to practice the invasion there, landing on the beach, and Slapton Sands was the ideal place. They had troop ships down there. Our division never participated in it, but the British subs and some British gunboats or something were supposed to protect the US Army on this invasion, because they had U-boats all over the place, see. Well, the British fell asleep and we had a U-boat come in, I guess one U-boat, and they had something like PT boats, something like that come in and kill 700 of our men! We had 700 casualties, US Army, okay? Far as I know, none of the 101st, and they kept it all quiet. Oh, it was a real disaster.

Swift-moving German torpedo E-boats darted in among the lumbering LSTs packed with men and heavy vehicles under cover of early morning darkness, sinking two immediately and heavily damaging a third, and then disappeared into the open water. Nearly 750 soldiers and sailors were killed, and hundreds more were missing, many succumbing to hyperthermia and drowning before they could be plucked out of the water. The magnitude of the disaster was not known for years, as the Normandy landings could not be compromised. Corpses washed ashore for weeks as the high command sweated it out until all the bodies of officers killed who had top-secret knowledge of the upcoming invasion were accounted for. One veteran later recalled, 'In comparison to the E-boat attack, Utah Beach was a walk in the park.[5]

Normandy

Well, now we go back to getting ready for Normandy. We were down there about ten days before. My job of course wasn't what you call really important for administration or anything like that, and they sent us, nonessential, sent us down there first. I had to turn in my jeep at a compound, and I said, 'I don't like doing this.' And the MP said, 'Don't worry about it. It'll be over there. It might be there before you get there.' That's the last I saw it. [*Laughs*] And we wandered around. We'd go here, we'd go there, all walking, okay. We were supposed to originally go by glider and they told us the British ran out of their Horsa gliders; they're made out of balsa. And they took some of our gliders, and we wound up going in by boat, so let me jump ahead.

I took seven glider rides while I was in the 321st Glider Artillery, and I saw four smash-ups, and we had smash-ups in training. They were for strange reasons, and so anyway, we were glad to go by boat. We took the risk with torpedoes and mines; we said we'll take our chances. And we wound up on the *Susan B. Anthony*, headed toward the Utah Beach area. Now what we were doing down off the shore of Omaha, I don't know. But somewhere along the line I lost a whole day. I thought I landed the sixth, and I found out about six months ago, [it was the seventh].

It was off Omaha Beach, we hit a mine, and sunk, but we didn't lose a man, and we had about 2000 on the boat.[10] It was a converted cruise ship, and we were transferred onto a British destroyer and British corvette, and as I say, the story goes we never lost a man. This is Omaha; we were supposed to land at Utah.

---

[10] *It was off Omaha Beach, we hit a mine, and sunk, but we didn't lose a man*- The ship *Susan B. Anthony* was sunk June 7 by a mine while cruising through a previously swept channel; all 2,689 people aboard were rescued with no fatalities.

They moved us west of where we were supposed to be, Utah Beach, and we were trying to signal some landing craft to come and take us there, Utah. Well, once these guys got to the beach, they turned around, you know the Navy, they turned around and got the hell out of there. They didn't want to pick us up, see, and take us to the beach. They'd already been there; they didn't like it. So finally we got to the beach and we landed, and it was a quiet area compared to the rest of it. There wasn't much artillery coming in or mortars or small arms fire, machine gun yes, and we got up on there and we ran like hell. There were dunes, and tall grass, and we went uphill; it was soft and you couldn't run too fast through the soft sand. And then we ran down, because we get up near the top and the machine guns open up, so we ran back down again, crouched low, and started to run toward where most of the action was, because our battalion and division was supposed be landed up in here, except the jumpers; they went in the night before.

So finally, we got a break and there was only two of us now. We had this one lieutenant who says, 'Follow me,' you know, he says, 'On the way, grab a crate of supplies.' So a couple of guys went, me and a friend of mine, we went out to the beach, we weren't going with this guy. We got up over the loose grass, and we got into like an orchard, and we wandered around here, there, and the supplies were coming in, see, and they were stacking them. They were trying to grab us to stack this stuff, see, and we'd take off, and finally we got to our outfit, and we had one gun. That's all we had, a 75 mm pack howitzer, the barrel on it is not too long.[11] Of course everybody's not sitting around; we're moving and trying to keep from getting shot. We moved around, and we finally got another gun. I was like a two-legged mule, carrying stuff on my back, under my

---

[11] *75 mm pack howitzer*-artillery piece designed to meet a need for a howitzer that could be moved across difficult terrain. It could be broken down into several pieces to be carried by pack animals.

arms, going here, coming back, going over there, changing positions. We were support, for the 2nd Battalion of the 506th, which we did most of the war, and if you had read or seen the movie, 'Band of Brothers,' that was Easy Company. We supported Easy Company, and in the book, not so much in the VHS tapes, but in the book, Dick Winters started off as platoon leader, and it said that he would claw for artillery and the British would support him [with his] artillery... We supported him, okay, the 321st supported him, and I recognized most of the names of these villages they were trying to capture, they'd get into and hold, and finally one day my captain says, 'Look, are you tired of lugging this stuff?' He says, 'I am.'

I said, 'Yeah.'

He says, 'I didn't tell you this, but see if you can find a truck or a jeep, will you?'

So he says, 'It doesn't make any difference if it's enemy or what, we'll somehow paint it over or something.'

So I went, and I wound up back near the beach. Things were hot, but I caught a glimpse of a jeep down by the beach see, not real close, maybe 50 yards from the water; it was buried, all four wheels, up to the hubs. So I went down there, and there was a beachmaster—they're bad boys, you don't want to cross them up, especially the British. He was up there yelling orders and everything, so I go running down to this thing, you know? It's in good shape, it's not wet or anything. I can see it's not going to move, but I popped the hood up, everything looks all right. Slam the hood down, buckle it. I get the shovel off the side of the jeep and I started to dig, you see, so like it'd go a few feet; I figure you get a quick run, I could get out and get right up on the high ground. I moved maybe a foot or two, then along comes a 6x6 truck, I think it was three guys in the back, and two up front.

He says, 'We'll give you a hand.' He says, 'Take this rope.'

I took the rope, they tied it, I tied it, out comes the jeep, and they took me for a ways. But they took me the wrong way, you know, it was going into the heavy fire! The beachmaster is screaming his head off at all of us, at both of us. I pulled the rope and the knot out of the rope, and I took a left turn, and [took off].

I thought I was going to get stuck again, buried, because the sand now was soft and dry, you see. Down near the water where it was wet, and it was packed. But I hit some hard pan, and I got up over, and anyway, I got back, I found the captain, and brought the jeep back. But on the way back, I had stopped. Now these bumpers on the jeep, front and back bumpers, had 'ENG' on it, and it had a number, which is an engineering battalion.

I stopped and put some mud on the front bumper and back bumper, [over it], and away I went. It had a whip antenna, which we needed. It had that on it. It had a radio and it had some stuff in the back. Full of gas, full water radiator. I had that jeep up until we went back to England, just after the Saint-Lô breakthrough. We were shipped back to England for R&R. But now we were called the Carentan Commandos. [*Laughs*] It was because we got as far as Carentan, I think. You gotta understand something, I never knew a whole lot about what was going on, you know? Because I was on the run, like almost 24 hours a day. I'd go here. Some officer would say, I need a jeep, I need you to drive a jeep. Well, Captain says, take him, go ahead. So I knew some of the names of some of the towns, some of the villages and hamlets. But, where they were, I didn't know exactly, I don't know. I'd have to look at a road sign or something. I did a lot of running through the fields. Of course, the roads were zeroed in, artillery had the roads zeroed in, even the little roads, you know, hard to hit the pavement. Anyway, we got back to England in July, end of July. Never saw that jeep again. They tell you it'll be there, it'll be there. You know?

I went back to being a chauffeur, and part-time truck driver. Then we'd go on what we'd call bivouacs and field maneuvers, make-believe war, to keep us in shape. We did a lot of calisthenics, got a lot of lectures. They were looking for pathfinders, and I was going to sign up for it. Everyone told me, 'don't do it, don't do it.' But I didn't ever do any jumps until after the war was over.

Mr. Sheppard went on to participate in Operation Market Garden (the airborne invasion of Holland), the enemy siege of Bastogne, and the Southern Germany Campaign, which will be detailed further in a future volume of this series. He was awarded the Purple Heart for combat wounds received at Bastogne and helped to liberate the Holzhausen concentration camp in 1945. He died in 2004 at the age of 79.

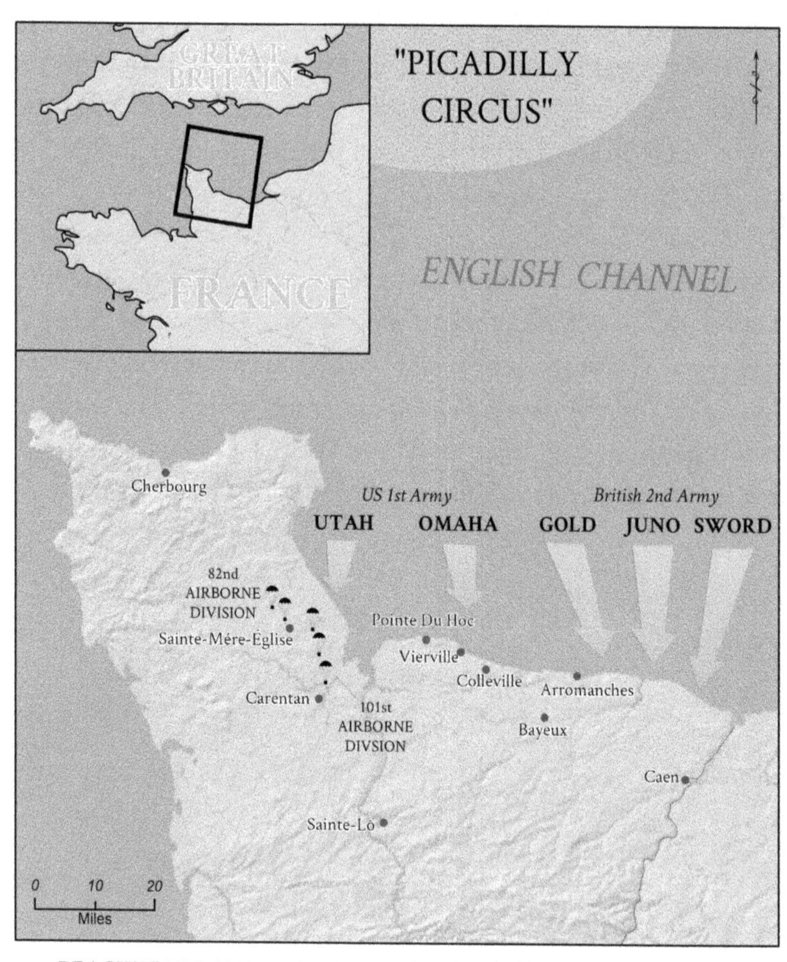

BEACHHEADS AND PARACHUTE DROPS: JUNE 6, 1944 - JULY 1944

The Invasion of Normandy. Map by Susan Winchell.

PART TWO

INTO THE SKIES

"You know, Oyler, the Germans have been kicking the hell out of us for five years and it is payback time.... [and] you'd be a damn fool not to be [scared]. But the trick is to keep moving. If you stop, if you start thinking, you lose your focus. You lose your concentration. You'll be a casualty. The idea, the perfect idea, is to keep moving.'

—Gen. Dwight D. Eisenhower to a paratrooper on the eve of the jump into Normandy, June 5, 1944[6]

CHAPTER FIVE

Airborne

In the first half-hour after midnight on June 6, 1944, C-47s carrying three Allied airborne divisions took off for their respective drop zones on French soil, followed a few hours later by troop and equipment-bearing gliders towed across the Channel. The American divisions, the 82nd and 101st, were tasked with descending on the Cherbourg /Cotentin Peninsula to carry out specific objectives and secure vital outposts and crossroads. Just over 13,000 paratroopers made the nighttime jump, but very few were close to their targets; only one of six regiments were delivered close to their objective, and thus able to fight as planned.[7]

The main objective for the 82nd Airborne was the crossroads town of Sainte-Mère-Église, which would become the first French town liberated by the Allies. Linking the vital port of Cherbourg in the north with the city of Carentan to the south, planners concluded that a sustained operational offensive in the region would be almost impossible. The jump was widely scattered; some landed in the Atlantic, and some were as far as 25 miles off course.[8] Closer to the town, some men were hung up in trees and slaughtered; one trooper of the 505th Parachute Infantry Regiment had his parachute caught on the spire of the town church and pretended to be dead before being cut down and taken prisoner.[12]

The 101st's objective was the high ground between Utah Beach and the peninsula's interior. The Germans had flooded the marshlands between the beach and that region; many paratroopers drowned before they could cut loose their heavy gear and chutes, and many who drifted far afield of the drop zone were captured. Still, despite disorientation and darkness, troopers rallied and managed to take the objectives, fending off counterattacks and awaiting those who would join the fight from the beaches. They would jump again into Holland in Operation Market Garden in an auspicious daylight mission three months down the liberation road, and be called upon to defend the major German siege at Bastogne during the coming Battle of the Bulge.

[12] *parachute caught on the spire of the town church*-The soldier was John Steele (1912-1969). The two sticks of paratroopers who descended over the town were illuminated by a fire caused by a stray incendiary bomb; many were killed. Steele was wounded and taken prisoner, but escaped 4 days later. He was awarded the Bronze Star and Purple Heart, and returned to Sainte-Mère-Église several times after the war.

CHAPTER SIX

The Paratrooper

Ellsworth Joseph Jones was an officer with the 101st Airborne Division, 502nd Parachute Infantry Regiment. Their mission on D-Day was to secure two of the causeways leading inland from Utah Beach and destroy an artillery battery on the coast.[9] *He was wounded on the fifth day of the attack. In a 2004 interview, the former mayor of Saratoga Springs, New York, gave his thoughts on the battle for the Cherbourg /Cotentin Peninsula, on being wounded, and the nature and folly of war.*

Ellsworth J. Jones

I was born in Albany, New York, on January 6, 1918. I attended St. Mary's Academy in Glens Falls, New York; I graduated from there in 1936, I believe. I didn't continue any other education and I joined a National Guard unit in 1940; I had the distinction of being the first one, I was living in Corinth at the time, and quite a few fellows came down with me after that, and it was Company L, 105th Regiment, 27th Infantry Division.

We were all assembled. [The troop train] stopped at Whitehall first, I believe, and picked up the unit there, and the train came on down with Company K from Glens Falls, but as it came around a little bend where the station was, a young girl somehow got out on the track and got killed. We didn't see any of it, we knew there was a lot of commotion and so on, and they hustled us into the train. We went down to Fort McClellan in Alabama. I was there until I was accepted for officer's candidate school at Fort Benning, Georgia.

[Pearl Harbor was attacked when I was at] Fort McClellan, I think. There was panic for a little while, everybody was running everywhere, and nobody knew what was happening, they just said 'Get back from your leave,' and so on. At first, it was just a lot of excitement, nobody really knew which way to go, but that soon ended, because the officers got back and the calm [settled in]. They said, 'This is it, fellows,' you know, 'They're not fooling now,' and 'Here's what's going to happen. We're going to get our orders and we're going to move outta here and we'll find out about it, and you'll know about it soon enough, so just keep cool.'

[I was at] Fort Benning for officer candidate school for 90 days, they used to call us '90-day wonders'; I don't know that it was any wonder, but I was there 90 days. And while there, I met a gentleman, who later got killed in the service, but he wanted to go join paratroopers, he was all set for it. He had made some jumps out of private planes up in the air, and he prevailed on me, saying, 'Come on, let's go over and see what's going on.' I said, you know, 'I'm crazy enough,' but anyway, you got special pay, $100 a month, and we wore special hats and uniforms; we were in a class by ourselves—we were the best trained troops in the world, bar none. You know, it wasn't at our behest, it was the people that they had training us, and you got in shape, and you obeyed the rules, and it turned out that I was assigned to the 101st Airborne, Screaming Eagle Division.

We trained at Fort McClellan, Alabama, where the parachute school was. [We] had to go through a series of tests, endurance, mostly, you know, run until you fall down almost, run up and down those stairs until we thought we were wearing them out, or whatever, and we had good noncoms, no fooling around. You know, 'If it's too much just walk out the door and go, and go back' to Company L, or whatever you're going to do, but, 'We don't have time to baby you, so get in or get out.' And that was a great attitude, because we knew where we stood. I had to make seven jumps to qualify, five day jumps, two night jumps, that's seven; much later, I became an instructor, and that's a tough job. If you got a guy in the door and he balks [going out], I never believed in throwing a guy out the door. You know, if he got killed or something, I would feel responsible. So I would say, 'Let's talk, come on, sit down here.' I'd tell the crew chief, 'Tell him to go around again, will you?' I said, 'Look, if you don't want to be a paratrooper, that's no problem, but go out the door and quit down there, don't quit up here, because if you quit up here, that's a mark on your record,' you know, all the forms and everything else—'You're a quitter,' and 'In combat [the guys]won't trust you,' and so on. I would say, 'I'll go with you. Hang on to me, I'll go with you, but let's get out, and get down there, and then you can say I've had enough and nothing will happen.' We had three guys do that.

Well, I went around. I had the experience and so they loaned me [out] to get them oriented, make them feel at ease; I was a good psychiatrist, I guess. I was a salesman of a sort in my own business, and instead of threatening them with court martial and all this, and losing their stripes or whatever, just say, 'Sit down, let's talk this over.'

[We went to England and] we trained with British troops. Training for D-Day, we had pictures, we had sand tables, we had everything they could give us. I landed right exactly in there where the sand table said I should.[13]

The Jump

My platoon was 30 men, and two officers. I was a first lieutenant; I had a second lieutenant. We were in one of the early planes, fortunately, [because the ground fire was intense as the Germans got their bearings]. We could see the German trucks and soldiers going to their positions, and I said to the crew chief, 'Kelly, what the hell are you trying to do, kill us all?' He got us down where I could step out, and I said, 'Give me 250 feet at least, will you?'

He said, 'Jonesy, shut up and get back there, I'm running the plane, I'll give you all [the altitude] you want,' and he did.

In the C-47s there are seats on both sides, and then there's a cable that runs down and comes right back to the exit door. There are two lights right down by where I sat, there's a red one and a green one. The red light would go on as you're approaching, you got three minutes or four minutes, so I'd stand up and say, 'Stand up and hook up.' Everybody gets up and they hook up; now, some place way back in the history of it, somebody was nervous and jumped out without hooking up. I would give the command to sound off for equipment check. 'Number 20, okay, 19, 17, 18, 16,' so on, and I'd always say, 'Give me that again, I didn't hear it'; I wanted to make sure. [And] I figured we're going across the Channel, and I don't want to jump in the Channel, because with this stuff on, I ain't going to make it. And now I can see, and it's just as plain to me now, I can see every farmhouse, I can see every road. I saw the river, though it wasn't much of a river that ran by there. I said, 'Stand up and close in on the door,'

---

[13] *sand tables*- Since ancient times, sand tables have been used in military planning and preparation, modeling terrain, obstacles, and other factors that troops will contend with in combat.

so they got in just as tight as they can, and I'd say, 'I want this plane emptied in two minutes,' or something like that—which is impossible; the guys on the other side of the plane, not the exit side, have got to go way down and come back, make a big U-type line. But they knew what they were doing.

Now, flak started to get a little heavier, and I think it was more ground fire than it was flak, I don't know, but it looked like we were starting to take some. So, I said to the pilot, 'Come on, Kelly, get me down there, let me walk in there anyway, will you? Give me a shot.'

He said, 'Jonesy, you're a worry wart, shut up and get back there, I'll take care of you.'

Now, these C-47s don't go too fast, and because the pilots were great, they'd slow the plane [before the jump] because the faster they're going, the more that propeller's going, the greater the shock. You get out, man, it hits like that [*slams fist into open palm*] and then, you know, if he can cut that engine a little bit ...

I had to get my guys out, I had to see that everybody got out, so I'm the last guy [out the door].

We jumped and came down around Sainte-Mère-Église; the force of the impact [can be tempered] when you're coming down, just before you get twenty-five feet or so, you have some control if you can pull that parachute down towards you; it will slow you down because it's full of air, but you're pulling it down and you can steer them a little bit. I thought we had had the best indoctrination that was possible. We had those sand tables, and the little houses and the streets, and it was like, you know, open your eyes, here you are—I could recognize every tree; that was highly successful.

We didn't get all of [the men together right away], some of them landed too far, but it only took us about eight minutes [to assemble]. And we had the Cricket.[14]

We had pathfinders in there, [but the opposition had been] pretty well documented, I mean, they took pictures, and they had everything that we wanted before we went, you could go and look it over, and we knew what our objective was. We had two. I guess you would call them anti-aircraft guns, and they're tough. We had hand grenades and it was a daring exploit, [with another platoon], I'll tell you that, for the American Army. We got the anti-aircraft guns. We had casualties, no question; I lost some good men there, every officer did, and I still have shrapnel in my diaphragm.

Our platoon took two casualties. We could see the German trucks going back, they were retreating, going back, and right down the road, and it was a beautiful moonlit night, beautiful night. You could see the tracers; I was happy, but the resistance wasn't what I had anticipated.

We were twelve or thirteen hours in that vicinity, I wasn't keeping time but I had my platoon leader, I had an assistant platoon leader, and I'd say, 'Find out what you can.' It was mass confusion, I don't know who, really, was to the right of me. I had a radio operator, but you got to be careful with that because everybody's on the radio, 'Where are you? What's your position? What's the situation?' So I had an assistant, a runner. I had a guy there and I didn't have to write it down, just say, 'Tell them here's where we are, here's what we're doing, we're getting low on ammunition, get something up here, and we need some relief,' and he'd go back by the beaches, and

---

[14] *Cricket*- The Cricket was a 2-inch brass signaling tool that made a sharp clicking sound when pressed down upon. Paratroopers could communicate under cover of darkness, regrouping with a single click answered by two clicks.

he was a pretty good salesman in civil life, because we'd get stuff when the rest of them didn't.

Wounded at Carentan

[I was fighting in the hedgerows for five days]; it was murder. [But] psychologically, we were the best troops in the world. There was nobody [like us]; I had all the training that they could give us, but [nothing prepares you for some things]. You know, in my platoon, the assistant platoon leader got shot right through the head, right through the helmet, dead, right there [*points to the ground just in front of him*]. That affects you, doesn't it?

My colonel was Robert G. Cole, Congressional Medal of Honor winner. We used to say, 'He has no fear, no nothing, he don't know nothing,' you know. He wanted us to win the war, and we weren't going to win it backing up or sitting down in the foxholes. You're going to win it by getting to Berlin, or wherever we were going to, and he got killed.[15]

On D+5, I got hurt; I still have the shrapnel in me. The enemy came out with an all-out effort, bombers and everything. They either had to get us back in the ocean or else it was all done for them.

We got by the college at Carentan, there was a college near a wooded area, and I was concerned with my platoon that they would have tree bursts.[16] One of my scouts got hurt and he came back and

---

[15] *Robert G. Cole*- (1915-1944) Cole was awarded the Medal of Honor for leading a famous bayonet charge near Carentan on June 11, facilitating the capture of that town on June 12. He was killed by a German sniper the following September in Holland; the award was announced two weeks later.

[16] *Tree bursts*-artillery shells that detonated on impact with treetops, causing hot metal shrapnel and wood fragments to rain down with deadly effect if men instinctually took cover by hitting the ground and spreading out.

he said, 'Lieutenant, there's something back over in there, and these guys have got a bead on us, they know right where we are.'

So I said, 'All right, let's see what we can do,' so I went back and got the guy on the radio and said, 'Get me some air support or get me some guns on the plane or the Navy,' because they're in there. At that time, we're trying to expand the beach and let the guys get off the LSTs and walk right up.

The Germans were firing at us and I said, 'We got to get up and see where it is.' Well, I went too far, and the Luftwaffe came over and bombed the heck out of us and I caught one of the pieces of shrapnel. I lost two good men there, both of them were killed, and I got hurt.

I got hurt and, man, they took great care of me, jeez, the guys risked their lives to go to get me, pull me back, put a plug in where the wounds were, I was bleeding so bad, got transfusions, and then I was sent back to the beach, and then back in an LST, and back in an airplane, back in a hospital, doctors coming in, you know, and nurses, and reassuring you, 'You're all right, you got a piece of shrapnel in your diaphragm.' The guy that dragged me out of there at risk of his own life deserved a medal, [and I got him one]. And then once we got back to the hedgerow a little bit, [there was an aid station nearby]. [I was able to breathe with this hole in my diaphragm], but it made a very peculiar sound, you know, the blood is rushing out. I spent that night there, and then the next day, I was taken to the beachhead and put on a hospital ship. I had two hand grenades, and they had the LSTs, the landing ship tank, and that could run right up almost on dry land, and they'd let that door down and the nurses were there, and the doctors were there, [classifying us], 'this one goes here, that one goes there,' 'give him a blood transfusion.'

Hospitals

Back in England, the doctor that came in; I was an officer, I had a private room, you know, big deal. They've got the X-rays, he said, 'You got a pretty fair-size piece of shrapnel in there. We're going to give you three or four days, and we're going to take that right out, okay?'

The nurse is in there, he goes out, so she says, 'Would you mind if I had a friend of mine come in and talk to you?'

'No.'

So, the guy comes in, he was a doctor. He said, 'I understand they're going to operate on you and take that out.'

I said, 'That's what they said.'

He said, 'Don't tell them I said so, but if it was me, I wouldn't let them touch me, I'd just say no, I want to just leave it there.' He said, 'You have that right, you tell them.'

He said, 'They go in through your ribs, a rib resection, and no one'll guarantee they'll get it either when they get in there, because of where it's located, so why don't you let it ride? [When you get stateside], you can go to the VA or you can go back to an Army hospital and have them take it out, no problem, but I don't think you're physically fit now either. You've just been through this shock.'

I said, 'What'll he say?'

He said, 'I don't care what he says, you just tell him no way.'

The first doctor was a major, and he came back and said, 'Well, tomorrow morning at 10:00, [we will do the operation].'

I said, 'Whoa, hold up. What do you mean? You're not going to operate on me, major.'

He said, 'What? I'm the doctor!'

I said, 'Yes, and I'm the patient.' I had to sign the waiver relieving the federal government of all responsibility, so I still have the piece of shrapnel [there today]. Every once in a while, I have a hemorrhage, but not often; I think it's been months since I had one. If I sneeze, my diaphragm expands and pushes it up.

I had two doctors come in [a while later, after transfusions and therapy], who asked me, 'How do you feel?'

I said, 'Great.'

'What do you want to do?'

'Well, go back!'

'Well, no, you can't,' the doctor said, 'I'm not going to sign off and send you back to being a paratrooper; I don't think you should jump again at this time.'

What could I do? I want to go back to the infantry, that's my home, but I can train soldiers, I can show them what I did wrong or what not to do, and I'm an asset, I'm not a liability anymore.

Then I got several assignments. I got assignments for indoctrination for troops that were just coming in, I got assignments of the general headquarters for offering information and suggestions, not to the general himself, but [questions from] his aides, 'What did you think of this?' And 'What do you think of that?' There were three of us, sometimes we didn't agree, but we would come to a consensus on what was the best way to do something, and the paratroopers were the best way. We were pretty tough troops, I'll tell you that.

[I did a stint as a commander of a PoW camp], not for long, but I did. And then I wanted a transfer, I wanted no part of that. I was prejudiced, I was, I really was prejudiced. I had lost some [good men], so let's skip that part.

'He Shouldn't Have Been There'

When we were discharged, we went through a process, which was great. They had psychiatrists and they'd say, 'How do you feel, how do you feel about the war?' And, I lost a brother, and I'm bitter, you know, he was a lot smarter than I was, and younger, and shouldn't have been called. He was in the Pacific theater, he was a pilot, his plane got shot down; it was never found. He shouldn't have been there! He was six years younger than me, he was just eighteen when he got called. There were two boys in our family, then I was gone into service, and then they put him in. I called my congressman and told him this.

He said, 'Well, we'll see what we can do.' The next thing you know, my mother gets the telegram [that he was killed].

*

After I was hurt, there were lots of casualties in my platoon, I didn't know the exact number. But we were scattered to hospitals all over England, like, I mean, I had a chest injury, I went to one hospital, it was really practically all chest wounds. Somebody else might've had a head injury, there was another one. Several of the men came back together after some years, I've had several meetings with some of them, and we re-fight the war again. I've been to a [couple bigger] reunions since, but it's different, see, and I suppose it sounds self-serving, but the group that I was with, most of them either got hit, or are dead, or are not interested anymore, or are incapacitated or something. I am one of the fortunate ones, really.

[I had gotten called back for Korea, and I left service in '52]. [Looking back at the war], oh, it changed my whole [outlook]. War is not an answer to anything, I don't care which side it is, it's never, you know, 'they hate us, we hate them,' it's that they're jealous because we have such a prosperity, and they don't, and I don't know what the solution is. War is no solution for anything, but it seems like it's just a brief respite between wars and peace, that's all it is now. And some way, some way, we've got to find out a way to be able to sit down at a conference table and express our positions and then come to [an agreement]. When I was in business, that's what we had to do; I couldn't have my way every time. And if I went to sell you something and I couldn't, I had to try to get your friendship then. That's the way I try to do it, to see what a good fellow you are, and we don't do that today. War, you know, I can't condone it. They know what the situation is and what our liabilities are and what could happen, but I just hate to see these young guys having to go to war, and, you know, the ring, the doorbell, and the telegram.

What fools we mortals be, I mean, really. I was in business and we seem to believe that might is [more important], and it isn't, and you lose good men and women...

Try to live your life and be as generous as you can.

Ellsworth J. Jones was a recipient of the Bronze Star, Purple Heart, and Croix de Guerre. In 2005, he was inducted into the New York State Senate's Veterans Hall of Fame He passed on December 31, 2006, at the age of 88.

CHAPTER SEVEN

The Glider Pilot

'They were the only aviators during World War II who had no motors, no parachutes, and no second chances.'

—General William C. Westmoreland on the glider pilots

The use of gliders in airborne combat operations in World War II was pioneered by the Germans in their invasion of the West in 1940, particularly in the Battle of France. Impressed with the stealth and swiftness of conducting troops to the battlefront, Great Britain and the United States embarked on their own development programs. In the age before helicopters, the engineless Waco CG-4A combat glider was built to be towed up into the skies by the C-47, carrying assault troops and cargo to strategic targets behind enemy lines. A canvas skin stretched across lightweight steel tubing for the frame, and the honeycombed wood floor could support the pilot, co-pilot, and 13 men, or an equivalent weight up to 4000 pounds. Dubbed 'flying coffins' by the men who flew in them, there was scant room for parachutes or any kind of protection, and little margin for error. Six thousand men were trained as pilots, and Meyer Sheff came into the training program via a typical Army miscommunication; another 'snafu' put him in the pilot's seat of a much larger British-built glider he had never flown before, on the eve of the Normandy D-Day landings.

Meyer Sheff

I was born on March 2, 1918, in the Lower East Side in Manhattan and I grew up there, my first 15 years in Manhattan. Then we moved to Brooklyn. From there, right after Pearl Harbor, I enlisted.

I was quite a reader as a kid. I read about trench warfare, where some sergeant blew a whistle, and everybody jumped out of the trench and were mowed down, a bloodbath. To my way of thinking, the generals still had the trench warfare syndrome [mindset] of running that war. I also read that no army moved more than 500 yards in either direction during the whole war. I was not going to be part of that bloodbath. I went down to Whitehall Street, told them I wanted to join the Army Air Corps because I was a mechanic, my father was a mechanic. I figured I'd work on airplanes. I had to take a test. Did very well, and they took me into the Army Air Corps at Selfridge Field, Detroit.

I didn't do any training. The Army being what it is, while I was being processed in Fort Dix, somebody looked at my record and said, 'You did extremely well on the test. There's no point in sending you to school.' They bypassed me on the assumption that when I got to the next base, I would join a team and become a crew sergeant and work myself up. When I got to Selfridge Field, I wound up hauling coal, cleaning out the kitchen, the grease trap, fire duty at night; you had to walk up and down to make sure there's no fires at the tents and camps.

I was miserable. I explained to the captain, 'They told me I would be on the line.'

He said, 'I'm sorry, son, but if you don't go to Army schools, you're considered an idiot. You're going to be doing this the rest of the war.'

I was sorely disappointed. One day, I passed the bulletin board and I saw an advertisement, 'Wanted: glider pilots.' You had to volunteer. The only way I could get out of that outfit was to sign up to be a glider pilot. That's what I did, and that became my career. The bulk of my training was at Dalhart, Texas, in the panhandle of Texas, right near the New Mexico border. You could see the horizon, make a 360° turn—nothing. Nothing but tumbleweeds. That's where I graduated. Of course, by that time, I was a staff sergeant. You had to be a staff sergeant, so I was promoted from buck private to staff sergeant for training. Apparently, from what I hear, you were not allowed to send a pilot overseas unless he was an officer. They came out with a rank called flight officer rank, a temporary rank. It said, 'The appointed will continue in force for the duration of the war and six months thereafter.' They don't have that rank anymore.

The first phase of training was in a single-engine Cub Taylorcraft. I don't remember how many hours, but we had to learn how to fly it. I remember the first lesson we got. The instructor took me up about 5,000 feet. Prior to that he said, 'I'm going to show you that this airplane is smarter than you are. It flies better than you can.' Took me up to 5,000 feet and put it into a spin. We're going down this way [*makes hand motion downward*]. He said, 'I'm going to let go of the controls. You don't touch anything.' Came right out of the spin; very stable airplane. I graduated from there and then we went into the sailplane. I tell you, that's the greatest thrill going. You're flying and all you hear is 'shoooosh'—you're riding air currents, thermals. I don't remember how many months we were at that, but maybe a month or two. Then we went into advanced training. Cargo gliders carrying troops, ammunition, guns, cannons, jeeps, things like that. I graduated from that and became a flight officer.

We trained on CG-4s, which is the American gliders. When we get to the part when I was at the D-Day invasion, I flew a Horsa glider. That's an interesting story by itself, but that's the training we had.

I remember a couple accidents. We were segregated into groups. One instructor had six or eight student glider pilots, he was a second lieutenant, an 'eager beaver' [type of] guy. He always wanted to be the first on the line early in the morning, the first one to take off on the training flight. What would happen, six guys would sit in there, one guy would sit in the controls. Then another guy would sit at the controls, take off, and the sort of thing like that.

While we're in it and ready to take off, another officer, I think he was a first lieutenant, commandeered the first flight. He made the second lieutenant and the glider pilots get out, because he wanted to be the first one off. We're talking about Dalhart, Texas, semi-desert, not a tree in sight. Tumbleweeds, but in the middle of all that, there was a brick building, like a shed made out of brick. Something happened on the flight and this guy ran into that brick shed and killed all the pilots.

Later, in North Carolina, Laurinburg-Maxton Air Base, I was on a training flight there, and made one of these landings where somebody 'saturated' the field and I ran into something and I got banged up, but nothing big, hardly worth mentioning, really. The only time I really slammed in is when on the D-Day flight into France. I ran into a hedgerow. They had to chop us out.

Overseas

We went overseas to England. [On leave], I avoided London, because it was much too expensive and I couldn't afford it, the halls and the nightclubs and the pony steaks. They called them pony steaks. I don't know what the hell kind of meat it was. I would go to two places. One was a place called Weston-super-Mare, and the other was Cardiff. Cardiff was a beautiful, beautiful town; it seemed like it escaped the war. What I was impressed with was it seemed like everybody had red hair. I don't know why, I just remember that, and beautiful speaking voices and beautiful singers, they sang beautifully. That's what struck me most. I did like the locals, I sat down at the pubs and I talked to the women and walked around. Nothing much, I didn't get involved too much. They were very nice. Very nice. We had what they called 'pinks' in those days. The girls, if they saw you in pinks, and no less wearing wings, they mobbed you. I didn't go for that sort of thing.[17]

I was with the Ninth Air Force. The Ninth Air Force had bombers, and we had the Troop Carrier Command within the Ninth Air Force. I was in the Troop Carrier Command. I didn't get to see many of the pilots, because they were the tow pilots, the C-47s. They worked their end, and we hung around with the glider pilots, because we were always in training, always taking off. You just didn't sit around. We were always in training. Taking off, landing, loading, and God knows what all.

Come D-Day, I remember they locked the base, nobody in and nobody out. Some officer came around, said, 'Go see your pastor, your rabbi, your priest, whatever, because we're taking off.' Next morning, we come out for briefing, where we're going to land, what we're going to find. I come out to the flight line. Number one glider, a Horsa glider, and I was to be the pilot. I almost died. I ran back to the operations. I said, 'How come you put me on a Horsa glider? I never flew one.'

He said, 'We have you on record as a co-pilot.'

---

[17] *pinks*- 'Officers' pinks,' so-called for the pinkish hue of the stripe on their American uniform khakis.

I'm thinking way back to what happened. I remember one Sunday everybody was running to London and whatever, but I didn't have any money because I sent a lot of it home, so I hung around the airfield. The British were flying Horsa gliders. I walked up to one of them and I said, 'Can I go for the ride?'

He said, 'Yeah.' So, I sat in the co-pilot's seat. Now if you're in a pilot's seat, there's a 'form one' [to fill out]; I had to enter my name in there because I'm sitting in the co-pilot's seat. They used that to say that I had trained as a Horsa pilot! I tell you, I almost died! I'm standing in front of this big monster, it's a big, big, big glider—I think it holds 36 people.

I'm looking at it and I said, 'A glider's a glider,' the controls, things like that. I had one saving grace [for making this maiden flight on the eve of the invasion]—I was to be the first one on the lead. When I have to make a landing in France, I'll be the first one down. In a glider, once you land, you can 'saturate' a field; two gliders can saturate a field quickly because [the others following may not be able to land] because wherever the [first gliders] stop, that's where they stop.

During the briefing, they said, 'We're going to Sainte-Mère-Église.' Our landing zone was to be Sainte-Mère-Église; I was supposed to land there. My troops were all infantry, probably the 82nd.

So I'm flying a glider I never flew before, so I was a busy guy, because the characteristics are not the same as the CG-4. It's tremendous, big, and you had to keep away from the downdraft. I was so busy, all I noticed was when I crossed the Channel, I saw a million, million, million boats heading towards the shore. I tell you, we were supposed to release when we got to a certain point; you got a signal from the tow plane. So I'm flying and I'm looking down, and I see out of the corner of my eye, everybody's letting go before they even got the signal! Right away I say in my mind, 'Ah, they want to get down there first before somebody else saturates the field.' You know what I did? I released [from the tow plane] and I went into a steep dive. Really, a steep dive, because I wanted to get ahead of everybody else. Then I leveled off. I was flying so fast that it wouldn't go down. I kept sailplaning.

We went over one hedge, another hedge. I think I went over the third hedge, and I hit the ground and slammed into another hedgerow. By the way, the glider is made out of whole wood. When I slammed into the hedgerow, all the wood splintered. I had a mouthful of dirt, they chopped us out. The troops were all right, and they chopped us out, but I don't remember who my co-pilot was. I never saw the guy in my life. That's one of those things. That was the only accident I ever had, near-death.

I got out, I didn't know where I was. All I know is I saw cows in their fields, munching on the grass. I saw farmers walking like nothing is happening, an unbelievable sight. A couple of farmers and, I don't know, maybe a woman. I'm not sure if I saw one walking down the road, just like a Sunday stroll with all this going on, gliders coming in all over the place.

I worked my way back to the beach. What I remember about that is shells were coming over from the Americans. They were shelling the mainland, the beach. Every time I heard a shell, I'd drop to the ground. There was another infantryman next to me. He said, 'If you hear it, don't worry about it—the one that gets you, you'll never hear.' So, I just kept walking right to the beach. I flew the mission; I ran into some hedgerows, but I'm alive.

The Last Mission

Back in England, I went back to training. My last mission was the Bastogne mission. On that one, I was tailing Charlies, CG-4. I asked the guy what I was flying. He said, 'Blood plasma,' but I didn't believe him; [the containers] looked like gasoline jerrycans, although I didn't smell any gasoline, so I don't know. We were being towed, we're approaching Bastogne, and I see a cloud of flak, anti-aircraft fire. I said to myself, 'I'm not going to make it.' There were a couple of groups ahead of us, so now [the anti-aircraft batteries] are zeroing in. Every time a new group came over, they kept zeroing in. My outfit had, I think, 95% casualties. I became a prisoner of war then. A couple of my friends were killed, and a couple of friends were PoWs. I spent the rest of the war in Germany. [I had to land the glider outside Bastogne]; I never reached Bastogne.

When I landed, the Germans were shooting at me, because I could hear the bullets ripping through the glider material, it's made out of canvas and pipes. There was a forest down there, and I was concentrating so hard on my flying. You have to be lucky to find an opening where you can land your glider. I came down and I stepped out of the glider, I'm looking down in the snow—the snow is popping up. I see somebody shooting at me, so I dropped to the ground, I held up my carbine; I had a .45 and a carbine. I held my hands up and a couple of German soldiers came out of the woods towards me. I saw they had the 'SS' on their collar. They started to fight over the .45 I was carrying; they each wanted the .45. Then a captain came, and he settled the argument because he took it. [*Laughs*] He took the gun. He sent me to an interrogation post. On the way to the interrogation point, because I was Jewish, I pulled off my dog tags, which had an 'H' on them. I dropped them on the ground. I had to, because I already knew what the score was.

I wound up at the first interrogation point. On the way there, I'm feeling a peculiar wetness in my forearm. I look down, open up [the sleeve], and I had either a bullet wound or a flak wound. It went right through the muscle. [*Points to inside of left forearm*] It didn't touch the bone, but the skin [looked] like an opening of a flower. They sent a medic over to me. He had a pair of tweezers, and he's digging in there, looking to see if he can find a bullet or whatever.

Didn't find anything. Put on a Band-Aid or something. I don't remember what he did. Then they took me to another interrogation point.

I had those propeller and wings insignia on [my uniform], so they sent all the air corpsmen or air force men to one side. Apparently, what I learned later on, they were looking for navigators. They wanted to talk to navigators, where they came from; I don't know what they had in mind. A German asked me a question. I said, 'I don't know. I don't fly bombers or anything like that.'

He said, 'You better tell me, because I'm going to send you outside.' By the way, this is December 27. It's cold. He said, 'I'm going to send you outside naked until you tell me more.'

I said, 'I don't know.'

He spoke to somebody in German. I thought they were going to take me out and take all my clothes, but no, he just took me outside, and I joined a couple of other prisoners, PoWs.

Prisoner of War

They started to walk us towards Cologne. There was no food, no water. If you wanted to eat or drink, you had to pick up the snow and put it in your mouth. The trouble with that is the snow had a lot of cordite and soot on it, whatever they use for ammunition. But everybody was drinking it; I was, too. We passed a farm; somebody would dig up some frozen carrots from the ground, things like that.

All of a sudden, I'm getting dysentery and a guy ahead of me is getting dysentery. This guy was a big guy. He died in three days; water just came out of him. I figured, 'I'm next.' I started screaming, hollering at the officer. I was thinking, 'What the hell can I lose?'

I said, 'I'm an officer and I want you to obey the Geneva Convention. I'm sick, and you've got to put me in the hospital.' I'm screaming at him. What have I got to lose? He sent me to the doctor. They put a green tag that said 'KRANK,' I think it means sick.

They put me in the hospital, and would you believe they gave me opium? I think it was opium to stop the crapping, stop the water. In three days, it stopped. However, there were other GIs there that were having their toes and feet amputated. The reason for that is we had to walk in the snow during the day and then we'd have to stop off at night. I remembered my training [where] they had a big room and there must have been a million guys there, when all the other guys were playing craps in the back, I was a good little boy. I was a good soldier; I listened. One of the things I remembered, [the instructor] said, 'If your feet get wet at night, no matter how cold it is, take off your socks, put them under your armpit. In the morning, put them on,' which is what I did. These guys didn't, and they lost their toes and their feet and their legs. It paid off for me. [*Chuckles*] Oh, God. [*Shakes head*] Those are the memories I have of that [march].

[They took us to] Stalag VII. It was somewhere near the Dresden-Leipzig area. I just don't know where. I left the hospital. I got the name of the hospital in my records here. The Americans were advancing, so we left there and we walked all the way to Munich. Moosburg, they called it. Munich. That was a two-week walk. Walked all the way. When I got there, that was Stalag IV-F. That's where I stayed until I was liberated.

It was so cold. So little heat that we slept together, two men. I never took off my clothes in the three and a half months I was there. Never took them off and neither did anybody else, because it was so cold. We had nothing to do. They wouldn't let us go out on work details, because the Geneva Convention said officers are not allowed to work, but all the GIs managed to work on details and do some business with the locals. They had soup made out of potatoes that were peeled. We had one kilo of bread, it came in one kilo size.

It had a date stamped on it, and it was made from wood and flour. That's what I had. It's made out of processed sawdust. Not all of it. They use it as a filler. By the way, it tasted pretty good, but it left you flatulent. You had gas all day long. Terrible, terrible. First it was one kilo for four men. As the war wore on, it was one kilo for eight men. As it went on a little more, it was one kilo for twelve men. Now, if you have one kilo of bread for twelve men, somebody has to slice it. The guy who sliced it, believe me, spent time measuring exactly, because you're hungry. Every little grain has value. The problem was the guy who cut the bread got the last piece. You understand what's going on? Then the Red Cross packages started coming in. Again, two prisoners on one package and then four. Towards the end, I guess they were stealing it, all of that stuff.

The cigarettes were what you traded for bread with the German guards. The guards, they were pretty good; they were old men. They were farmers, so they were pretty good. The younger guards, they'd get you out 4:00 in the morning for roll call. What the hell did they call it? Used to holler 'appel,' there was another word for roll call. I don't remember the word. They make you stand outside while they're counting you. You're freezing. The older men, they were pretty good.

The only thing of interest [to me was that] somewhere in that compound, they had a radio. The higher-ranking officers were in a certain building and outside they had a map of Europe with the lines of the Americans and the Germans. I never did find out who or what or where, but we used to pass by to find out what's happening and how we're looking. We'd look good. The other interesting thing is they made whiskey; the Red Cross packages had prunes in them. I don't know how they did it, but they wound up with tin cans, they made little fires. I guess they distilled the prunes and they wound up with whiskey. I never got over that. They're making whiskey. I'm not a drinking guy, I didn't care for that. I could imagine it was rotgut. Got to be all practically pure alcohol, I would imagine.

Liberation

[The day we were liberated], I got up one morning; not a guard in sight. About a half hour later, you hear the rumbling of tanks. In about 20 minutes, the Americans rolled in with the tanks and we were liberated. However, they wouldn't let us out. You would think, 'Here, we're free. Go running around.' No way. Nobody moves, nobody leaves the area. They had Red Cross wagons come in with big pots of chicken à la king, [creamed chicken]. They gave you a plate and said, 'Get on the chow line.' As you pass by, they put in some chicken à la king. They said, 'You can eat all you want, but only what you have on a plate. You want more? Go back in the line.' The reason for that was you could eat yourself to death. By the way, I didn't see it, I heard that a couple of guys escaped to a nearby farm. They captured a pig, roasted it, ate the whole pig, and died from overeating. I never saw this, but this is what I heard. Maybe there's truth in it. I don't know.

They shaved our heads and they sprinkled, I guess it was DDT powder all over us. Then they sent us to a camp called... they were the names of cigarettes. I was sent to Camp Lucky Strike.[18] This is where they fed us. It was a fattening-up camp. Walk around, eat all

---

[18] *Camp Lucky Strike*- The so-called 'Cigarette Camps' were located in the Le Havre, France, port area, set up immediately after the liberation of this area following D-Day as depots and supply camps for combat staging. Mr. Sheff arrived as they were transitioning over to repatriating American GIs and PoWs. Camp Lucky Strike was probably the largest of these, a tent city that reached nearly 60,000 at its peak. Other camps included Old Gold, Chesterfield, Pall Mall, and five others. The code names were designated primarily for security reasons. See www.skylighters.org/special/cigcamps for a good discussion.

you want as often as you want, and then I guess when you gained a little weight and looked a little better, they shipped us back home. Then they sent us to R&R for returnees only, Atlantic City. A hotel for three or four days with your wife. We got there, and then I went home.

After I got home, I had my own shop for a while. I got tired of that. I wanted to become a teacher, so I applied for a teaching position. I had to go back to college again, take courses how to teach. I took an awful reduction in pay. I had two and three jobs, Fuller Brush man and all kinds of things. Then it occurred to me to join the reserves, because I can get two weeks' pay in one weekend a month. So, I joined the reserves.

[I don't recall experiencing] any antisemitism in the service; if there was it wasn't overt, but I was never directly confronted with it. I had what's called the 'Jewish antennae,' you know, I can hear something on the side but nothing was directed to me particularly; I just shrugged my shoulders and did my thing. Now, while I was at the PoW camps I heard about the German army sending in Germans that spoke English in American uniforms, [so I was cautious about my Jewish identity]. The fact is, the first guy who interviewed me at the interrogation point was a Coca-Cola salesman from Ohio; he spoke English, you would say he was an American, no doubt about it, or at least was in America since he was a kid, but I guess he joined the German army, figuring he would be on the winning team. In the PoW camps, I wouldn't tell anybody I was Jewish, so when we had Sunday services, I joined in. I remember singing 'Rock of Ages,' would you believe it, and I purposely didn't get close to anybody, figuring that somebody in the group—whether there was one or not, I'll never know—but I figured on a chance that there was a German soldier there who spoke English like an American-born guy, ferreting out information on who's who and what's what. So I kept to myself, I didn't make any close alliances with anybody, I kept my mouth shut and I waited, that's how I survived.

Do I think [World War II] made a difference in my life? Yeah, absolutely; I appreciate life. I'm in the pursuit of happiness, yeah, and I don't take anything too seriously. [*Chuckles*] I've lived a fairly good life, and a lucky life, and so I'm happy.

Mr. Sheff taught automotive mechanics for 22 years and served in the Air Force Reserve until 1972. He passed away on March 15, 2010 at the age of 92.

Engineer John Webster's reconnaissance photo of the beachhead at Omaha.

Beach obstacles appear as small dots; hedgerows inland plainly visible.

Courtesy John Webster.

PART THREE

ON THE BEACH

"If we can't throw the enemy into the sea within twenty-four hours, then that will be the beginning of the end."

—German Field Marshal Erwin Rommel to his generals, Normandy, June 1944

"Two kinds of men are staying on this beach, the dead and those who are going to die. Get up! Move in! Goddammit! Move in and die!"

—Colonel George Taylor to the men of his regiment on Omaha Beach, June 6, 1944

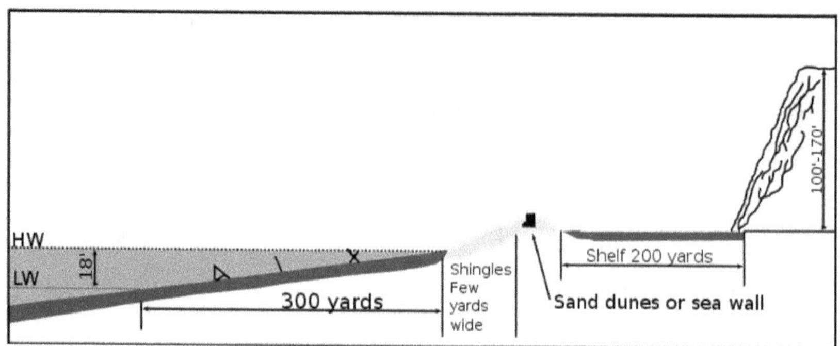

Omaha Beach cross section. Creative Commons Attribution: Share Alike 1.0 Generic license.

CHAPTER EIGHT

The 'Great Wall of Hitler'

After the German invasion of Poland and the declarations of war by Great Britain and France in 1939, an eight-month lull dubbed the 'Phoney War' set in as the western Allies scrambled to prepare for the war at home. In the early spring of 1940, the blitzkrieg turned westward; one by one, western European nations were rolled up on German terms—Denmark and Norway in April, and the Netherlands, Belgium, Luxembourg, and France in May and June of 1940.

France had fallen in a stunning 45 days. A collaborationist government was set up in the south as General Charles De Gaulle and his Free French forces took up residence in London, seething with wounded pride and vengeful aspirations; 100,000 Germans would be on duty in occupied France by the time Germany declared war on the United States on December 10, 1941. After the ill-fated Dieppe Raid in August 1942 on the northern coast of France—the British commando foray to test the idea of taking and holding a French port—was crushed in six hours, Hitler moved to beef up coastal defenses from the sub-Arctic to the Pyrenees along nearly three thousand miles of Atlantic shoreline. Fifteen thousand fortifications were to be constructed using conscripted and slave labor as contracts were carried out by private enterprise—the German Todt Organization, which built the famed Autobahn and designed the crematorium ovens at Auschwitz—and in France, where two-thirds of the fortification work was to be carried out, French business profited as well.[19] The collaborationist Vichy regime pushed over a half-million French workers into compulsory labor for the massive project. Since the Germans expected a cross-channel attack at the narrowest point, the Pas du Calais area, it was the most heavily fortified, but 50-mile stretch of beaches along the invasion coast of Normandy were not neglected. In the first half of 1944, as the writing appeared on the wall, half a million beach obstacles had been installed at low tide including the 'Belgian gates,' ten-foot-high steel frames tipped with anti-tank mines, Teller mines on angled posts projecting seaward, mine-tipped log ramps, six-foot-high hedgehogs resembling giant child's jacks murderously designed to disembowel flat-bottomed landing craft.[10] The deadly shore was strung with miles of barbed wire and seeded with six million buried landmines awaiting the invaders; GIs who entered France from the liberated beaches for weeks after D-Day were admonished to stick strictly to the taped lanes where mines had been cleared. At the seawall, concrete pillboxes protected machine gun crews at the ready to cross stitch soldiers wading through the surf; steel-reinforced concrete bunkers housing the dreaded 88mm guns were dug in atop escarpments and cliffs a hundred feet high, with walls and roofs many feet thick.

To add to the logistical nightmare, the mercurial tides at Normandy had never been encountered before. Twice a day the tide rose nearly two dozen feet at a rate of a vertical foot every eight minutes. Four hundred yards of open Omaha Beach appeared at the

---

[19] *French business profited as well-* Several French construction companies benefited in the construction of Hitler's Atlantic Wall; these companies have yet to answer for the profits engendered by this work. Source: Prieur, Jérôme, *Le mur de l'Atlantique : Monument de la Collaboration.* 2010. Like many of Hitler's grandiose undertakings, the wall was never completed.

lowest point of the tide, but just six hours later the same point would be under twenty feet of sea; engineers tasked with blowing obstacles for landing lanes would have only a half hour of working time before the cycle hid them again.[11]

Beyond the beaches, more anti-tank obstacles, booby traps, low-lying flooded plains, and fields awaited the soldiers who lived to get there; on June 6, 1944, nearly 2,500 Americans did not.

CHAPTER NINE

The Cryptographer

Harry Rosenthal was drafted in 1943 out of high school. From an inauspicious start, he rose to being selected as a courier and decoder aboard an important Navy flagship, the USS Bayfield, *during the Normandy landings and afterwards. He was anxious to sit for this 2002 interview.*

Harry Rosenthal

I was born on March 20, 1924 in Brooklyn. I had a high school education; I didn't go beyond that, and I had plenty of jobs up until the time the war broke out, then you couldn't get any jobs because you were eligible for the draft. Oh, I remember Pearl Harbor, but I didn't know it was a U.S. possession. I didn't know what it meant, Territory of Hawaii, until I got to Pearl Harbor. This is about three years later. I was stationed there for a year from 1944, I think, September to September '45. I was in the streets when I heard about it, but I don't know what I was doing. Maybe I was playing ball or... I know it was a Sunday, I remember that. And when we heard that we said, 'Where's that?' So we found out later where it was.

So, I waited [for my turn]. And then when it came my turn, they sent me a letter, 'Greetings and salutations.' At the time, Grand Central Terminal was the induction center, so we went there, the big station, and there was an Army officer, lieutenant, and a young second lieutenant from the Navy, a JG, junior grade. And there was a Marine lieutenant. When they saw all the blue marks on my health chart, they [wanted to] put me in the Marines or the Navy. And I said to them, 'No,' I said, 'I want to go to the Army.'

He said, 'I'm sorry, son, you have no choice. You can either enlist in the Navy or the Marines.'

I said, 'I can be drafted?'

He says, 'No, not at this time.'

So I went to the Navy, and I enlisted. They gave me a week off and we went down to, I think it was 20 Whitehall Street, not far from where the World Trade Center was. It wasn't there then, of course. And then they had the people, the inductees... in the Navy there's regular Navy, I think there's USNR Naval Reserve, and there were Seabees. So, I didn't know what to do. And I found out later, never volunteer. I raised my hand. I said, 'I want to go into this Seabees,' which is construction battalion. And I found out that there, you fight and you work. Well, if I have to fight, why should I work? So I got out of it, took me two hours before another lieutenant says, 'You're in here now, you stay in this group here.'

I said, 'No, I want to go in the Naval Reserve.'

So he said, 'Okay, get back with the other bunch.' By that time, I was regular Navy, so I didn't go to the Seabees, because I knew the Marines and the Navy were in the Pacific, and it was pretty bad there. I didn't know I was going to go to Normandy. I got my share, anyway.

I think it was February '43. February 19, they sent us up to a boot camp in Sampson, New York, right near the Canadian border. And we were in boot training for about three months, but they were well equipped. We went around the drill field with a full sea bag, and that was pretty heavy walking around there and marching cadence. And then what we had to do was learn how to use whaleboats, which are aboard ship, and they're used for safety when a ship is going under. Well, we didn't have any whaleboats to practice on, so we had beams to sit on and something in the shape of a boat that was arched like a whaleboat, it was about 25 feet long, I think. And then we had two by fours used as oars, so eight of us on one side of the two by fours and eight on the other side. And it was snowing, and the guy at the helm was hollering, 'Heave-ho,' something like that, and it looked like Washington crossing the Delaware with the snow coming down. We were on grass that you couldn't see, and it's full of snow, and here we were, 'Heave-ho,' just to get the idea.

So we did that a few times, and then I wasn't used to that kind of life, washing clothes. [It was my first time] away from home. Well, there were some good times in it, but that came later on. But over there in boot camp it was very cold, and I wasn't used to eating that kind of food. I don't know. I don't know what SOS was. Oh, you know what that is, right? So, and then I never had any of that food before. I used to go to the PX. Well, the Army closed the PX. We didn't call it that. We called candy 'pogey-bait' and ice cream 'gedunk.' We had that. I used to go there to eat the candies and the ice cream instead of the food. Whenever I had money in my pocket, I went over there to eat. I couldn't stand the food, unless sometimes on a Sunday they'd bake cake or they gave you eggs, but I got used to the food later on in different parts of the world.

We stayed three months, and then they shipped us to the *USS Alcor*, a training ship. That was in Norfolk, Virginia. The ship never left port, it stayed there. And well, we were on there for about three months, I think. We used to get liberty weekend passes or liberty by the day. Place was full of sailors, loaded with sailors; nobody liked sailors there. They couldn't wait for us to leave, couldn't wait to get rid of them, and then another batch would come in from different training stations. So yeah, I stayed there, and then they shipped us out.

Crossing the Atlantic

They sent us from there on an LST pulling out of Norfolk, Virginia, to Halifax, Nova Scotia. Well, we don't know what we were going into, but there were ten or so LSTs. I was on LST 531, and there were six British corvettes convoying a 72-ship convoy across the North Atlantic. There were German U-boats there, and it was freezing. The guy in the forecastle along the bow of the ship, he had about 40 pounds of gear on him, and you couldn't even see his face and his eyes. And he was always at it, he's looking out there for subs. And then they would give us duty, 24 hours on and 24 off on the watch. We had about a 30-foot tower to scale, it's like the firemen use. It's a long pole, and it's got bars on the side to grab on. Out in the North Atlantic it was stormy and ice cold, and you couldn't see anything at night. I don't see how you could see a sub with a periscope then, impossible. And the weather was bad, and the ship would pitch at a 25, 30-degree angle, and you're up there and knocking on the door, and he's a lieutenant JG. He says, 'All's well below, sir.' 'Aye-aye.' And you climbed back down there, and you go below decks, you know, where it's warmer.

The LST was loaded with tanks, trucks, jeeps, ammo, everything. So about 500 miles out, two LSTs turned back, they had problems. Well, we were now about 1500 miles, the point of no return. And we had to hobble into Glasgow, Scotland, because the rudder was broken. They had three of us, they were calling down degrees of where to steer the ship, and we'd all take turns. So we did that, 1500 miles into Glasgow, but we stayed and dried out overnight.

*

We went down the English Channel via the Irish Sea, and we went to Plymouth, England. That was March of 1944, and when we got there, well, we saw a bombed-out city. They put us in Quonset huts or barracks, and we saw these balloons up there with cables attached and realized they were filled with hydrogen. And that was for the German Luftwaffe, so they would not come in and strafe the city, which they did [anyway].

We stayed there, and I was a courier there, but I didn't know how to drive, and I didn't want to learn how to drive. So there's this other sailor, he was from upstate New York, and I used to wake him, Haran. I used to wake him up every hour as long as I was on duty, because I needed a car driver. So he got disgusted, and he says, 'I'm going to teach you to drive. So I got behind the jeep with him, and I didn't know how to shift with the clutch and all that. And we were jerking. We had to go about two or three miles away, just a little letter, but it was high security, and it was [for] the British about two miles away. Well, I stepped on the gas, and he almost flew out. And I was going fast and slow, and I finally got there and he was with me. Then he says, 'Next time, don't wake me up anymore.'

So I was really nervous: Don't wake him up anymore. So I got the .45 on my hip, and I got a jeep. I used to go to the motor pool, and each gate was about 20 feet wide because they have trucks and weapons carriers. So one day he didn't have any jeeps, and he doesn't know anything from anything, this guy on duty. I give him my pass and he gives me a weapons carrier, and that thing... well, they look amphibious, they're huge, and 10 forward speeds. I says, 'Where do I start?' And I was embarrassed. I couldn't wait for him to go inside. I feel he was hidden from my view. So I got up, I drove there, but I was really nervous with that big thing. And I got there and I got back, and as I progressed, you know, I got to be a little bit better. So I ended up learning to drive, not too well over there, but we stayed there about three months. And the city was all bombed out, and they ran dances in the local church, and we didn't have too many good times. And you couldn't get any sweets, no candies, nothing at all. And I love the sweets.

So after that March, April, May... the LST 531 went out for maneuvers, and it was sunk by a tin fish, a torpedo. It hit the LST midship and the thing went down because that thing is hollow. I knew some of the men on board, I met them when I was going across on the LST, but they were assigned. I was lucky I was off, because I was that courier. They told me it sunk immediately, and then I saw the names on the roster, and they were in burning oil, I heard.[20]

Now we didn't know where we were going, but it was June. When it came early morning, it was June 6, [but we may have] left June 5 and we were in the English Channel. I know it was June 6 because I was assigned to Admiral Moon's staff. There were forty of us, and we were assigned to the *USS Bayfield*. It was a hooligan ship. A hooligan ship [in our lingo] means it's a Coast Guard ship. And we were passengers, and they were ship's company because they were attached to the ship. So we were doing our jobs decoding messages. They called it a HAG machine, H-A-G, and we were doing whatever we were told to do.[21] There were other Coast Guard guys on the *Bayfield* with the .50 caliber firing at the planes. And someone said, 'They're ours!' So the guys [shooting] said, 'Who knows whose it is? They just [better not] fly over here.' And they kept shooting at them, no matter who came over.

---

[20] *LST 531 went out for maneuvers, and it was sunk by a tin fish, a torpedo-* His former shipmates were killed when LST 531 was sunk by German torpedo boats during the ill-fated Exercise TIGER in April 1944.

[21] *They called it a HAG machine-* The U.S. used a portable rotor-based encrypting device, the Hagelin C-38, which they designated the M-209. Designed by Swedish cryptographer Boris Hagelin, it worked on the same principle as the German Enigma machine.

Omaha Beach

When we were attached to that ship we were in the Channel, and we hit the Omaha Beach. I never left the ship, but there were big water mines with tentacles. They were huge. They looked like eight to 10-feet-tall ones; you could see that half of it with the tentacle sticking out. Some of the men didn't even get a chance to go down those ropes to get onto the small crafts. But they weren't hitting us with the shells because we were about three to five miles off the shoreline.

But [later] we were pulling up the American soldiers, sailors out of the Channel. On these small craft where they were wounded, they would put six or eight stretchers and they put a cable or a rope, like a V, and they'd lower the boom with a hoist and pick up eight at a time and put them on the quarter deck towards the bow of the ship. And there was hardly any room to stand. You couldn't stand there. So we had everybody aboard.

[Later we were transporting German PoWs] and one of the Germans, he had a hole in his back as big as your fist, and he was asking others for a cigarette. I says, 'Nope, I don't'—I wasn't smoking. And [there were so many] aboard, there was no room for anything. And I realized later—I saw them baking bread before, I don't know if it was on land or aboard ship, but they were baking bread and putting it in the freezer—one day we were sewing these stiffs up in canvas, and they were putting them in the freezer and I realized the bread is there. So I lost my appetite for the bread, but men did what they had to do.

And finally it was D+5, I think, and we left the English Channel, and we thought it was over. Now my case, I don't think my experience was so severe as some of these men who hit the shoreline, they really got it bad. I felt bad for that, I really did. And the guys aboard ship [had it rough too] if they were sunk or they hit a mine, [and soon after] was the worst storm of the channel at the time. They had these big anchors with these chains—they're as big as my forearm, each side of the ship—and they were breaking loose from the moorings, and the ships were floating loose in that channel with the mines. So it was dangerous, but these guys who hit the beaches, they really took a beating.

The Flagship

Our ship was a pretty big size ship, it was the flagship. They had a few flagships, but Admiral Moon, he was the flag on the flagship. And they had medical people doing whatever they could but not nearly enough. We pulled out with the wounded. But it was D plus three or four when they sent over the V-bomb, I saw it on the HAG machine. We didn't know what the V-bomb was yet, but it was jet-propelled, [and] they could hit Britain. So you know, we started to realize that we're not [shooting back at] anybody who was firing a gun, and whatever they hit, they hit.

We ended up pulling out, we went down through the Mediterranean Sea and we stayed in Oran, North Africa. And it was stifling, like the desert. Our sheets, the Arabs were buying them for $25 a sheet if you wanted to sell. We stayed there about a month and we were walking in the streets around there, and [my friend] had his sunglasses stolen. An Arab kid runs over, picks it off him, and he started to chase the Arab kid. I says, 'You better not.' I says, 'Look behind you,' because you don't know what they're carrying in under those sheets.' So he stopped running. I says, 'Let him keep the sunglasses.' So he stopped. But we didn't know where we were at because it was new for everybody. Five cents a beer, but I don't drink. What a shame. [*Laughs*]

So we stayed there about a month in the heat, sweating into our sheets, and they put us aboard ship, and we went to Southern

France. There was another invasion there. And we didn't know that, they told us later, but that was easier because it was only about two days because the Germans were moving inland. We already hit them from Utah and Omaha Beach and on the Cherbourg Peninsula.

When we got to Southern France, I got off the ship. We stayed there, I think it was about three or four days only. They anchored, and then they let us swim off the ship. They tied a line out to a life preserver at about twenty-five feet out. And you can jump off the side of the ship and swim in the Mediterranean and then you come back. And we did that and we got aboard ship and we went to Naples.

We stayed in Naples about two months, I think. And Admiral Moon, we were still on his staff... I was a courier and I used to go with an LCVP, a landing craft vehicle personnel. It was a square type of thing, probably 30, 40 feet long, I think. And I used to go get the mail. Well, at one time while aboard ship Admiral Moon put a gun to his head, and he committed suicide. They called it battle fatigue. We don't know if it was or not, but that's what I was told.[22]

So we stayed there for a time and I remember cartons of cigarettes were 50 cents a carton. So now I'm going to make a confession. I was selling cigarettes maybe for $3 a carton if it was Raleigh, Lucky Strike; I got $5 for Camels and Chesterfield. I had a mailbag. I gave the guys a buck a carton. So I would wait inside a public toilet in Naples, and I had the Italian customers I sold to for three to five dollars a carton. I was making a profit, the start of being a businessman. And when I got enough, I used to go shopping, I forgot the

---

[22] *Admiral Moon put a gun to his head*-(1894-1944) On August 5, 1944, Rear Admiral Don Pardee Moon shot himself in the head with his .45 aboard his flagship *Bayfield* in Naples harbor. Some attributed his personal hell to the ill-fated Exercise TIGER disaster that had occurred under his watch back in April.

name of that fancy street, but I bought the leather gloves for my relatives back home, ladies, and I bought tortoise shell combs, $5 a comb. Well, when you don't pay much for it, sell it pretty cheap. I came back with some prizes.

And after a while I got tired of eating the food aboard ship, so I wanted to go have some eggs, and you couldn't get eggs nowhere. Ah, some girl offered me eggs. I says, 'Yeah, where's the chicken?' She took me to the building, they're big courtyards, the houses there, the tenements, and she says, 'You stay here.' She went, I don't know if she got a frying pan and she gave me two eggs. I think it was a penny, a lira. I got $5 worth, two eggs, 500 lira. And I got eggs and it was a real treat.

And there were girls around, plenty of girls, but you don't know what you were getting. You took your chances. Well, I didn't get anything, I wasn't sick. But brothers were pimping their sisters. The mother and father would be in the living room, not caring, offering you wine. If one British or American would go with the daughter, the other one would be waiting, and it wasn't like a typical turnstile, but it was war. So people were very hard up for money. Grandmothers were picking bricks out of the streets for pennies a day just to make ends meet. Getting something, some money. An American dollar meant a lot.

Harry Rosenthal passed on September 25, 2012, at the age of 88.

CHAPTER TEN

The Combat Engineer

John Webster was a 1st lieutenant serving with the 20th Engineer Combat Battalion, fighting and building his way through North Africa and Europe. He landed in the second wave at Omaha Beach on D-Day. He also was in the thick of it during the Battle of the Hürtgen Forest and the Battle of the Bulge, receiving a Bronze Star and Purple Heart. He visited my classroom and veterans' symposium several times, bringing with him his curled up 8x10 black and white aerial reconnaissance maps that he used to find beach obstacles on D-Day. The photographs had been taken only three weeks before the landings. This 2002 interview was conducted after school in my classroom, with interested students in attendance.

'I got hit in the face with shrapnel. Yes, it knocked out my upper teeth and I still have a piece of shrapnel left in the side of my face that they didn't take out. It moves around a little bit, but it doesn't go very far. But when I shave every morning I can tell where it is. My brother Charlie was in the Eighth Air Force, he completed over 25 missions from England and didn't get a scratch. He was really lucky.'

John O. Webster

I was born on January 13, 1920; I'll be eighty-two soon. Grade school was a one-room schoolhouse in the Town of Queensbury district, Number 4 on Ridge Road. Then, in high school, I went to the Glens Falls Academy, which is no longer in existence; Queensbury didn't have a school system that was for higher education. I had an older sister, and a younger brother a year younger than me, and then a younger sister. There were four of us in our family; we all went to the Glens Falls Academy; it was a tradition. My mother had gone there, as well as my aunts and uncles. It was one of the major schools in its day in Glens Falls; it was located on Chester Street, and it's now the home of the Salvation Army. I graduated in 1936 when I was sixteen. Those were the days when you could take several years together in grade school, such as your third and fourth, or seventh and eighth. If you passed your Regents exams, you went into high school no matter whether you were eleven, twelve, or thirteen! It didn't make any difference. So, I was able to get out at age sixteen—it's harder to do that now; it may be just as well.

[Now, I didn't know what I wanted to do, because this was] right in the middle of the Depression, in 1936. The subject of college was never even mentioned—it was unheard of for a farm boy who didn't have any money, so we were just hoping to go out and find a job. [*Gets emotional, shrugs shoulders*] No, college wasn't even discussed, really. I suppose I should have had ambitions to do it, but I realized the family didn't have the money, and I didn't really have the know-how, or the actual ambition to find a way. If I had been Abraham Lincoln, I probably would have. [*Laughs*] So after I got out of high school without any particular plans, I had an aunt and uncle who lived on a Navajo Indian reservation, and they wanted me to come out and live with them. So I did. They put me on a Greyhound bus, and I went to Houck, Arizona, on the Navajo reservation. I spent a year out there, and then my family sort of talked me into coming back home to the farm, and I did.

When the war started over in Europe in 1939, I was working, clerking at a grocery store on Ridge Road in Queensbury for a dollar a day, six dollars a week, with one day off.

That was the pay then, yes; I don't even think my father earned any more than that. This is the Depression I'm talking about—people were starving to death, and it was really hard to make a living at that time, except for those who were comfortably well-to-do; almost all working people were really living from hand to mouth. To get through the winter, my mother and father would get one of their parents to come up with a couple hundred dollars to buy groceries to help us out. It was really, really tough, [but it seemed like every family was like that]; we didn't know we were poor. Everybody was in the same boat. But anyway, the war was looming. You talked about the war in Europe—Germany, France, and England were at war, but it looked more and more like we couldn't help but be involved. We were already becoming the 'arsenal of democracy,' supplying things that England and France needed. So the opportunity for work at General Electric in Schenectady came and I applied, and I got accepted. I went to work in the induction motors department, where we built motors for ships, and gears and hydraulic controls. By then, we were in the war. I went to Schenectady and lived there. I moved to Schenectady, rented a room, and got my own meals and I registered for the draft in Schenectady because that's where I was living at the time. For a fellow used to earning a dollar a day, to start working for General Electric during that period when they were really laying on employees for the war effort, I was getting more money every thirty minutes than I was sitting at the counter all day long where I was working before. So, yes, to a young fellow off the farm, it was just a glorious opportunity to earn money, but I found that I didn't last long enough for me to amass any great fortune. [*Laughs*]

When Pearl Harbor came about on December 7, 1941, it didn't take very long for my number to get called; the next month after Pearl Harbor, I was inducted into the Army on January 10, 1942. I wasn't eager to go, but I accepted the fact that it was my patriotic duty to do my part.

The 20th Combat Engineers

I became part of the 20th Combat Engineers [although] I didn't start out as an engineer. When I first was inducted into the army, I was assigned to Fort Knox, Kentucky, to become a tanker in the armored force, and that is where I took all my basic training. Then I went to Camp Fort George G. Meade in Maryland, and took more training as a tanker, and I was a tank driver with the rank of corporal. The war in Africa was going full force. General Rommel, a German commander, was chasing the British in North Africa all the way from Tunisia to Egypt, and through Libya and Algeria. So they sent our outfit by train, tanks and all our men and equipment, out to Southern California into the Mojave Desert. There we trained for six months under General George Patton to prepare ourselves for going over to Africa, and fighting Rommel, but after about six months out on the desert, I was urged to apply for officer school. So I did, and I was accepted, and I became a second lieutenant in the engineers.

Engineering was building bridges, doing construction, building roads. It wasn't just that, though—it was picking up mines, and it was assisting the infantry; it was combat engineers acting as infantry whenever they were needed to be. We had to have all the weapons and knowledge that a combat infantryman would have, to be a combat engineer, but we also had to have a certain amount of engineering skills as well. It was sort of a mixed bag; some of the times we were in combat in Europe and in other places where we were, we were doing engineering work. We worked on roads and bridges, especially in Sicily. We had the Germans in retreat in front of us in Sicily and they did a lot of demolition of bridges and highways, and it slowed the American advance down; we had to do a lot of work like that. But in France and Germany, we were acting as infantrymen more than we were doing engineer work, although on D-Day, our mission was to remove mines and obstacles from Omaha Beach so that the landing craft could come up onto the beach and discharge succeeding waves of troops without getting sunk by obstacles piercing the bottoms of the boats. We made three D-Day landings, by the way—one in Casablanca for the North African campaign, one in Sicily, for the Italian campaign, and one in Normandy, at Omaha Beach, in the main campaign. Each time we were assigned with the 1st Infantry Division, The Big Red One, to assist them and give them more engineers.

My 20th Engineers outfit landed D-Day in North Africa at Casablanca, which is in Morocco on the Atlantic side of North Africa, right on the Mediterranean Sea, but I wasn't with them yet. A few weeks later, I got to North Africa on a convoy, landing at Oran, Algeria, in a replacement depot—to take the place wherever an officer would be needed. While the North African campaign was still going on, I moved from the replacement depot to Bizerte, Tunisia, and was assigned to the 1st Platoon of A Company of the 20th Engineers and took the place of a lieutenant that had been seriously injured by stepping on a mine there. I took over his platoon, and three days later I was on my way to Sicily, landing on D-Day in Sicily with my new outfit, but I hardly knew the men's names; at the time it was all so new. I was in charge of those men, but as their replacement officer. They hardly knew me, but we did our jobs. I got to know them pretty good very quickly.

In Sicily, we did not have a difficult beach, and initially, the Italian army was facing us, not the Germans at that particular place—

in fact we found that the Italian army liked us and was awfully happy to frequently surrender to us. They didn't like the Germans any more than we did. So, we didn't take very many casualties, but we took a few, and we captured hundreds and hundreds of prisoners. We easily got to Palermo. Then, the route from Palermo to the Strait of Messina where Sicily touches the mainland of Italy was where the Germans threw up ferocious resistance all the way back—delaying actions, blowing bridges, dynamiting everything. It was a long, tedious, bloody operation to clear the Germans out of Sicily, but it was done.

Right after Sicily, without very much rest, our outfit and the precinct from Division 2 were put on boats again and we were moved up to Glasgow, Scotland, and then down into England through Lands End, which is heading way out in Cornwall for training, getting ready for the landing across from the channel on D-Day. We did all our training there. I only got to London once, for one brief pass... I don't even remember if I stayed overnight. It wasn't a vacation. I was probably there six months or so.

Everybody knew it was inevitable we would cross the channel. But whether we were to go to Normandy or to Cherbourg or to Le Havre or the streets of Calais, nobody knew for sure. We even trained so realistically that we would be put on our boats, and then we would go out onto the English Channel, and then we would attack the English coast instead of the French coast; we would put on a landing on English soil instead of French soil to get us experienced. In fact, there was one training exercise where there were more casualties than some outfits took on Omaha Beach, because of the English Channel's terrible weather, the boats capsized, and there was a lot of drowning—all just in training for Normandy. But most of the training was just on land; being proficient with your equipment and knowledgeable with your weapons and being physically fit and ready for discipline to take over as needed. Good armies have to have soldiers that do what they're told.

There are some things that are sort of hazy about exactly the time of when we did certain things, but certainly we were ordered to go to the embarkation point. We still didn't know where we were. We didn't know anything about our mission specifically until not only after we'd gotten on the boat, but until the boat had gotten away from shore, because security had to be very carefully controlled. We also didn't object because we didn't want the German command to know where we were going to be hitting the beach any more than any of our side did. If your own safety demands discretion and care, you're willing to put up with it. And all through the war, we were subject to censorship as far as what we wrote in our letters. I never told my family one single word of where I was all the time I was overseas; they had to figure it out for themselves.

After we got on the boats, and went out a ways into the Channel, then we were just inundated with information. I was told exactly what part of the English Channel, what beach I was going to land on, and I knew who was going to be on my left and who was going to be on my right. I knew every section of the beach had a name, and I had aerial photographs. We knew just exactly what the Air Corps was supposed to do, just how many bombs they were going to drop on the gun emplacements, the size of the bombs, the number of bombs, the time they were going to do it. We knew just what the Navy was going to do, what ships they were going to have bombard the coast before we got off our boats and went up on the beach. We had these aerial photographs, given to us shipboard, of the placements on the beach. For example [*points to photograph*], this is the beach with the English Channel waters below here, and here's the beach, and this patchwork [back] here is hedgerows of Normandy that have been well prepared; this is actually a tank trap, dug by the Germans to protect their position from enemy tanks coming in. But here on the beach there were obstacles, you weren't able to figure everything out [from the aerial photographs]. The date on those photos is 10 May '44, taken about three weeks before, and it was about as current as they could come up with for something like that.

H-Hour

My main objective was to, well, get off the boat! And not necessarily get off the beach, just to get off the boat and get on the beach and carry out a mission of clearing obstacles on the beach. We landed low tide. I landed in the third wave of boats, which was 30 minutes after H-Hour. H-Hour was when the first boats landed. Fifteen minutes later, the second wave landed. The third wave came 15 minutes after that, and I was in that wave. The low tide was still in low tide, thankfully, because that's when the obstacles were exposed. They were these big metal angle irons, railroad rails welded together so that from the air, they'd look like harmless little jacks that kids used to play with. Of course, there were mines, too. We were supposed to try to make for safe lanes for succeeding waves to come up even when the tide was in farther, because then these things would be covered up if they weren't removed. Then, when the tide was higher, a boat would come up, and if they didn't have a safe lane, they would run up on one of these obstacles and get pierced in the bottom of the boat with a piece of angle iron, or hit a mine with the boat. We had equipment to blow up the obstacles and to neutralize the mine. We had bangalore torpedoes that you would ignite, and they would clear a path 100 feet long; we had material to mark lanes. After saying all this, and maybe I've said too much already, things don't always go right. Certainly, even in battles, things don't always go the way they are supposed to go. Omaha Beach is an example of that. [*Pauses*] All of the Air Force bombs didn't land where they were supposed to land, all of the naval shells didn't go where they were supposed to go. When we hit the beach, the Germans were firing at us with machine guns [*makes impression of machine gun fire*] even before we got out of the water. Right in the water, they were shooting at us! It was absolutely impossible to carry out the whole mission, because if you were out here planning to blow an obstacle, you'd be dead in minutes. I mean, as a matter of survival, there was just no way to do some of the things we were supposed to do. Many of the American troops who got up on the beach went up as far as what is called the shingle—the first big dune where the high tide of a beach is—which gave us protection from the machine guns that were firing right over our heads all the while, at anybody who got out on the beach. Then the Germans brought up more and more artillery, so that with each succeeding wave that came in on boats, their artillery was more and more accurate and knocking out whole boatloads of soldiers. So with me coming in 30 minutes after H-Hour, in the third wave, I was lucky, I got up to the shingle. If I had been in the seventh, eighth, or ninth wave, I wouldn't be here now, they probably would have blasted me out of the ocean like so many of the boats were.

By noon on Omaha Beach, there were still obstacles on the beach that should have been knocked out, but after the tide came up we couldn't get them anyway. Most of us hadn't been able to get even over the shingle, because if you stuck your helmet on a stick [and raised it], somebody would have put a hole through it the minute you did it. They were that close, they were that accurate, so we were there until the tide became high and we had to go someplace else, and we finally went over the shingle [*gestures with hand, gets emotional*]. I went here to this antitank ditch [*points to reconnaissance photograph*] right there with my captain and some of my men, and we moved right up to a pillbox area and I captured my first German prisoner. I was wounded at about 1:30 that afternoon, but not very bad, a piece of shrapnel glanced off my hand and arm. I didn't have to be evacuated; I was able to stay right with my men. That very first night I still hadn't gotten in to where we were supposed to be, but I could see the whole panorama of what was going on, the boats, the Navy, the troops going in, German prisoners going back out, being taken back to England, the wounded being evacuated, just this enormous panorama. It was almost awe inspiring, but it was also something that nobody ever wanted to see again, you know.

We were right near a little town called Colleville-sur-Mer, it's the American cemetery on Omaha Beach. [I have never been back there], but I have a feeling if I went back to Normandy, I could trace my steps on that beach to the place where I was wounded. Years later, my 20th Engineers outfit went on a special tour, but at that time, I didn't feel that I could afford the cost of the trip. I wish that I had now, of course, but I didn't go then.

The Tankers

Incidentally, in the States, when I was a tanker, I was training in the Mojavi Desert [for the invasion of North Africa], and I was with the 741st Tank Battalion. And I was a very happy tanker with the training I had received, but I had the opportunity to become an officer, and in ninety days, I became one. On graduation from the officers' training program, they gave me a 10-day pass to go home, and then I went back to Washington DC and they put me right on a boat to North Africa. So here I was in the combat zone, and my old tankers were still on the Mojavi Desert! After the African and Sicilian campaigns, we went up to England, and then lo and behold, the 741st Tank Battalion arrived in England as the major tank support for the Omaha Beach invasion! These were medium tanks; the Army had developed a plan where collapsible canvas sides would be attached to the mediums so that you could put them on an LST boat out in the English Channel and drive them right out, several miles from shore, drive right off the boat into the water. They were boats because of the added sides to the tanks. The tanks themselves were down in the water. The canvas sides were supposed to make them floatable until the tracks hit the beach, the land, the ground, the sand. Then they would propel themselves up onto the beach and the canvas sides would be dropped down. In this way the American Army would put medium tanks on the beach that very first day to support the infantry. The 741st had this mission to do that. You probably have heard that the weather wasn't as good for the landing in Omaha Beach as it was hoped to be, and the Channel was quite rough. Well, as it turned out, almost all the tanks were swamped and sank in the English Channel, because these canvas sides wouldn't support them under the weather conditions. Whole crews of these tanks were lost, but some were saved by crawling out of the hatches in time and getting into life jackets and into small boats. After that [disaster], there were only three or four of the 741st tanks on the beach in the front of where we were on that first day; all the rest of them failed to make the beach. Later, I contacted my old 741st outfit in France and it was surprising to see how many crews actually did survive D-Day. They got new tanks, and the 20th Engineers were close to the 741st Tank Battalion through France and up through Belgium. Even though I was with the tankers on the desert, they were still associated with us in the action on D-Day. They had a difficult mission on the beach just like we did.

*

You know, D-Day was famous, it was very important and very crucial, and it set the stage for our winning the war, having the successful landing back in France. But there were other battles in World War II that individual units, individual divisions, and corps undertook that were even more grueling and more difficult from a standpoint of hardship, loss of life, and injuries that the public hardly knows about. Everything you hear about is something like D-Day.

Mr. Webster's story continues in Part Four with the longest battle fought in American history, the lamentably virtually unknown Battle of the Hürtgen Forest.

CHAPTER ELEVEN

The Demolition Man

James E. Knight was in the first assault wave on Omaha Beach as an engineer with the 299th Combat Engineer Battalion, most of whom hailed from central and western New York. On D-Day, eight assault teams were tasked with blowing 50-yard gaps in the beach obstacles under heavy fire with no cover; they sustained heavy casualties. Mr. Knight was in the Omaha Beach sector for two nights after landing.

'Now there's men going down, and you can hear them hollering and screaming that they're hurt. I take this last step off the boat. Now I'm right even with this Element C. I look, and the damn thing is loaded with [mines] all around it. The fuse is floating in the water, and smoking! My heart is right in my mouth; I know as well as I'm sitting here, there's no way in hell, whether it goes off now or 10 seconds or a minute, there's no way I can get far enough away to miss out on this.'

James Knight

I was born on August 7, 1924, in Fulton, New York. I got out of high school, but I dropped out for six months because I had an operation, and before I got a chance to get to the next semester, Pearl Harbor came.

I heard about Pearl Harbor when I was on the way to the local skating rink, and as we went by a house where some other person was just coming out, they told us they had just heard it on the radio. It was about noon. I just knew that it sounds like a bad deal, but you didn't have any of the details yet. But they came along not too long afterwards.

The Tuesday after Pearl Harbor Sunday, I went up to Syracuse to the post office to enlist in the Navy. I had been there three months before for four hours and it looked like I passed everything. But as I put my shirt on, the guy standing beside me noticed psoriasis on my elbow, and he said, 'I don't know if we send you up to Albany, they'd take you, so you go home and see if you can get rid of that.'

So I did. I went back and I took X-ray treatments and after about three of them, the spot being treated was gone, and they switched to another spot. About the second week into that, the first one was coming back again. Well, by then, this was several weeks, I didn't know just what to do, and I didn't get too much time to think about it. It was only two weeks later Pearl Harbor came along.

So I went back to set up there the Tuesday after Pearl. And you walk in that post office and the stairs are as wide as this room, going up to the second floor. And I looked and there's just room for people to go up and down quick, because there's about 12 or 14 people on every step, all the way up. And I got on there, and it took a long time to get to the second floor, and there was a line like a city block long down that wide hall to that room—I was three hours getting into that room that I'd been in three months earlier, I don't think I could have fell down in there! They looked us over and they said, 'You'll get vouchers in the mail, [for] a train ticket to Albany, lodging, and a restaurant.' And I got them two or three days later.

[I got to Albany], but that night, I didn't sleep too well. I'm thinking to myself, 'Am I rushing this a little too much?' One thing led to another, but I had to make up my mind pretty quick because I had to be at the post office down there at 9:00. Well, at 7:00, I decided I didn't think I'd go back, I'm going to get drafted anyway, so I didn't. I went up the main street and hitchhiked home.

I went back to my job. I was a manager of the dairy department of one of the first supermarkets, I went back to work there for two or three months. Then I had a chance to go steeple-jacking out in Cleveland, Ohio, which I did for six or seven months. And I knew I was about due to get drafted, I kept thinking that all along. Finally, the weather started getting bad, not too great for steeple-jacking, and so I went back and I worked in the local missile plant for two months and then I got my draft notice, a three-cent postcard from 'your friends and neighbors.' [*Laughs*] And the following Saturday, I went up to Syracuse. They took two busloads of us, we took the physical, and they said, 'You'll hear within a few days.'

Three or four days later, I got a notice to report over to the local train station Saturday morning, which I did, and left there for Syracuse and Fort Niagara; we were only there three or four days getting fitted with clothes and stuff, shots and what have you. And we boarded, Pullman cars no less. The only time that ever happened.

We boarded the train there and we headed west. We had no idea where we were going; we went through Canada and crossed over at Detroit, and on to Chicago. And if I remember right, they fed us in the terminal and we took off again, and we'd been moving along for a while before we realized about half of the people that had been part of this group weren't with us any longer. Come to find out later, they went to Texas.

We continued west, no idea where we were going. Finally got to Portland, Oregon. They fed us in this terminal again, and we swung south to the southern part of the state, Camp White, right outside of Medford, and that's where we wound up.

There was another trainload [of soldiers] that had arrived a few days earlier and were already there, and a cadre from an existing combat engineer outfit in California had been sent up there to form the new 299th Combat Engineers. We were the last section, bringing the strength up about 660 people. We trained there for about three months, basic training, a little bit of everything, and then they sent us up to the desert up in Central Oregon. We didn't even know there was a desert in Oregon. They sent us up about a month ahead of others who had maneuvers scheduled, to prep the area the best we could. We did a lot of cutting trees and stringing telephone lines, what have you. And then the maneuvers started and they lasted almost three months. And at the very end of the maneuvers, we were still in the area, and about half of us got furloughs. And I left there, came home to New York for 14 days. The morning we left it was still dark, real early, and the trucks were all beyond a little wooded area, and I was running a little late, I could hear the trucks revving up, so I was running through this little wooded area and I slipped and fell. I didn't realize until we had been on the trucks a little while, that somebody had decided to use that area [as a latrine] during the night, and I went down in it. You could almost get shot if you got caught doing that!

Anyway, when we got to this city, we had a couple hour layover to get buses up into the state of Washington. I had a chance to get somebody to take my clothes to the cleaners. Now I'm all set to go, and we get on a bus. I don't know how far it was, just across the border and where we're going to pick up a train, we had about an hour wait until the train backed in. Well, we found out they'd oversold the train by two tickets. So all the way to Chicago, me and another guy are trying to sleep in between the backs of the seats. We no more than get there and the conductor booted us out a little bit, because you couldn't block the aisles, see? All the way to Chicago.

And when I got off in Chicago, I looked like I'd come out of a coal bin.

While I was home, I got a telegram to report to Fort Lewis, Washington. We trained there for about a month and all of a sudden, the training stopped and we were making up wills and insurance stuff, bringing everything up to date. We knew something had come up. We figured that we were getting ready to ship to the Pacific out of Seattle. Finally, one night after chow, they said, 'Get a move on. We're moving out in two hours.'

We got ready and they had backed the train right up on the base. We loaded, on to Tacoma and onto Seattle. We got there and our train stopped and jockeyed for over a couple hundred yards and moved back 50 feet and fooled around there for quite a while. All I could think was they're putting a donkey engine on to get us down near the docks, when all of a sudden, the train moved again but this time it kept going a little farther, a little faster, and the first thing we know, we're going full board. We don't have any knowledge and the conductor came down the aisle, so I said, 'Hey, you got any idea where we're going?' He said, 'I'm getting off in Chicago. I have no idea where you're going.'

We get to Chicago and we swing south. Every time the train stopped, the guys would pull out their maps or atlases, see if they can find a fort or a camp in this area; about the time they'd spot one, train would be moving again. I don't know how many times it did this.

We finally got to Florida and we did this [exercise] with the maps and the atlas on a couple of stops. Finally, one morning just before daybreak, we stopped and we sat a long time. We came to the conclusion that this has got to be it no matter where the hell it is, and it was Fort Pierce, Florida. Well, now Fort Pierce might've been a fort 100 or 200 years ago, but I never saw one that was just a city. It had a harbor, small harbor, so the island that runs along

Florida for many, many, many miles, it was cut there because of the harbor. One was called South Island, and the other one was North Island. Then there was a causeway just a few feet above water on each end of town, both the islands. We slept in pyramid tents on South Island and the Navy had a small contingency of personnel there. They had a few landing crafts and stuff for themselves. We lived there. We had to go through town to get over to North Island, go up there a ways for the training, experimental demolition work and practice assault landings, what have you.

Demolition Training

They were building obstacles to the specs that they thought [we were going to face] on the beaches of Normandy, and we were re-testing them to see where's the best place to put the explosives and how much. I guess most of everything had a little bit of overkill to it; they wanted to make sure that when that thing got blown up, whatever it was, that it practically disappeared, couldn't interfere with anybody anymore. During that period, we'd load up these assault boats. We carried two 20-pound sacks of high explosives each and about 36 or 38 of us would run off the boat and there was a block of concrete, not quite as big as this whole room, about the same height, almost the same width [*gestures with arms*]. We'd lay these charges down, stack 'em up, and the last guy with the fuse would pull it, and of course, once we'd dropped our charges, we scattered as far away as we could get—it must've been close to three-quarters of a ton of high explosives, just lying up against that concrete, probably as big as a half a freight car, and it made a hell of a bang when she went, and you'd go up and check it and all it did was scab the front of that thing; after you'd done that several times, the scab got a little deeper and that's it! I don't know how many times we did that.

Then we got involved with what they call a shape charge, which really makes your eyes open, couldn't believe it, 40-pound shape charge put up against a similar wall of ten feet of reinforced concrete. I don't know if you know what a shape charge is. It's about the size of a five-gallon bucket with a pointed front and a hollowed reach. You put the fuse in the opening at the front of it, put the hollow side up against that concrete, and your eyes get awful big when you see what happens when that thing goes off. There's a hole this big [*gestures with arms*], through ten feet of reinforced concrete.

In the course of that training, about the third or fourth day, we went and made all the landings. I come back in and I had made up my mind, no question, if we ever have to do what this training looks like we'll be doing, we're not going to have a prayer, and I was firmly convinced. I spent about three, four weeks working on everybody I knew and even people I didn't know, trying to join the paratroopers, because to me, as bad as that is, I just felt at least you have a shake, whereas this deal is a suicide mission. I couldn't get anybody to go with me, they'd look at me like I was crazy. All kinds of answers but none of them, some of them, they'd say, 'Hell, the war might be over.' But Christ, it hadn't even started over there yet. I couldn't get anyone to even think of it.

Finally, I figured that if I'm going to try to do it, I better do it soon because this training's going to come to an end, so I went in one day before we went out in the morning, and the first sergeant looked up at me to recognize I was there, and he said, 'Yeah?'

I said, 'I've come in to see if I can volunteer for the paratroopers.'

His eyes opened way up wide. He said, 'You what?'

I told him. He said, 'Are you sure?'

I said, 'Yeah or I wouldn't be here.'

Well he paused for a while. Finally, he said, 'All right. I'll see what kind of paperwork's involved and I'll let you know.' About not quite a week later, he called me in. He had an order for me to go to

West Palm Beach to what used to be the Breakers Hotel. Well, the Air Force had taken that over entirely and made a hospital out of it. I was to go down there and have a physical, which I did.

I asked the guy when I was all finished, 'You have any idea how long before I'll hear from this?'

And he said, 'I would say probably a week.' Sure enough, the following Saturday on the way to evening chow, walking on little sand streets with pyramid tents, as I headed for the mess hall, the first sergeant came out of the CP and he spotted me, and he motioned to come over.

He said, 'Did you hear that we received a shipping alert?' Well, every three days there was a rumor, had been for weeks ever since we got there, some of the damnedest rumors you ever could imagine. After a couple of weeks, nobody paid any attention. I'm thinking to myself, 'He knows I heard it,' and before I got a chance to answer him, he said, 'Well, that's not why I called you, but your paratrooper papers came in this morning. The old man signed them, put them in the mail bag, but when we came back from chow this noon, while we were gone, we received a shipping alert. He had us dump the mail bag and go through it and see if anything was going to make any difference, and he pulled your papers.'

So that was the end of the paratroopers, and just a day or two later, we got shipping orders. If that shipping alert that day had come in 20 minutes later... See, they used to come back from the noon chow and take the mail bags across the causeway to Fort Pierce Post Office, and again at 4:30. If that shipping alert had come in 20 minutes later, my papers would have been in the post office, and that would have been it. They would've got them at Fort Benning, and cut me an order, sent it to my outfit, and in fact, if I was on the move, those orders would have chased me anywhere in the country, no matter what outfit I was in, as long as I wasn't walking up a gang plank, getting ready to go overseas. So that was the end of the paratroopers.

*

We shipped out of there shortly after that, Camp Pickett, Virginia. While we were there, we were training, routine training, and all of a sudden, I got an order that I was being transferred from the 1st Platoon, which I'd been in for a year, to the 3rd Platoon. Each platoon had 12 men in each squad, and they all had a classification, which carried a code number. They might be a jackhammer operator, or a bazooka man, a machine gunner, a rifleman, all different in each squad. For some reason, I never did find out exactly, but they switched us. Well, ten weeks later, it would make a big difference in my life.

We were only there about a month, and then, we went up to Camp Kilmer, New Jersey, which was a kickoff point for heading over. And we tested gas masks and brought papers up to date. We were only there three, four days, and it's just a little ways down to where the ferry runs to New York. Went down there, got on the ferry, went over to the dock area, and boarded a converted troop ship. We left there the following day. It formed a convoy, and either later that day, or the next day, another convoy joined, making this one even bigger.

We were about ten days in crossing, and during the crossing, there were two submarine alerts, where everybody comes up out of the belly of the ship, and onto the deck. Both of these were at night, darker than dark, and everybody's out on deck. Nothing happened.

But anyway, we get to Cardiff, Wales, and it was quite a few hours before we got off. We got off, and the train, took us by train down into the Barnstaple-Ilfracombe area. It's not far from the beaches, and they were all Quonset huts. We were in Quonset huts there, every day, we'd drop down to the beach. I don't know where the landing craft came from, but they would be there, too.

Then we'd go out [to sea] and come back, and still all practice on some more experimental stuff with the demolitions. And this went on for, oh, I'd say, four or five weeks. Finally, we knew we were shipping. We had no idea where to, but the assault troops, which was the bulk of the company, they're ready to ship. And we knew the rest of the outfit was going to be shipping a few hours later, but to a different place.

So we shipped over to near the port of Weymouth, to an old British fort. The rear echelon, all the truck drivers, and two corporals, and supply, all non-combat, they had shipped a few hours after we did, God only knows where; we'd had no communications. We were here, I would say, several days. About all we did was physical training and looking at the plans for the assault and watching movies. We had all our explosives with us; I was in a building that had been a gymnasium, but a lot of double bunks, and we had all explosives underneath the bunks.

Loading Up for the 'Real McCoy'

We had no communications with the rest of the outfit at all. We heard about the people that had been over there for a year or two, every now and then, having a practice alert, and they wouldn't know if it was the real McCoy until it was over with. But something about this one, at least to us, seemed like it must be the real McCoy, because when we made that little bit of move that we did make, civilians were out in the street, almost as if we were a parade going by, waving and everything. We'd never had any real practice runs like they had had over there prior. This was our first one, if it was practice, but it didn't turn out to be a practice. We loaded up one morning; it was only a few miles to Weymouth, and we got down there and got off the trucks. They would go from the road, the land, down to the water, and then to the ships.

There were a lot of big ships there, loading up with big equipment, and right beside them was a half dozen or seven or eight LCVPs. So we loaded up and they took us out in the harbor to a British converted freighter called the *Princess Maude,* and when we got there, they lowered the davits for the lifeboats down. Then they took the LCVP and brought it up. We got off with all our equipment, and the LCVPs stayed there. And after a while, I got to thinking, 'Are those what we're going to go in [to the beach] with?' Because, if they are, it's a radical change, because they don't carry the same number of people.' Nothing was certain, and there had been no mention about LCMs and LCVPs.[23] See, the LCM is bigger, and they would carry about 40 men. I don't know how many the LCVP [would carry], I would say, maybe 25. But they definitely were smaller, they wouldn't carry as many men. Shortly after we boarded this ship, word came over the loudspeaker: 'The last mail launch will be along at 4:00.' I had a couple letters, routine letters, one to my folks, one to my girlfriend. I had wanted to do something more [in writing the letters], but I just couldn't. So I put them in the mailbag, and when the launch came by, the bag went in there.

Shortly after the mail launch pulled away, it came over the PA system: 'The operation has been postponed for at least 24 hours.' Boom! Just like that. So, since I had really wanted to write a lengthy letter home, I decided, I'll give it a try, but I didn't know what to

---

[23] *LCMs and LCVPs*-The landing craft mechanized (LCM), also landing craft mechanical, is a landing craft designed for carrying vehicles. (LCVP) landing craft, vehicle, personnel (LCVP) AKA 'Higgins boat' after the designer, was used 'extensively in amphibious landings in World War II. Constructed from plywood, this shallow-draft, barge-like boat could ferry a roughly platoon-sized complement of 36 men to shore at 9 knots (17 km/h). Men generally entered the boat by climbing down a cargo net hung from the side of their troop transport; they exited by charging down the boat's lowered bow ramp.' Source: en.wikipedia.org/wiki/Category:Landing_craft

say, or how to say it, knowing this might be my last letter. Well, I worked five hours on these two letters. I was laying it out so they would know what I knew, or what I thought I knew. I didn't say it quite [flat out], but if you read the whole letter, you'd have to figure, there was a damn good chance that I wouldn't be coming back.

I wish I could remember what I said, but I think I said everything. On the outside of each letter I wrote, 'Please forward as addressed.' I figured if I'm lucky enough not to get blown totally apart and they find [my body] intact, somebody might pull those letters out and forward them to my family. Otherwise, my people are never going to know what happened from beans. I carried these letters in my inside shirt pocket.

They woke us up to feed us about midnight, I think, and I would say, a little after 1:00 AM we started getting ready to load up; this was at Piccadilly Circus, they called it, out in the middle of the Channel. I knew that these LVCPs were staying there, [to load other infantry], because along the side of the ship came an LCM, which we towered over.

Originally I'm still thinking, 'How in the hell are we going to load these things, when we're going to leave men here? They won't fit [in the LVCP].' So that settled it. We're going in, the same thing we've been training on. And we had our explosives, in these 20-pound sacks, all the way from midship to the bow, stacks that fed out several feet high. They all got to be put in the LCMs.

So, we started. They'd pass them to you, and the two guys, in this big old thing, on the side of the ship, you could get them, and we had two men in the LCM. You'd toss [the charges] to them, at two or three, four feet away, you'd get the next one, you're going to toss them, but good God, [they were lowering them] 30 feet down! Well, we waited for this about three times, and I thought, 'Good God, if we have to do this for all these local boats, we're never going to make it on time.'

Now we were [using the type of explosives] that don't go off just because you bang it. You could drop it on the deck, but it takes a charge to make it go off. So I figured, 'No reason why we just can't toss this stuff.' Otherwise, you'd be waiting here forever because the thing's got to go all the way down, and all the way back up, before you even load one [boat].

So I told the two guys in the boat, 'Get to the end of the boat,' and I didn't get a chance to tell them why, because they were already going down, but they knew why shortly afterwards, when these 20-pound things started getting tossed down. Anyway, we told them, it made a big pile. When it was all in, they moved it around, and we went over the side [of the big ship].

And that was no picnic, on account of those swells. You go down and there's the boat, and you're about ready to move on [the landing craft], and it's [bobbing up and down]. You be careful. Thousands of people were doing the same thing, on different ships, and there were many cases of broken legs and what-have-you. And if you fell in between the [ship and the landing craft], that might be the end of you, because that [net] didn't go all the way down.

So, anyway, we finally got in, and once we got it loaded with our gear and our personnel, the boat pulled away, went way out in the Channel, making a big circle, we just circled and circled, I don't know how many times. We paid no attention, because all the other ships had to be loaded the same way, and after a long time, we finally broke from the circle and started in.

Starting In

You didn't have to be in that boat over five or 10 minutes, and you were just soaking wet—every swell, or every wave, you get sprayed—where there's a big wave, you get a big spray, everybody in the boat was wet after a few minutes. We had OD wools on, with denim work-type clothes over them, and they had been impregnated with chemicals for [a potential] gas attack, and they were stiffer than starch. But once you got soaking wet, they softened up. Then we also had the carcass belt, with eight clips of ammunition, and a canteen, and a First Aid kit, and a bayonet, and a couple other things, and a bandolier over each shoulder, two of them, each with eight clips of ammunition, and the M-1. We had a special type of gas mask that served as a flotation belt as well, and rubber tubes vulcanized together for the life preserver, with each tube having a CO2 capsule in the buckle, which activated when you buckled it.

The sea was dark. All this is done in the dark but as it started to get light, you could see when the swells were just so, off in the distance, the cruisers, battleships, and then, of course, you'd dip down, and they'd be out of sight, but they'd come back into sight, and when they started [signaling], you didn't have to be in sight of the ships, you could see the flashes.

It was just a long, cold, dreary ride for quite a while, and a lot of people were getting sick. I'd ridden in many of these things, and I never got sick, and I don't think anybody else ever had before, but the first guy gets sick, and then another. It's quite a few of them, and they learn quick, that you got to know which way the wind's blowing when you go in your helmet and decide to throw it over the side, because the first couple guys who did that wound up wearing it; it came right back on them. I came about as close as I ever had to getting seasick during this run.

We finally hit a point where there were two Coast Guard boats, good-sized boats, but not real big naval ships. They were there to more or less make sure we were in the right area, and then we swung out of the line of ships so that we were now parallel to the beach. On signal, we all started in. We'd been in single file, for about 12 miles.

The boat was tilted a little bit. Didn't even realize it, and why? God knows why. While I'm thinking about this, all I can think of is something's amiss.

I looked out again and I could see water again. That means we've turned twice without realizing it. This machinist had been behind the coxswain's tower. He walks around the coxswain and goes down in the engine compartment. I nudged the guy next to me and said, '[Something's up].' Nothing I could do about it.

All of a sudden, here he comes up. He's got a mesh bag, like the ones that onions come in. He leans over towards the port side, and I follow him. As he gets close to the port side, I can tell the bag's full of corks—I'm thinking, what the hell is he doing? I pull myself up and lean over. He's putting corks in bullet holes, and you can see half a dozen further back that he put in while he was down below. We must've got hit when we made one of those turns, because you couldn't get hit that way otherwise, coming straight in. Up until that point, I knew Higgins boats originally were made out of plywood, I knew the ramp was metal, and I'd been on a lot of them, and I got to where I figured the whole vessel was made out of metal. We had a 40 to 45-foot boat, and two-thirds of it was carrying 30 to 40 men. The other third is the engine compartment, and that took 10 or 12 bullet hits, but where the personnel were, no hits. Anyway, I thought it would take a bullet until this happened; that shocked me because I was so certain that it would [deflect] a bullet.

Now we're getting close. The wood comes out, I don't know how to do it, the ramp's going down. That means you can be ready, because when that's down, you're supposed to be out. I reached, as the ramp was going down, I reached down to get my chargers. When I did, one of the C02 jackets in my belt squeezed, it went off. It's no big deal, it just inflates one section. I've got to unbuckle it. That was it, it wasn't no big deal.

The Belgian Gates

When the ramp went down, it was directly in front of what they call Element C, have you heard of them? I don't know where these names come from. They called it an Element C or Belgian Gate. It's a big, heavy gate, so to speak. The top of it's tilted a little bit, and then in the very center is an eight-pound German teller tank mine. At high tide, all this stuff's under water. If the landing craft touched that mine, it's going bye-bye. Anyway, if I walk straight off the ramp, I'm going to walk right in the middle of it. I've got to go one way or the other. I said to my partner—everyone had a partner—I said, 'Red, pull to the left, will you?' I watched him. He took like a couple steps half left, I went that way too. That means we're going to come in on the left of this thing.

I've got no idea if there's any engineers out in front of us. Bound to be a lot of men, but they're going to be all infantry, as far as I'm concerned. Way up ahead, there's a guy who turned around, facing us, jumping up in the air, hollering and screaming and waving. I can't tell what he's screaming; I'm not even sure who he's screaming at. I had to ignore him, because shells are going off, artillery and mortars and machine guns coming through the water, no matter where you look. I take a few more steps, and he's up there, acting worse than the first time; what I thought at the moment is this guy must've been hit and he's going crazy. I had to ignore him.

Now there's men going down, and you can hear them hollering and screaming that they're hurt. I take this last step off the boat. Now I'm right even with this Element C. I look, and the damn thing is loaded with [mines] all around it. The fuse is floating in the water, and smoking! My heart is right in my mouth; I know as well as I'm sitting here, there's no way in hell, whether it goes off now or 10 seconds or a minute, there's no way I can get far enough away to miss out on this. If that had gone off, it would have killed dozens of us. Well, the outcome of that was, it fizzled. It never went off.

Anyway, I got to forget about it. I go maybe 20 feet farther, 30 feet, and I hit a runnel, you know, that's a little cavity in the sand underwater, they're usually only a few inches, or a foot deep, for a few feet; if you step in it, you step right out of it. I stepped in one and it was about four feet deep! Years later, I thought maybe it was a shell crater. Anyway, I stepped in there, and when I realized how deep it was, I thought, I'm going to try and stay down like this, to just keep my head out of water for a moment or two and see if I can determine what in the hell I ought to be doing next. I'm trying to squat down in the water up to here [*motions chest high*], and my legs are kind of drifting out, which means I'm going to fall and go underwater if I don't correct it. I'm still trying to stay down, at this point, and my leg goes out again; I correct it.

This all happened within a moment or two. In the meantime, I noticed way up ahead, [on the beach], all these guys had exhausted themselves and just had to drop until they could catch their breath; there was a bunch of 'em ahead. Then I realized they must be dead, because the machine gunners were spraying all around, and they'd always come back and hit that area with a good pass, and you could see where they hit because everything was wet, and it would splat when the bullets hit, and I'm thinking, good God, if I'm lucky enough to get that far in, how am I going to get beyond that?

The Vision

Anyway, I'm still in that runnel, and this sounds ridiculous, but I had a vision, if you want to call it that. At my home, the mailman would walk up towards the front porch, but he wouldn't go up the front steps; he'd go around the end of the porch and along down the side of the house to what we called the milk house. That's a side entrance, and he'd put the mail in there—never went up the front steps.

Well I got this vision, just as clear as if he's standing beside me—I see his blue jacket and the blue cap and the leather mailbag. Here he goes up to the house, but he doesn't turn. He goes right up the front steps. This happened so fast, probably a matter of seconds, but the first thing that came to mind, that's the way my folks would find out what happened to me.

I wouldn't want to guess how long these few things took. The next thing I know, I kind of come to, and I'm in the push-up mode. I'm half up, and I'm trying to figure out what the hell happened [to those prone figures on the beach] and all of a sudden, I realized I'm in amongst those bodies! Oh boy, when I realized that.... It had to be 50 yards between the runnel and the pile of bodies. I never did piece it together. I don't know if I was exhausted, or passed out, or what. I think what really shook me was when I envisioned that mailman.

Omaha Beach

I didn't go straight in, because those [sand ridges], they were only this high [*moves hand to knee],* and they gradually went up, but they started a few yards over this way [*gestures to his left],* so I didn't run in straight. I ran like hell for the cover, in case I was lucky enough to get there, I'd have some protection. I got out of there, and now I've got some cover, and there's other guys already there, and there's guys still coming in, and now we're looking around trying to find out who made it so far and who's missing. I noticed two guys had lit these little one-inch paraffin cubes [we carried] for lighting or heating something, like your canteen cup or something. They had got one going on the rock in the [sand dune], sitting there trying to warm their hands, because even though this is June 6, it was pretty damn cold and windy that morning. I spotted them; I realized it was a no-no. I said, 'For God's sake, put that out! The German mortar crews will spot it!'

Now, the smoke was about the equivalent of a cigarette, and Christ, you couldn't see very far for all the other smoke, and they looked at me like I was out of my mind, and at about the same time I realize I'm smoking two cigarettes...

Anyway, after two or three hours, you looked down along that cliff. It gets higher and higher, you know; for two city blocks there were men. They made the cover, but they had to keep moving, but boy, after a while, there was a lot of them. A group that wasn't our people put their hands together, and they give this guy a boost up to have a look-see.

Because it was kind of slanted there, he fell over backwards but they caught him. The second time they angled themselves, and they boosted him up, and something damn near took his head off—helmet came flying off and a good chunk of his head with it! See, the Germans were up on that slope, and they have witnessed these people coming in that area for the last several minutes, so they knew they weren't in sight, but they knew where they were. Somebody puts their head up, and boom.

The Tanker

I looked down to my left maybe 40 or 50 yards. There was one Sherman tank that had pulled right up to this dune line, and all of a sudden the turret opens, and you could see somebody coming up out of the turret, and whoever it was, it looked like he was putting field glasses up, and he didn't get 'em all the way up, that tank took a direct hit on the far side from me! Big cloud of black and orange smoke went everywhere, and out of that cloud, towards the back of the tank, came a big bundle or something. It fell there, probably 12,

14 feet from the back of the tank, and I never seen anyone else get out of that tank. For several hours I watched that bundle. When the tide finally started coming in, long after it happened, for the last 20 or 30 feet, anything floating would just roll up and roll back, but with a net outcome of getting pushed closer to the high-water mark. Little by little, this bundle got closer, and closer, and finally, here it is lying here, and it don't make sense, because all I'd seen is this guy come up out of the turret, which you could see him from here up [*gestures waist high*], and he had been pulling his arms up, and then, boom. I look down, but the top of him isn't there. Now if it was the other way around, it would make sense. But the bottom section of him, which wasn't even out of the tank yet, that's all that's there. I don't know how in the hell that happened; I never could piece that together. Out of the pocket there's a little photo [wallet] hanging, and it's not going to stay there long with the tide, so I reach down, pick it up. And the first picture was a guy in uniform and what looked like probably his wife and a little two or three-year-old girl. And I snapped it back and I put it in his pocket; I reached in and there was nothing in there. This guy doesn't have some other I.D. on him; his dog tags went with the top of him.

The battalion teams continued on into the afternoon and evening working on clearing the beach in their assigned sectors of obstacles.

The Medics

It took a long time because the tide was much farther in. Here comes an LCI, you know what they are? And he's pretty well in when he hits a mine. And there's a hole about yea big [*gestures with arms*] above the water line, probably just one big blow. Bingo, just like that, a mattress went in there [to plug the hole]! And [the landing craft] doesn't go very much farther, and it grounds. And it's not far from me, and they drop the ramps, and all of a sudden, the men start pouring out; out of the sides of that center section, men start running down the deck and down the ramps.

And the first half dozen on each side of the ramp wound up in a pile from machine gun [fire]. And as that happened the rest of them slowed down, turned around, and ran back and got inside. They all had red crosses all over them, every one of them [*slaps arms for Red Cross armbands, taps head indicating Red Cross helmet*] And I read something years later that described what I saw, they referred to it as the First Division's Medical Detachment. I guess about everybody on that thing—and they carry a couple hundred men—I think they must have all been medics. I don't know why the ship didn't have everyone like the hospital ship has, but anyway, we watched it trying to get off. He revved those engines up, and it wasn't moving a whisker. And every moment or two he'd try it again. Of course, the tide was still coming in, and after it must have been 15, 20 minutes before that thing moved. And he edged it back, right straight out and out of sight. According to the article I read, he unloaded all the personnel, the wounded and the ones who were all right. And not long after he finished unloading the personnel, it sank. I'm pretty sure it's the same one.

Now finally [with the tide going out] I realized that elements, the Belgian gates in the sea out in front of me, are still there. We'd been there a Christ-long time, and I reckon that's the first time I realized it didn't go off! In fact, we stripped it later that day to get the charges, to take them down [the beach to] where they were needed more than that.

And we stayed pretty close to this area where we were, because we had no equipment; other than the explosives, we had absolutely no engineering equipment at that moment. So, we were waiting to find out what the story is, and against the mortars; we're not going to stick our neck out piecemeal.

But anyway, it was now, I don't know, six, seven o'clock in the evening. It didn't get dark until close to nine or 10 o'clock at night. But here comes an LCM in, we can't see anything until the ramp comes down and here comes this big guy in denims. Clean, nice, he comes walking up towards us and he gets probably 20, 30 feet from us and he motions to the LCM. He said, 'You men get those litters off that boat,' and we can't see them from where we are, because we're down a few yards up close to the sand dunes.

But he could see [the wounded], walking up the beach from the ship. He said, 'You men get those litters off and load those wounded up.' He points over there where the wounded are. And we did. We went and got the litters and we brought in quite a few, but we still couldn't get them all on there. And as soon as he said that, he just headed for the other end of the beach and we never saw him again, but I did find out from a friend of mine, who was halfway down the beach, that the next morning they found this guy [dead], the rumor was this poor guy was a one-star general! The only thing I ever read was the fact that there was supposed to be no line officers of that grade in the field in Omaha, though [I know Teddy Roosevelt Jr.] landed at Utah and he died from a heart condition a week or two later. Anyway, I had no idea who the hell he was.

The First Night

That night we stayed in the same area for the cover [afforded by the dunes], but you couldn't dig in there because it was nothing but three inches of stone [where we wanted to settle down]. I [found a discarded ventilation shaft from an amphibious tank], one of these big gizmos [*gestures with hands wide apart*], which were five or six feet high over the back end of the tank—the purpose of them was so the tank can run if it's half underwater, but once they get ashore, they get rid of those. Well, there was one lying not far from me and

I had to pull like hell, I dragged it over close, but because of the [bent] angle of the thing, I was [struggling], as I was trying to load it full of stone. I didn't get very far, but I pulled it up close [to our exposed side] and left about that much space [*gestures about one foot*] between it and the cliff.

I lay there with my partner, and finally we went to sleep. And I knew that when the tide came in, we'd be in for a fight against the water, but it didn't bother us any; in fact, I don't even recall if I woke up, but I knew that at high tide I would be lying there in a few inches of water.

The next day we were out trying to cover the beach. You got three, four hundred guys on the open beach when the tide's out, in four to five miles, looking for explosives that had been jettisoned or lost the day before, and we found quite a bit of them.

During this period, I was with two guys from my outfit, C Company, and there was another guy who was a stranger, I thought he might be from A Company. They had also landed, and B Company landed on Utah. Well, come to find out, he was an infantryman. All I could figure was this guy that came in sometime that morning, somehow got disconnected from whatever unit he was with, or he decided if he could get 'disconnected,' he'd make himself look busy here instead of moving on. The 2nd Division, I think, was coming in that D+1. Any work with us was finding these explosives and moving them down the beach. Who was I to say that if [the guy wants to do it, I should stop him?]

So, they had blown one bunch of [obstacle explosives] we had brought down and were almost ready to blow another section. We moseyed up to the dune line again to where the ground pitched [back a little bit to form a hollow], took three or four paces down in there, and turned around and lay down facing the Channel, because you got a little cover there [from the beach demolition]. We're all lying there, elbow to elbow, four of us. They hollered,

'Fire in the hole!' We waited a minute, because they were hollering again, 'Fire in the hole!', and they let her go. We just held still in case there was any fallout. Then we got up and started over to that little path, three or four steps back down the dune line.

I was the third one out of the four of us. As I started to go over the dune line, I happened to glance back. This other guy, the stranger, he's lying there. He's not moving or anything. I thought, 'Jeez, something's wrong there.' So I moseyed back. As I approached him, I kicked his feet. No response at all. I thought, 'Oh no.' So I bent down, and lifted him. [*Hunches over, bends from waist in his seat, as if he is lifting something with both arms*] Christ, he looked like he was dead. I rolled him right over and his face was up now—he was deader than a doornail. Some damn sniper up the slope had timed his shot with our explosion, because he had seen the first one blow. He just waited until we blew again. He heard that, 'Fire in the hole,' and then shortly after that, that booming, he just timed it. Here you got four people he could see, but he could only get one of them. The guy next to me, right there close to me, is gone. I'm glad it wasn't anybody I knew.

[There was a lot of that]. We were picking up a lot of stuff, mines that had been on the beach, and moved them over into a pile. Helmets, trying to clear up the area a little bit, another pile. I don't know how many piles of helmets I seen that would cover the area in this room, maybe a hundred plus helmets. Many piles of them, here and there, all down the beach. The 1st Division landed where we were at, the 29th Infantry Division landed on the western half. They both had a big logo on the helmets; the 29th was something like the Union Pacific Railroad logo there. The 1st Division had the big red '1.' I don't know how many helmets that were sticking out of those piles that I saw with a bullet hole right through the logo [*points forefinger to forehead*], so many of them.

*

Artillery was still coming in late D-Day and the following day or two, but not as much—every once in a while, you might get an artillery shell or two, which wasn't much for the whole beach area, but they were still taking a crack. The Germans knew where we were and they knew a lot of activity was going on there, but they weren't wasting any rounds; I don't recall getting any damage [at that time].

The Second Night

The second night, we moved down towards the center section of the beach and dug some fresh foxholes. We had a little battalion command post down at the foot of the slope; it was probably 40 yards of grassy area to the dune line. I was brought down there to be a runner—wound up I didn't do any running, but I was sent down there because our battalion officers had foxholes down in there.

When I got down there, here's a monster tree, four feet thick, which had been felled and stripped, and the big trunk was still lying there; I think the Germans knocked it down just so it wouldn't interfere with their field of fire. Right underneath this thing is a full-sized foxhole; I thought, 'Good God. That must belong to somebody,' but there was no gear around it. I had my sack with me, and my helmet and rifle; I moseyed over there, and I put my things down. I figured nobody claims this, that's where I'm going to be, best hole on the beach.

I was in there and I was sleeping that night. Suddenly, I hear this commotion and we're being strafed. The minute I realized that we're being strafed, I started shaking—D-Day morning, when we got ashore, I was shaking like this, but I was half-cold and half-frightened at the time. Now I'm lying in this hole, stretched right out, my gas mask behind my head, and I started shaking again. My whole body's going like this [*does a shaking motion*]; I couldn't stop it. I think there were two planes that went over; first one made a pass, and then another one. After another little bit of time, they came over again, and my whole body was shaking hard. I took my arms and I forced my elbows into the side of the hole—if I was forcing it, I'd stop shaking. This happened three or four times. The last time I held my elbows out for a long time. Little by little, I pulled them away. I didn't shake. But I'd never seen anybody shake like that; that's the only time that ever happened.

That second day, there were a lot of wounded left over from D-Day. When we woke up in the morning, these barges made of four-foot metal cubes all welded together were half the size of a football field, big, flat. We covered the whole deck with wounded.

On the third morning, there were two real great big barges, where if it was on dry land, it would be 12 or 15 feet from the bottom to the deck. The deck's got another 10 or 12-feet-high stack of 10-in-1 rations. You know what they are? Big boxes, and five-gallon water cans, probably several thousand. We were taking them off, as many as we needed.

We jumped up onto a knocked-out LCI at low tide, and went through, never been on one, just snooping around, and I got a pair of real fancy binoculars. I didn't have them long. Oh, they were powerful. I found a case half full of what turned out to be pea soup, with a bottle-type cap. You open it, and you won't want to touch it for a while, I learned the hard way. I opened it, and I went to sip it, but in that length of time it was scalding! If you opened it and let it sit for a moment or two, it was all right, but boy, you put it up to your mouth quick, you get burned. We each took a couple cans, and I never saw anything like it afterwards. That would have been a handy thing to have all during the war.

I also saw something down in that area that I just couldn't believe. You know what an LCT is?[24] As we got down in the middle of the beach, there's one not too far out, upside down and the flat bottom was up, wider than two of these rooms [*gestures across the room*]. How in the hell that thing got there, I don't know, and there was one that had beached. It happened close to high tide because it was right up into the landing zones. It was full of halftracks with a quad machine in it. The first one that [had disembarked] went about from here to the bathroom [*gestures across the room*], and you could see it had been burned right to a crisp. And the next one behind it had caught fire; I think they all caught fire. Later I saw a picture of this, but you can't tell they are all burned because it's black and white—you would swear there's nothing wrong with these things, but they're burned right up. The one that had got off and went those few feet, the burned people were still in there, burned to a crisp. If you wanted to wander around that beach, you could see just about anything. You'd find an arm here or a leg there, half-buried in the sand from a tide or two.

'This was a Suicide Mission'

Shortly after the landing we got replacement soldiers in, even when we still had no equipment and were waiting on it. This one [replacement] guy who was in my squad, after a few days of talking with him, said that he had been [chosen as a replacement for our unit, even before the landings]! He had been in one of the biggest 'repple-depples' in England; there were 25,000 people there. He said they kept drawing men, they'd draw two men, they'd draw 20 men, they'd draw 100 men, all day long, every single day, and when his

---

[24] *LCT*- The landing craft, tank was an amphibious assault craft for landing tanks on beachheads.

name came up, he and others were assigned to the 299th Engineers, but that they were not going to embark immediately.

I got to thinking; I said to him, 'How big of a draw were you in?'

He said, 'Oh, God, there must have been over 400.'

And I thought, 'Jesus. Talk about giving us the shaft.'

We had no communication just before we left England between our rear echelon command and the assault troops. You know, the rear echelon knows [what's going on]. So, I discovered that two or three days before D-Day, this big draw-out from the repple-depple is assigned to the 299th, [even before we landed]! All I could think of was, boy, I was right when I was at Fort Pierce, [training on the demolition teams], and the [command] knew it; all the plans [for our part in the D-Day invasion] were generated after that—they knew this was a suicide mission! We're going to be replaced 100%, and our rear echelon isn't even going to be here yet! But nobody ever said 'boo'; I pieced that together—there was no doubt in my mind. They knew what the mission was. It was bad enough that the infantry was getting dumped off there, and they have to cross three or four hundred yards of open beach, hoping they can get to the dune line without getting killed or wounded, and it is going to be a hell of a thing; fifty percent didn't make that three or four hundred yards. Our objective was entirely different. We were supposed to land three minutes later, but these two waves, infantry and engineers, got all intermingled [in the confusion of the morning]. But our objective, [unlike theirs], was not to get over to the dune line. Instead, we would be going in, say fifty yards, and we would start working, two or three people standing still, working together. Our rifles aren't even in the position to fire, we need both hands to work with. We're not even facing the beach half the time, and we're standing still with all these machine guns playing out there... it's a wonder we had the survivors we did. In a couple of cases where the infantry had a late boat coming in, they dropped them off and they're scooting up to the beachhead like they should, but they're going through an area that's about ready to be blown by us. And it got to a point where the demolition guys are ready to blow an obstacle, and realize they're not going to be able to unless they want to kill a bunch of infantry guys lying there for cover, so they tried to make it in themselves.

It was many years later before I realized, the only reason that we had any survivors is because the whole landing—I say the whole landing, well, at least for ninety-plus percent of it—landed anywhere from a hundred yards to a thousand or two thousand yards, and in one case a mile or more east of where they were supposed to land. I had no idea how far east I was or from where I was supposed to land. We lost fifty percent of our men as it was, but if everybody landed where they belonged and we'd had that 150 yards on each side of us with no interference, we would have been able to stay out there to complete our mission, but in doing so we'd have been caught out there even longer; we'd have all gotten [killed]. Nobody's ever put that together, that I know of.

Today, a monument and memorial in Auburn and Cayuga Counties remind passersby of this day and the loss of their sons in the 299th Combat Engineer Battalion. James E. Knight went on to see more combat at the Battle of the Bulge and later fought into Germany and Central Europe. He passed away on February 3, 2012, at the age of 87.

CHAPTER TWELVE

The Tanker

'WE KEEP THE FAITH'—MOTTO OF THE 743RD TANK BATTALION

I first met Bill Gast at a reunion of the 30th Infantry Division Veterans of World War II in 2008 in North Carolina. I would get to know him that weekend, and even better when he and his wife and sons traveled to my high school in the fall of 2009 to our second 'American Soldiers/Holocaust Survivors Reunion' where he was able to reunite with seven survivors from the Bergen-Belsen concentration camp who were liberated from a train transport that the 743rd Tank Battalion had intercepted in the closing days of the war. Several years earlier I had interviewed a tank commander from D Company, Carrol Walsh of Johnstown, New York, who told me the story of coming across the train. That set into motion a series of events which led to the reunions of these Holocaust survivors and World War II soldiers sixty-plus years later. Bill's company was not in the immediate vicinity of the train, but I think for him and many of the soldiers, meeting the people their unit saved in person helped them to push some wartime demons to the background.

I sought Bill's testimony out for this book because he was one of the few soldiers who fought through all of the five campaigns the 743rd was engaged in across Europe after landing on Omaha Beach ten minutes before H-Hour on D-Day—Normandy, Northern France, Rhineland, Ardennes, and Central Europe. He was awarded the Silver Star and the Purple Heart during his tour and went on to marry his high school sweetheart Vivian, or 'Betty', who wrote him all through the war and accompanied him to our reunions. Bill rarely went to World War II reunions, and I think our 2009 gathering was his final one.

'At eighteen years old, I only completed half my senior year of high school, I'm just a boy. Really, I thought I was something, you know. You do all your training, you get tough, you're hard, you're all full of it, you know. But as soon as you see someone blowing up, that's an altogether different story... To see a pregnant lady sitting in a rocking chair with a baby in her arms being shot through the head, it's hard to understand.... How do you describe something like that? I guess that's why I don't come back to some of these things...'

William Gast, Jr.

I was seventeen, a junior in high school when war [began] on December 7, 1941. In order for the draft boards to meet their quota of men, the draft age was lowered to eighteen, and less than a year later on December 4, 1942, I was inducted into the army in New Cumberland, Pennsylvania, and was transferred to Fort Knox, Kentucky, for basic training at Army Armor School and learned mechanical skills. Then I went onto Camp Campbell, Tennessee, to learn to operate equipment. Camp Laguna was a barren camp in Newman, Arizona, and there I joined the 743rd Tank Battalion for desert training and maneuvers.

Originally our outfit was to be shipped to Africa to enter the conflict against the Nazis under the command of Rommel, who was known as the 'Desert Fox.' It became apparent that [the end of the conflict in North Africa] was imminent, so the 743rd was redirected to be shipped overseas, destination unknown, via Camp Shanks, New York, port of embarkation. It was top secret; no one was allowed on or off the base. We bordered the overcrowded *HMS*

Aquitania, the third fastest ship of the Allied forces, and crossed the Atlantic in seven days, unescorted.

The voyage was rough and there was extensive sea sickness, but fortunately I was spared that agony. I do remember one incident, however. We had been issued little wool knit caps to wear under our helmet liners. One night as another soldier and I were standing on deck leaning over the rail watching our ship cutting through the water, a gust of wind came along, and my cap blew overboard. The troops had to be on deck each morning for inspection, regardless of conditions; helmets were not required for inspection, but we were to wear our little knit caps.

'Gast, where's your cap?' Captain Phillips barked.

'It flew overboard, sir!' was my reply.

'Did your razor blow overboard, too?'

End of conversation.

*

The 743rd disembarked on November 24, 1943 in Scotland just in time for Thanksgiving dinner. After spending the night on rope beds with straw ticks, we traveled by train to Camp Chiseldon, Wiltshire, England. Our training was intense as we prepared for the invasion. I was a medium tank driver in Company A, and on December 3 we left for special assault training. During maneuvers, one soldier was killed by shrapnel fragments in a range accident, and eleven were drowned when the craft carrying their tanks overturned in the high surf off the coast in the English Channel. Their tanks became their tomb.

As we got closer to what eventually would become D-Day, we loaded our tanks onto LCTs, and went out into the Channel. Imagine having three 35-ton tanks jammed onto a little boat barely big enough to hold them and the 15 men that operated them, then leaving in the middle of the night for training—or the real invasion, we never really knew if it was an exercise or the real thing. [25] D-Day was supposed to happen on the 5th of June, but because of the extreme Channel weather conditions we got called back, and we got to do it all over again the next night.

The channel was very rough, cold, misty, and wet, and we were getting nervous. Because the hours were dragging on, we threw a tarp under the tank to try to get some sleep, [but there was just] too much tension. Through the night we became friendly with the LCT captain. We got to talking about getting the LCT in close enough to the beach so when the ramp was lowered, and we drove our tanks off into the surf, they would not be submerged. He promised he would get us close enough, and that is what he did, but many of our tanks never made it to the shore. The fighting was fierce, casualties were high, and a lot of our equipment was destroyed.

In the planning for the D-Day operations, armored support for the infantry troops was prioritized for the initial landings, with the 741st Tank Battalion and the 743rd Tank Battalion spearheading the effort. Some

---

[25] *35-ton tanks*-Mr. Gast described his tank: 'Our tank was a Sherman M4 Medium Tank that weighed approximately 35 tons. Each tank had a crew of five men—driver, assistant driver, gunner, assistant gunner, and a tank commander. Our first tanks had a cast hull with a 75mm main gun, a .30-caliber machine gun mounted beside it on the right, and another .30-caliber machine gun, known as a bow gun, which the assistant driver operated. There was also a .50-caliber machine gun mounted on top of the turret with a 360-degree traverse that the tank commander could use for direct fire or anti-aircraft. A little later we received a tank with a welded hull; it had more armor plate and a lower silhouette of the turret. Later this same tank came with a 76mm main gun. These tanks had four different engine configurations; we had rubber-cleated tracks, also steel-cleated tracks, and we were taught how to remove and replace tracks and cleats [as necessary]. The gas tank held about 250 gallons; I got about two gallons per mile, and out on an open, level, hard-surfaced road I could get the tank up to about 35 miles per hour.'

companies of the 741st tanks were equipped with inflatable rubberized canvas skirting and a duplex drive propulsion system (hence the name 'DD tanks') with dual propeller screws in the rear so they could be launched far offshore and 'swim' to the tidal flats. Unfortunately, out of the 741st's 29 DD tanks launched (in waters much rougher than what they had trained for), only two made it the three-mile distance to shore, the others foundering and sinking almost immediately and entombing their tankers inside.[26] *The 743rd landed much closer and was in combat all day, opening a draw to lead an advance off the beach later that night. At the end of this first day in combat, the 741st Tank Battalion had just three tanks operational, two in repair, and had lost 48 tanks. In contrast, the 743rd reported 38 tanks still operational, although Bill's A Company of the 743rd Tank Battalion had lost eight tanks and six tank dozers.*[27]

---

[26] *sinking almost immediately and entombing their tankers inside* -An interesting side note regarding the recovery of the remains of these drowned tankers: "For years, the tanks and the crewmen's remains sat in the seabed, where they were ravaged by the elements and scavengers. The French asked the U.S. 'to return the remains of the soldier-heroes back to their families for final and decent burial.' The Army refused to fund further search efforts, claiming its responsibility 'begins when the tanks are out of the water.' The Navy's position was that the tanks belonged to the Army. In 1987 President Reagan ordered a salvage effort in response to a French fisherman's complaints. It was too late. An Army scuba diver found the tanks and a few were brought ashore, but nothing remained of the crew. Today, the soldiers' personal effects and the salvaged DD tanks from Omaha Beach are in private hands. A few of the tanks are in museums. If you go to Omaha Beach, in Colleville-sur-Mer, you'll find an engraved plaque with images of the floating tanks of the 741st Tank Battalion." Source: Douglas, Alan M., "The Tank That Sank on D-Day", *The Wall Street Journal*, June 5, 2019.

[27] *At the end of this first day in combat*-Data figures here sourced at globeatwar.com/blog-entry/us-741st-and-743rd-tank-battalions-omaha-beach.

The Landing

Now it was just around 0600 hours in the morning and as we looked out over the side of our LCT, there were boats and landing craft as far as you could see.

'Mount up and get your engines started! This is it!' The captain of the LCT did as he promised. The front ramp was lowered and the first tank drove off. Then I drove down the ramp and I could feel my tracks turning, then they took hold of the bottom of the channel and I was able to move forward. I found out later that the water had all kinds of metal obstacles to prevent us from coming onto the beach, loaded with everything you could think of to keep us from advancing.

The [hatch above me] was closed and sealed, but in the middle of it there was a slit with a little hinged cover. I was able to push a periscope up through this slit by hand. Inside I had a little window about three inches high and about six inches wide for me to see outside, and for me to be able to look around I had to manually push it forward and backward to see up and down, and manually turn it left or right to see in those directions—all while driving the tank. I had two levers that came up from the floor. I pulled on the right one to go right, pulled on the left one to go left, and pulled on both together to stop the tank, and sometimes it took both hands just to pull one lever. In addition, I had to operate a clutch with my left foot and an accelerator pedal with my right foot, and I had the gear shift lever with five forward speeds and one reverse, and that also took both hands to operate. We had intercom radios in the tank that didn't work most of the time, so the only one who could really see was the tank commander who sat above me, who would have to stick his head up out of the turret. He had a very dangerous job. He told me where to drive by kicking me on the right shoulder to go right or the left shoulder to go left. He would have to hang on to the turret rim with both hands and put both feet on my shoulders for me to back up. Plus, he had to see from which direction the firing was coming to tell our gunner where to concentrate his firing.

'Throwing Marbles at a Car'

I could hear the machine gun bullets hitting our tank, it sounded like someone throwing marbles at a car. I could feel the big shells exploding in front of and beside us, and it would make the tank shake. By dusk we finally made it up to the wall, that's as far as we could go. Up against the wall we were protected from direct fire and started to get a little organized. We learned that out of the fifteen tanks of A Company, only five of us had made it. Now, I have something to say that bothers me to this day. The beach was covered with dead and wounded soldiers, and there is no way of telling if I ran over any of them with my tank.

Sometime during the night, the engineers were able to blast enough of the wall away, enabling us to exit the beach the next morning and get on top of the bluff.

Bill gently insisted to me that he be referred to not as a liberator, but as a fellow survivor of World War II. Now you know why. Mr. Gast's story will continue in Part Four.

Tony Leone's USS LST 27 loading for the D-Day invasion in England. Source: National Archives, public domain.

CHAPTER THIRTEEN

The Coast Guardsman

He sits behind a student desk, wearing a medal presented to him by the French government that he also wears to Mass every Sunday. 'I wear it with pride to pay homage to those fellows who burned alive next to me. I made it and they didn't. It still bothers me.'[12]

He rests on his walking cane and leans forward as he speaks. He is animated—he motions with his hands to emphasize his points. A prolific author and letter writer to the local daily newspaper, Anthony's mission is to educate the public about what his generation of Americans went through: 'It would be at least 25 years after World War II before I could begin to think about the experiences of that time. They were buried deep in my subconscious and remained there so that my mind and body could heal.'

Upon rediscovering the war journals he kept as an 18-year-old, 'the disorganized scrawl of a frightened youth stranded in the middle of hell,' Anthony decided to conduct research and write it all down once again to contextualize the trauma that he and his shipmates experienced. He put out several monographs and wrote newsletters for his brothers-in-arms, many of which were reprinted in the U.S. LST Association's official magazine.[13]

He came to my classroom to speak on many occasions. He had strong opinions, and he had things to get off his chest. He talked to anyone who would listen, and my teenagers were a captivated audience. He spoke rapidly, as if the words themselves were screaming to get out of him.

*

'I hate snakes, and I could feel the snake slithering between my legs. They were firing live ammo over our heads but I endured and the snakes didn't bother me... I didn't raise my head and get it shot off, so I'm here to tell you about what happened after that. We were the Suicide Navy, they called us. A very apropos title.'

Anthony F.J. Leone

I got assigned to USS LST 27. I said to myself, 'What the heck is an LST?' We boarded in Norfolk, Virginia. I carried my sea bag, along with the rest of the graduates of boot camp, up this long gangway. This was the biggest vessel I had ever seen in my life! If you had it up here on Lake George, it was 327 feet long, imagine that, and 50 feet wide. That's a big ship.

'LST' stands for 'Landing Ship, Tanks.' What we did is carry small boats. We sent the small boats in first loaded with troops and vital supplies, then we came in right up to the beachhead with the LSTs and opened the bow doors and dropped the ramps. But on D-Day, not even the small boats could get in among the obstacles, and there were mines all over the place. They were killing our soldiers like sheep to the slaughter.

*

We left Norfolk in March of 1944 and landed in Africa. We had gone through bad air raids by the Germans in the Mediterranean and U-boat attacks but we survived. One ship was hit and set afire, a ship carrying lumber, and incidentally the crews couldn't get the fire out; it was in the stern of our convoy. We got attacked by the Luftwaffe, JU-88s and Dornier torpedo bombers.

I didn't tell you this previously, but I almost lost my life there. I was the loader on a 20mm anti-aircraft gun; it's obsolete now, but back then it was a pretty good gun, pretty accurate, made in Sweden. I was about to get another magazine and load it when a bomb landed on the port side of the ship, a near miss, and it swung our LST over to the starboard. I was going over into the dark Mediterranean with a magazine in my hand and I said to myself, 'There goes Leone, you're done,' but the aimer grabbed me by the back of my lifejacket and pulled me back. That was close; that was my first baptism by fire right there. I was 18 years old, screaming hysterically and shaking a fist, but if a real German had popped up in front of me on the deck, I would have fainted dead away. [*Laughs*] I was scared; heroes are heroes, but most are scared. And we succeeded in almost obliterating the British anti-aircraft cruiser on our port side; I think some of the guys did it deliberately, some guys didn't like the British too much. They knocked the radar off, but that's a story I don't wish to go into.

*

We reached Africa without further incident and then we sailed for England. We landed in Swansea, Wales, and we got liberty [after] we unloaded an LCT from the ship. An LCT is a long, wide, flat-box sort of landing craft where the ramp drops down and the conning tower is in the back, and we had one topside. We carried it piggyback; what we did was fill the starboard bilge tanks with water and then chop the cables holding the LCT on, onto these greased wooden skids. By severing the cables, the thing would slam into the water with a big splash. We got rid of that thing because there were some heavy seas and we were top heavy. These were the craft that would land the men, later on.

About the end of May, about a week before D-Day, we went to Southampton, and then to Falmouth, to become part of the backup force for the D-Day landings. We took on units from the 175th Infantry, which belonged to the 29th Division. Everything was frozen in place, we couldn't move. The area was sealed off, we couldn't go on liberty, we couldn't visit the British girls, which was quite a sacrifice in those days, since they were all over the Yanks. We were like the invention of sliced bread; the British girls couldn't get enough of the Yanks. [*Laughs*] We had a lot of money I guess, and we showed up the British servicemen pretty bad. The American troops over there, their behavior was abominable. The British treated them really good, but the Americans were spoiled, had a lot of money, and... well, it's the same old story.

They sealed us off, and on the 4th and 5th of June we were ready to go. We headed toward 'Piccadilly Circus,' that was the code name of the circle in the middle of the Channel that we were supposed to rendezvous at; from there the flotillas would go towards the English beachheads [in Normandy] and we would go towards the American beachheads, Omaha Beach and Utah Beach.

We went out to the sea on the 5th, and it was really stormy. Eisenhower was really blown away by [the weather]. So, they waited, and I guess a British meteorologist saw a break, a window in the weather. Eisenhower had decided to go for it, he had his fingers crossed, he had a letter ready apologizing for the loss of lives and withdrawal from the continent in case it failed.[28] So, we went; the

---

[28] *he had a letter ready*-Eisenhower had hastily drafted a letter accepting responsibility in the event of a colossal failure at the Normandy landings: "Our landings in the Cherbourg-Havre area have failed to gain a satisfactory foothold and I have withdrawn the troops. My decision to attack at this time and place was based upon the best information available. The troops, the air and the Navy did all that Bravery and devotion to duty could do. If any blame or fault attaches to the attempt it is mine alone." National Archives.

first units moved up from the British ports of Southampton, London, Plymouth, and Portland. We were the second, the backup force from Falmouth.

The Americans had gotten off the beach by late June 6. Of course, [before that], the Germans had mowed them down like a wheat field. As I said before, there were German privates just sitting there with machine guns, just killing Americans and crying as they were doing it, 'Please go back, I don't want to kill no more!' [*Repeats this line in German*]. At one point, General Bradley was going to pull them off, take all the people at Omaha Beach and bring them over to Utah. Utah was a pretty successful landing—there, casualties were [far less].

By the time we got to the [Omaha] beachhead the next day, it was a mess. We came in with the LSTs. We had already launched our LCVPs [on June 6] which brought in the troops, the 'Landing Craft Vehicle-Personnel,' that is, a Higgins Boat. It was invented by Andrew Higgins, a boat builder from the United States. Then it was time for us to come in and unload the tanks.

It was now June 7; all you saw was a layer of white smoke on the beach. The [US Army] Rangers had gotten in behind the Germans, but when we [first arrived there with the big ship], it was still hot, there were still mines all over the place, hedgehogs and stakes driven in the ground with Teller mines sitting on them. At high tide when you came in you couldn't see them. Our LCVPs had to negotiate between them; this was impossible at high tide, you had to wait until the tide was way out, then the soldiers had to walk almost half a mile over bare land, no foliage or anything.

As we came in, it was pretty hard to negotiate because the mined obstacles were still all over the place and there were pieces of human bodies floating all over. The American soldiers had the life belts on that you activate, and they inflated because they had a CO^2 cartridge. But because the guys had heavy packs on, it would upend them and drown them because they couldn't get loose. We saw a lot of soldiers floating that way. Their life belts worked all right, but they killed them. Their bodies floated to and fro all day long.

After we saw that, we were not too enthusiastic about going in and hitting the beach—we said, 'If this is happening out here, what is going to happen there?' Even though it was a couple days later, we were all armed to the teeth. We had our clothing well-impregnated with chemicals to withstand a gas attack, and when your body got out of it, that stuff would drive you crazy.

'The Shadow'

We proceeded in. Now up in our conning tower, our officers had barricaded themselves behind a pile of mattresses up in the bridge, not that they were 'chicken,' they were just being smart about the whole thing, they didn't want to get hit with shrapnel.

We had that on and we were all ready to go over, life jackets and helmets, I was manning the 20mm gun and all of a sudden, the public address system crackled. I heard the damnedest noise, that scared me more than the enemy, really, when it first came on [*singing*], *'Mairzy doats and dozy doats And liddle lamzy divey/ A kiddley divey too/ Wouldn't you?'* It was the voice of our skipper, and he was dead drunk. [*Laughs*] Now understand that he was a very solemn-looking individual, dark, so dark that at night we couldn't see him, so we called him 'The Shadow'—when he walked on the bridge, all you would see was the glow of his cigarette. He would let it burn to his lips and then spit it out, he was [tough as nails]. So here is this guy who is fearless, and as we were going in, he is singing *'Mairzy Doats.'*[29] I would have chosen a different tune really, but everyone

---

[29] *Mairzy Doats*-A silly novelty song that hit #1 in the US pop charts in March 1944. As others have noted, the amusing sheet music lyrics sung by Mr. Leone are revealed in the song's bridge: *"If the words sound queer and funny*

burst out laughing, so it was a morale builder in a sense. It told us the captain was human after all, and he was just as much afraid as we were!

The 'Blast Furnace'

So we went in and hit the beach, started up the ventilator fans as we had big tubes coming out of the tank deck to suck the exhaust fumes out—and incidentally, both their vehicles were burning oil, don't know why, poor maintenance. They got them going and the trucks were towing—this was the 175th Heavy Tank Company, it was part of the 29th Division—they started to move out when the brake seized on the 57mm anti-tank cannon carriage they were towing in the back of the lead truck. Marion Burroughs, a friend of mine who was driving it, later told me, 'God that saved my life, that brake locking up like that, it never happened before in all my years of working with it.' That's the way things happen, you know. He motioned for the other truck to go back around him—it was an army wrecker, used for picking up tanks or wrecked vehicles. It went around and both of the vehicles went out; the wrecker hit a mine just coming off the ramp. They had it taped off where it was safe you know, I still think they went 'off the tape,' the taped-off lanes to distinguish between the mined and unmined areas... It blew up and there were bodies all over the place and the trucks were filled with Chesterfield and Old Gold cigarettes, I remember vividly; 'Lucky Strike had gone to war' with gold packaging—they had taken the green out of the cigarette wrapper to save the cadmium that was green, I think. Well, I remember those cigarettes just went all over

---

to your ear/ A little bit jumbled and jivey/ Sing 'Mares eat oats and does eat oats/ And little lambs eat ivy/ A kid'll eat ivy too/ Wouldn't you?"

the place, bazooka shells, the thing was loaded with ammo and gasoline and it went up, a flaming cauldron—it was like a blast furnace! These poor guys were screaming and they were pinned to the frame and you could see the rubber of the tires all turning to liquid and dripping. And their screams! It seemed like they screamed long after life left their bodies. I still hear them sometimes. If you ever hear a person screaming in agony when they were being burned alive... [*looks down, shakes head*]

We went out to see what we could do. I reached down and a piece of shrapnel came through the top of my helmet, punched it open, and broke some skin. I didn't realize it until later, when the thing fell off my head and landed on the deck. You couldn't get near the fire because the flames were so hot. A couple of individuals did rescue somebody, and I went out again to get another helmet. They were all over the place, like coconuts. I saw one with netting on it, and I went to get it and 'zing-zing-zing' [*gestures quickly, tapping the air in succession three times*], there were little bursts of sand right in front of it. Some German probably anticipated my move and said, 'Well, this guy's not going to get his helmet.'

One of our officers, a deck officer, a little fellow named Serge, went out and dragged somebody back to the ship. Now they had always made fun of Serge because of his size; he was puny, like another Don Knotts, all nervous and such. They all used to pick on him, like making him stand on a table because he was Jewish, things like that; that was World War II, you know. A colored steward would have to stand on the back of the bus—even though he survived a lot of battles, he had to stand on the back of the bus in Norfolk, Virginia. This is what World War II was really like.

He went out in the surf, the crazy [son of a gun, and rescued some guys], and he got back, I think he got the Silver Star or something for it. He was ten feet tall in our eyes after that. Finally, we closed the damn bow door; we lifted the ramp—it takes ages for that thing to come up on chains—and we closed the bow. We waited for the fires to subside and the flames went down, and we went out. We hated to see what was still out there. Things were still hot, fires were still burning, everything was gone—it was just bones sitting there, grinning skeletons.

The 'Suicide Navy'

[Later] on Utah Beach on June 19, a big storm stirred up a lot of mines. As we were coming in our lookout yelled, 'Stop engines! Wreckage in the water, dead ahead!' We slowed and stopped. Apparently, there was an LCT that had been hit earlier and it was lying there. Had we gone another 25 or 30 feet, we would have been impaled, practically stuck on the thing—so we couldn't move. We reversed and motioned for the LST in line behind us to go around us. When they went around us, and as they made that move alongside, they blew right in half; they struck a mine. Now try to picture a huge structure like an LST, 327 feet long, welded steel, 50 feet wide, blowing in two, [lifting out of the water and straight up into the air]. The crew aboard it had a motley assortment of pets. They had pigeons, and chickens—what the hell would you have a chicken onboard for?—chickens, and dogs and cats; this was strictly forbidden, but they let them get away with it. Just before, we had been waving to the guys and laughing at the animals. We were the 'Suicide Navy,' they called us. A very apropos title.

There were medical teams assigned to all the landing ships, like the LSTs, and they were composed of one or two naval doctors and a team of corpsmen. We had a surgical operating station in the back of the tank section, it was a complete operating room and they operated on the wounded there. At times we'd go back to eat, and we'd set our trays down in the dining room. They'd operate on the tables there, and our trays would slide in the blood—well, you don't feel much like eating after that.

We started out low, the fellows of the 175th took off with the trucks and the anti-tank guns. They didn't cast one eye towards the human barbecue—that's what I call it, that's what it was. They looked the other way; unbeknownst to them they were heading into a bad battle with the Germans at Saint-Lô. The [German] 352nd Infantry Division wasn't supposed to be there, but it was, and it hit them.

German Prisoners

On June 7, we started carrying wounded back, became sort of a hospital ship, because we made many, many trips back and forth across the Channel. Our tank deck had stretcher holders, metal things that clipped in and you hung bars and stretchers on. We had a lot of wounded. Among the wounded, we had enemy and our own troops together. We didn't differentiate when it came to surgery, they were treated the same, believe it or not, this is the way the American mentality worked. The Germans probably weren't that way at the time, but we treated everybody the same. One German boy, couldn't have been more than 13 or 14, had his arm blown off up to here [*points to above the elbow*]. I was out feeding the prisoners and I came to him and I had a can of creamed chicken, where you heat up the can. I proceeded to take a spoonful and put it in his mouth; he took it in his mouth and spit it all over me. He was Nazi, Hitler Youth. I was about to take the .45 out and kill him, I felt like doing it, really. The fellow next to him, a German prisoner, was my age, and my God, he looked twice as old and his hair was gray. He had apparently been through an awful lot, he was a member of the 352nd Infantry Division out there. They had been through bombing from the air, they couldn't come out in daylight. Our planes would hit them with rockets, knock out their tanks. This older fellow, 18 years old, looked old enough to be my father at the time. He said, 'You must forgive him, he lost his parents in Berlin, the American air attacks killed his parents, and his entire regiment was wiped out, and he is alone. Your mortars got him.' [*Makes a crazy lunatic circular gesture with forefinger to head and whistles*] That's the universal sign. But you know sometimes I worry about him, I wonder what happened to him, [even though] he was the enemy.

At the time, we hated the Germans, we had some [Nazi SS] aboard that slaughtered our GIs at Malmédy during the Battle of the Bulge. They were under double guard because the crew was all trying to get at them and kill them. In fact, one of the crew had relatives in the army who were prisoners of the Germans. Real bad feelings. We transported them back to England for trial, boy you want to see them, they were different, they were not typical German prisoners. They were arrogant. They were selected for height, blue eyes, blond hair, and they looked down on us—the SS, they were bad news. They had the death head symbol, the symbol of a skeleton, on their caps. All night long we had double watch on them. There were guards, MPs, and guards with machine guns. The crew was trying to get to them, all night long. I couldn't sleep, I'll tell you right now. I mean, a stray bullet, who wants to sleep with something like that going on?

We carried a lot of wounded back and forth. One of the first casualties we had aboard was off of the Coast Guard's LST 16; he was the coxswain of an LCVP, bringing in the soldiers. They hit a mine, blew both his legs off. They brought him on our LST and put him on the operating table: he died probably an hour later, he didn't have a chance. They brought in a Navy officer, his LCVP got blown sky high. He didn't have a scratch on him. That's what we got all day long. We got British paratroopers, English flyers, American flyers, casualties. Even before we hit the beach, they were coming on board. They were bringing them out to us on Rhinos. Rhinos were like a pontoon with an outboard motor on it. They put them on that and they brought them out on LCVPs too.

A lot of the time we couldn't sleep at all—all we could hear were the groans of the wounded, the screams of pain from the dying, and the gurgling of the dead. You noticed that most of all. They got that vacant look in their eyes, like they've left this world and gone. I guess the only good thing about that is they didn't have the pain anymore. I was 18 years old, I shouldn't have been there. It was a hell of a waste—quality time, no way. But [then I guess] I wouldn't have it any other way, because as I pointed out before, it was a 'good' war. We had our fleet sunk at Pearl Harbor. What would you do if somebody was coming into your house, grabbing your family? You have to fight. It was a good war because we were fighting for a cause. I fought against my own relatives in Italy. We had Italian prisoners on board who worked in our galley—they helped the cook, they saw to the ovens on board, [had the run of the kitchen]; they were the enemy and they ran loose, the German [prisoners on board] didn't like that. Italians were big lovers, not fighters—I know from experience. [*Laughs*]

The Hometown Lieutenant

Now I think of the most horrible thing that happened to me, next to the trucks blowing up. We had the dead on the fantail. I was on the bow watch, usually the bow watcher had good eyes, specially trained for aircraft identification. I got a call on the intercom that said the guys wanted to see me on the fantail.

'This guy from your hometown wants to talk to you...' See, before we went in and hit the beach, I talked to a second lieutenant from my hometown.

He said, 'If something ever happens to me, go see my parents.'

I said, 'You're going to be all right, don't worry about it!'

So I got that call and went back and a guy said, 'He's back on the fantail.'

I made my way back on the fantail, it's the stern. It was just starting to get dark and a guy said, 'There's your friend from Utica right there.' He had propped the lieutenant up, the guy I had talked to and reassured days before. They propped him up and pulled a blanket back. His face was bloodied from where a sniper hit him in the head, and it's the same second lieutenant, his mother and father owned a clothing store in Utica; Kessler, I think his name was. About that time I just went nuts. I went after those guys, they were running and laughing, it was a joke to them. This was the kind of mentality I contended with. When you live with people like that, it's not a good time. You sleep with people like that, and they come back drunk, bragging about their victory with the girls—I think their brains were where the sun don't shine. A lot of violence, one guy went crazy. These guys were sick to do something like that.

We were anchored up in Rouen after D-Day, to bring troops up there. A guy had been drinking an apple cider made locally in Normandy, it was a very potent drink. It'd really knock you out if you weren't used to it, and he had his gut full of it. I lay there and watched him—I didn't trust that son of a gun. All of a sudden, his eyes turned red, he was crazy, and he was on me. He came at me with his knife—he was slashing at me, jumping on me. Why me? I don't know. He cut this left foot right open, right through the shoe; I've got a big scar there. [*Points to foot*] It took about 20 of us to get him down. Do you know he got out of the punishment? He tried to kill me, but they probably needed men desperately. I would have shot him, you know, really, because he tried to kill me, pure and simple.

That is what I had to live with every day. The wounded, the dying, the death, it became a way of life. That's bad, that's real bad.

When I got discharged from the service, I got 100 percent disability because I was a basket case. I had to get some shock treatment, once or twice. I spent ten years at the VA hospital in outpatient treatment, I'm still going there in Albany. But I would do it all over again, because it was a cause. A cause célèbre, you might say. It's nothing like what's going on today.

War itself should be abolished, it should be outlawed. There can't conceivably be any winners, [with these nuclear weapons]. For me it was bad enough to see men die all the time. I'd hate to see, right now today, a dog die—if a dog got hit by a car, I'd die, I'd feel badly. But now think about seeing human beings die, and then you get used to it, to endure you have to say to yourself, 'This is a way of life, I have to live with it.' That crew became my family for two years, the only home I had. The medal presented to [us veterans by France] is the most beautiful medal I've ever seen, and I wear it with honor every Sunday. The priest doesn't like the medal because to him it speaks of violence and war, but this is the biggest argument against war there is. For kids to even think of settling arguments with violence and war, that just shouldn't be considered, because it is a foolish move. The innocent die.

After the war, Tony Leone ran a construction business with his son. He passed away on July 3, 2010, twelve years after our first interview.

CHAPTER FOURTEEN

The Infantryman

Like many World War II veterans, Joseph Dominelli was born shortly after the United States entered World War I. He sits in a leather chair in his office, a D-Day calendar on the wall at the time of this interview in 2004. He is relaxed, the picture of a man content with his life, and where it has gotten him thus far. An award hangs on the wall behind him; his office is probably bursting with them, given all of his life achievements and the three Bronze Stars and three Purple Hearts he brought home from the war. At the time of this interview he was 87 and had met presidents and governors and traveled the world on behalf of the law enforcement organizations he led over his career.

Mr. Dominelli's life's journey commenced after high school as the Great Depression was still rearing its head and he had to find work. Soon he was married and found himself at the crossroads answered by millions of American men—the draft notice from Uncle Sam. On June 6, 1944, he went ashore on Omaha Beach in Normandy with the 29th Infantry Division.

'Bodies were lying all over, all over the ground, in the water. They wiped out the whole goddamn regiment; it was a terrible, terrible thing. Well, you see, when you don't have intelligence about what you're really going to walk into, you're caught with everything.'

Joseph S. Dominelli

I was born in Schenectady, New York, August 11, 1917. Oh, I can remember very clearly [the day Pearl Harbor was attacked]. It was such a shocking thing that people were running out of their houses where I lived, on 8th Avenue in Schenectady. And people were saying, 'Oh, what's going on?' They thought they were bombing this country, that's the truth—people were very frightened. Police cars came up the streets, I mean, they thought we're getting bombed here, you know? But when we analyzed the whole thing, and settled down, the bombing was [just at] Pearl Harbor.

I was drafted [and was sent to] Camp Croft, South Carolina. I can't use the word I want to say to describe it, just hot and rural, and the only city nearby was a small city of about 10,000 people, Spartanburg. Today it's a metropolitan city. My biggest problem was my wife had just had a baby; we had a little baby and they still took me! I was married, and when you're in basic training, you don't have so much time to write. They work you night and day, they're transforming you from a citizen to a soldier as fast as they can. Discipline—taking care of your own self, your body, your clothing, your bed. Going out in the field, taking you out in the woods and leaving you there to find your way back. Teaching you how to read a compass, and of course, a lot of time spent shooting on the rifle range; various weapons you shoot. Then they put you on trial runs, you know, they form teams; you know, like actual combat. And you do that for maybe a week or so. But it's what it implies, it's just a basic training course, to train you from a citizen to becoming a soldier. And that's a tough thing to do.

I completed my basic training. They shipped me home, and they sent me to New Jersey, which was like a port of embarkation. I asked to be transferred to the Rangers; I was twenty-six years old, and I was in excellent physical condition—I used to work out all the while. I played professional basketball, and the guy said to me, he said, 'Well, that shouldn't be hard for you to do.' Then he said, 'You married?'

I said, 'Yeah.'

'You have any children?'

I said, 'Yeah, one.'

'Well, you're not going to be no Ranger.'

They wouldn't take married men, they wouldn't take men with children, because the Rangers were the group of people who were going to really get killed.

They had a special patch that indicates that you are a recruit, ready to be attached to a division, and they call you a replacement. I ended up with the 29th Division; I was a replacement. I went over on the old *Queen Mary,* which is now docked out in California. Fifteen thousand people on one ship. Slept like a rat, you know, just on top of one another. It was not pleasant.

I arrived in Scotland—Firth of Clyde, they call it, between Ireland and Scotland—and they put us on trains, about a day, a day and a half. We went to a real rural area and they put us in trucks and brought us up on [to] old farms, they took over the farms from the people. They just took them over. And in one day, we built a tent city; I bet we had 50,000 guys there. In one day! And they fed you. Can you imagine that? That's where I was. They moved us out of that area to Southampton area, the coast of England, you know? Huge replacement depots, huge. They took over the whole city, really. Cities! Moved people out and put them up in the woods. That's what they really did. They took everybody's home. Let me see, that probably was sometime in the first part of May. And we trained in boats, cargo nets off of ships, and getting you ready to go to the landing craft, you know?

'Move, Move, Move!'

And we did that until I think the last part of May; I was sent over to the 29th Division, which I didn't know was an assault division. And the only fortunate part of it was I was assigned to the 115th Regiment; the 116th Regiment was the assault regiment. And whether you know it or not, they were wiped out right on the beach, just about the whole regiment. We were laid offshore, and they kept telling us, you know, we were lucky guys, we were laying offshore. 'You're not going to be committed for two or three days. The 116th'll go in there to clean the whole area out, and then you're going to walk in.' Well, that didn't happen.

They went in early in the morning. And about nine-thirty in the morning, we were committed.

Bodies were lying all over, all over the ground, in the water. They wiped out the whole goddamn regiment; it was a terrible, terrible thing. Well, you see, when you don't have intelligence about what you're really going to walk into, you're caught with everything. Once we got in there, we developed [better] intelligence.

One of the bravest men I've ever seen in my whole life—in fact, I think he saved that beach—was a man, a brigadier general named Norman Cota, probably was in his fifties. Tough guy, carrying a walking stick, walking around that beach encouraging soldiers to 'Move, move, move! Lay down!' He was trying to save their lives and was never hit once. And he saved that beach, he finally got us against the cliff. Now, you had to go up that cliff to get to the top of the hill. The Germans would drop hand grenades on you; they'll just drop them down, roll them on you. Terrible, terrible scene. People—so many people died, so many men got killed there. It was pitiful.

'Bodies Floating in the Ocean'

I was on a Liberty ship that was taking me out. They take you out halfway, almost, then they drop cargo nets down. You crawl down on that and get into a landing craft, that's how they do it. Landing craft by the thousands, thousands! I looked and I couldn't believe what I was seeing; in your whole life, you're never going to see anything like it. Thousands and thousands of ships. You look around, [thinking], 'Oh, my God. We ought to be able to overwhelm that beach in no time!'

And the 116th was already in. And we didn't know they were getting slaughtered on that beach; we had been told we wouldn't go in for two days. Maybe 9:30, 10, 11 o'clock in the morning, they said, 'You're committed. You got to go.' What the hell happened? That's when we saw bodies floating in the ocean, all over the place. And the guys driving the boats, you know, they want to drop you quick and get the hell out of there, see? So they drop the front down, so you got to get off. Now you got a full pack on your back and a rifle. I saw guys that were maybe 5'8", 5'7", 5'6", and they drowned! Right in the water, they would disappear.

I was six-foot, lucky. And that's when we started screaming. One guy took a gun and pointed it at the [coxswain]; 'Move this in close, or I'll shoot you.' So, he moved the boat in closer. He would've shot him.

When I got off, I was in up to my waist. I was fine. And I could see all these bodies, [I think some of them had tripped] landmines; actually, they cleared [a path] for us, really, so we were able to get to the front of the hill and lie there. That's when the general, walking up and down all over the place, said, 'We got to get out of here. We got to get up on that hill!'

I said, 'Yeah, you go first!' Son of a bitch, don't he lead us up that hill. I've never seen a man like him; he wasn't a physically powerful-built guy, he was a fifty-year-old man! But he got us up the hill. And when you're up at the top of the hill, then we were running into all kinds of machine gun fire, mortar fire, all that kind of thing, you know? Artillery fire, it never stopped, never stopped. They knew they had to get us out of there or forget about it.

We walked through a swamp; I'll never forget that god darned swamp—terrible, terrible stink. We were dirty, all wet and coming out of the water on top of [all we had been through] ...

Mr. Dominelli's story will continue in Part Four.

CHAPTER FIFTEEN

The Military Policeman

Jacob Cutler became a military policeman with the First Army. He participated in the Normandy landings on Omaha Beach and elsewhere, as you will read. In this 2002 interview, Mr. Cutler also talks about the appearance of a new secret weapon, the German V-2 rocket, a last-ditch effort by Hitler to terrorize England.

Jacob N. Cutler

I was born on February 17, 1924 in Brooklyn. Pearl Harbor was a Sunday afternoon; I had finished one year of college. I was listening to the New York Giants football game on the radio. They interrupted and announced that Pearl Harbor had been bombed. I said, 'Where the heck is Pearl Harbor? I never heard of it.' Of course, later we learned it was Hawaii, and the war was on. I was 18. I enlisted in the Army Signal Corps. I was interested in electronics and radio. I used to build radios as a kid and whatnot, so I thought that would be something good. Of course, I didn't know what the Signal Corps did. Not what I expected... I was called into active service in April 1943. I reported to Fort Dix, New Jersey, reception center. There I was collared by someone who asked me if I play a musical instrument. I was drafted into the Army reception center band only for about two weeks because it was a temporary thing. I was shipped out to Signal Corps camp in Camp Crowder, Missouri, where I took basic training for about four weeks. Then, I was shipped to Fort Monmouth, New Jersey, for Signal Corps training. I was there for about three months or so, I guess with all the training and whatnot, and I was assigned to a unit to go overseas. I landed in England in November 1943.

We crossed in a tub that had been a former cruise liner, the *Capetown Castle.* The food on it was absolutely awful. The ship rocked and rolled because it was a small tub. We crossed in a convoy escorted by one of the ships, which I'll always remember was the battleship *Texas.* I have a reason for remembering it. At one point, they thought there were some submarines. The convoy stopped and the battleships and other escorts got in closer, but it turned out to be a false alarm.

I believe we landed in Southampton, England. Then, I was assigned to a Signal Corps battalion, 59th Signal Battalion with V Corps, First Army. We were stationed in Taunton, England. That was south of Bristol, which was a large city. Bristol was bombed very, very heavily by the Germans. We heard them regularly. Almost every night we could hear the bombers coming over; we could actually hear the bombs coming down. They took a terrible beating. The people of England were very friendly, very nice. If you found the pubs in the back roads, they would give you liquor, which was not available. I wasn't much of a drinker, but I started to drink gin and soda there. Gin and lime was what they drank. That hooked me on that.

I believe it was the 1st or 2nd of June, they told us, 'Pack up. The invasion is coming. The intel is just where, when. We're moving out.'

I forgot to mention it. While I was in this Signal Corps camp, a new military police platoon was being formed to be security for the

V Corps headquarters. They asked for volunteers, and I volunteered. They say you should never volunteer in the Army, but I thought it would be a good change for me, so I volunteered. Actually, when the invasion came, I was in the military police.

I believe it was very early, June 1 or 2 or maybe the last days of May, when we moved out to a marshaling area where they then briefed us as to exactly what was going to happen. We were scheduled for D-Day H+3. We couldn't understand why they needed MPs there on D-Day, but they explained to us that you'd take positions on the road and guide all the straggling troops and whatnot to their units. Just didn't work out that way.

I crossed the channel on an LST, tank landing ship. The invasion was supposed to be June 5. We started out on June 5. The Channel and the weather was so bad that it was canceled. We went back to the ports. Of course, we were terrified because at this time we thought, 'How could the Germans not have seen us?' We expected an attack any minute. I slept on deck under a truck. I figured that would be the safest place.

The next day, we started out and we got to within wherever we were supposed to get off and get on to small landing craft. They had these big nets over the side of the ship, had to climb down with a 60-pound pack carrying my tent and food and rifle and whatnot and climbed down to get to the landing boat. The water was still very rough. When I thought the boat was down, I jumped from the net. Then, a wave lifted the boat up. I just hit and my legs just buckled under me, but I was unhurt.

The Landing

Then, we started in towards shore, at about the early afternoon, I would say somewhere between 1:00 and 2:00 p.m. We were supposed to land probably at 8:00 or 9:00 a.m., original plan, but we didn't complain about that. We were briefed and told we would land, at most, knee-high water they would let us off, that we'd have to wade in. Didn't work out that way. Partway across, again, our boat got pounded so hard by the waves and there was a lot of shelling around us. Other boats were being hit, and our boat got a leak. They took us back to the tank ship; we had to climb back up the nets. We thought we were probably lucky because we were delayed a couple of hours till another boat came to get us.

The same procedure; down we went. This time we made it except that the Navy guys were afraid they would get trapped near the shore or get hit by shellfire or whatever, so they dropped us off in chest-high water. A lot of guys were floundering—they didn't know how to swim, and they were so taken by surprise, some went under. Fortunately, nobody in my group drowned. We all managed to get ashore. We just raced across that beach, Omaha Beach, Easy Red sector, just to the left of the cliffs that the Rangers had climbed to try to take out the pillboxes.

The beach was a horrible mess—bodies and bodies all over the place, bleeding and bloody, dead bodies. They didn't have time to remove them. We just ran. On the end of the beach was like a little bluff, maybe eight feet high or whatever; we took cover under there and had to clean our rifles. We didn't have any dry clothes, so we just stayed wet. Luckily, it was warm.

Later in the afternoon, we moved up the road; the Germans had been pushed back a couple of miles. Along this road off the beach, the Germans had built a long trench with interior dugouts that they had been using as a headquarters. We stayed about two nights in this area. We started moving inland in Normandy very slowly, through the hedgerow areas. We were bogged down for quite a while until July. Troops are moving very slowly. The Germans were putting up very fierce resistance.

Finally, the time came when I guess they felt they had enough armor and big guns. Incidentally, going back to the invasion, they had these amphibious boats that were called DUKWs, which was an acronym for something, had to do with landing amphibian. They were carrying most of our artillery for the first day. Almost every one was sunk, so we had no guns on the beach. The battleship *Texas* cruised back and forth shelling the German positions. I think they and the other ships that were shelling saved the day, but I always remember that battleship just cruising back and forth, back and forth, from about five miles out, firing shells into the German positions. The aircraft did a very bad job. I think the weather, they couldn't see the targets. They didn't take out everything they were supposed to.

Anyway, we started moving inland. We were bogged down. Saint-Lô was the big strong point for the Germans. Finally, the time came for the breakthrough. I was sleeping in a, I guess you'd call it a trench. I was about a foot underground, below ground or so. About 5:00 in the morning, the shelling of the German position started. It was so intense, the ground was vibrating. These shells came overhead, sounded like a subway train screeching around a corner, it's the shrieks.

It was so heavy that the Germans finally broke. Many of them surrendered and they were shaking and terrified. They thought we had invented automatic cannons because there were so many guns being fired in sequence non-stop, just rapidly like it was a machine gun. They broke. Then, the big breakthrough came. The troops moved through.

We were always a few miles behind the front. We never got into real combat. D-Day was our worst day, but I was lucky that way. We moved through. We eventually reached Paris. The infantry marched through the famous march. We were right behind them. We stayed in the outskirts of Paris for one night and then continued to move on. We went through France. At this point, we began moving fairly rapidly compared to before. Finally, France was completely liberated.

We went into Luxembourg. Then, we went down into Belgium. We went through and we stayed one night overnight in Bastogne, which was later under siege. It was never captured by the Germans. We moved south into this village in Belgium a few miles, maybe two, three miles from the German border. It was the first place we finally had indoor quarters. The first night we spent in a movie theater. We slept on the floor. I was really very thankful for it. The floor was a great comfort.

The next day, we moved into a building nearby, which had apparently been some kind of a school, and they had dormitories. We moved into there. We slept on folding cots, which, as far as we were concerned, were the most comfortable things in the world at that time. We're just waiting to break through into Germany.

Mostly, [my responsibility as an MP] was security guard duty. We took over outposts and just did guard duty watching out for German patrols that might break through and to sound alarms if that happened. We were called 'combat MPs' because we never were in the villages with the white hats and whatnot. Never had those. We wore camouflage nets on our helmets. More or less, we were security troops.

The 'Vengeance' Rockets

A week after D-Day, the Germans began launching a new type of weapon—a small, medium-range cruise missile—from bases in northern France, the Netherlands, and western Germany. It was the forerunner to the modern rocket; indeed, some of the German scientists involved in the program later worked on the U.S. space program. The loud noise that made by the primitive pulsejet engine of the V-1, or 'Vengeance Weapon 1', could be heard approaching from more than ten miles away. Over 9500 were launched at England through the next five months, sometimes more than one hundred a day until the launch sites were knocked out by the advancing Allies on the continent.[14]

Hitler kept saying he had a secret weapon, a secret weapon that was going to destroy us and win the war. We had reason to believe that the Germans were working on an atomic bomb. We were fortunate we beat them to it. [The German] buzz bombs were small, I have a picture of them. They did have a cockpit which could hold one man, but I don't think they were ever piloted that I know of. They were like robots. They went up and they just landed almost at random at areas in France. I think they were more of a terrorist thing than anything else. If they hit anything, of course they were powerful bombs.

One went over a hill where I was on guard duty in Belgium and exploded. I heard it and I hit the ground. I didn't know where it was coming down because you heard this awful noise. When it stopped, you know the engines died and it was coming down. It came down and whistled like a bomb, just shrieked coming down.

[Another time] I was on guard duty near a field where we had stopped. One of them came down and it hit the field and didn't explode; it kind of pinwheeled across the field. It crashed into a barn and then it exploded and blew up the whole barn. It was maybe 50 yards or so from where I was.

They just came over and it got to a point where they were pushed back far enough where they really couldn't do anything anymore but then they discovered the first rockets. The Germans were way ahead of us in rocket launching. They had these V-2 rockets that were really huge. I have a picture of that, too. They were huge. They would take off, all you would see was a vapor trail, a blue vapor trail. Then, they just disappeared. You couldn't hear them coming because they were faster than sound. They were actually hitting London till they got pushed back too far where they couldn't reach anymore.

Mr. Cutler's story will continue in Part Five.

CHAPTER SIXTEEN

The Navy Signalman

Fred Harris was a friend of mine, a man I knew from our joint interest in local archeological efforts at British military sites along the Hudson River in New York State that pre-dated the American Revolution. He was a quiet and unassuming volunteer in many excavations; he became aware of my interest in World War II and D-Day in particular, so he told me of his involvement, and I had him up to the high school where I taught to sit in on a veterans' symposium for students on that topic, along with Anthony Leone and John Webster, in 2001. He also sat for this 2005 interview at the New York State Military Museum.

Frederick G. Harris

I was born in Hudson Falls, New York, on July 12, 1925. I had just finished high school in 1943 and I immediately enlisted in the Navy. That was in June 1943.

Though I was born in Hudson Falls, I grew up in Queens in New York City. My father had taught at the Lexington School for the Deaf in New York. The school moved up to White Plains and that is how I ended up graduating from there. I was living in White Plains then and heard about Pearl Harbor on the radio. Like many people, I had no idea where Pearl Harbor was; later you heard more about how serious it was, and fellows were enlisting. My father had been born in England, and he served for a brief time in the Royal Navy during the First World War. Now, I used to hear some of his stories—he was in the merchant marine also—so I had a natural preference for ships and therefore, the Navy.

I had my basic training in Newport, Rhode Island. I arrived at boot camp in July 1943 and finished in September. After basic, I went to signal school, also in Newport. We learned Morse code and signal flags and other things; it was mostly flashing lights, and different procedures for flag hoisting.

We finished signal school at the end of the year. Then, in January 1944, I expected to be assigned to a ship, but we were assigned to a naval amphibious unit called 'Drew Unit One.' We were sent by train to New York City, where we boarded the *Queen Mary*, which was a troop ship at the time—she was the second largest liner in the world. We were just a group of several hundred Navy men among Army men; most of the men on the ship were Army. The *Queen Mary* was capable of carrying the equivalent of one Army division—that was nearly 15,000 men, and we Navy guys thought we were in the Army there for a while.

The ship sailed alone because it depended on its speed and secrecy. You never knew when it was going to sail. We made the crossing in about four days; that was an adventure in itself because she was so fast—she really rolled at that speed! She would roll over to one side and hang there a few seconds, and then roll over the other way.

We anchored in the Firth of Clyde, I think, in Scotland. We were assigned to an advance Navy base at Rosneath. For a while there, it didn't seem to be well organized. We had muster every morning, but we were given leave quite frequently while we were at Rosneath. We would go down to Glasgow, which was only about an hour away, by either bus or train. It seemed like we could go back and forth more or less as we pleased; there was no special training at that point. We had a lot of fun with the Scottish people, especially in their pubs, where they would sing; they were very friendly.

'A Unique Situation'

In the early middle part of May, we were sent by train down to the southern part of England, where all preparations for the invasion were getting into high gear. We went over to Edinburgh first, and then by train down to the southern part of England where the massive build up for the invasion was taking place; here were thousands of men, supplies, and ships—it was really something! We ended up at a place called Lee-on-the-Solent. The Solent is that body of water between the southern part of England and the Isle of Wight, and that is where I was separated because I was in a unique position. I had a unique situation, a navy signalman on an army tug with a merchant marine crew, a civilian crew of maybe eight or ten guys. The captain of the tug was a car salesman from Buffalo, I think. He knew something about tugs or ships. Of course, they had their crew of engineers and such; I was the signalman [for communicating with other ships].

We knew the invasion was near and we were just sitting around drinking coffee most of the time. Of course, the weather was terrible then, rainy and windy. We were just wondering what it was going to be like. Everything was very informal. I didn't have a regular uniform. I just wore my navy-blue shirt and dungarees. There was no drill or anything.

When we finally got orders to sail, the invasion had started. We joined a large convoy crossing the English Channel. That was when there were ships in every direction as far as the eye could see, from where we were, mainly supply ships of the auxiliary class. They were trailing barrage balloons all about. We arrived off Omaha Beach in the last couple hours of D-Day, just after dark. We were just off shore and you could still hear the gunfire of artillery and the flashes in the sky. At that time on D-Day the beachhead was barely a mile deep, so you could still hear the action going on. We were just waiting off shore to see what was going to happen.

Hundreds of Bodies

I can remember when we reached Omaha Beach, it was just about getting dark on D-Day. The beachhead was barely a mile deep after midnight on D-Day; and that night all you could hear was the gunfire, the shellfire, the flashes in the sky. I was on watch the next morning, which was D+1, and it was just getting dawn. We were very close to shore, maybe fifty or one hundred yards off shore. We were just a couple hundred feet off shore and could see bodies of the fellows that had fallen the day before. They were piled like cordwood against the sea wall, waiting for burial. Boy, we just kind of stood there and stared. That's when it really hit me because you could see the hundreds of bodies piled against the sea wall waiting for burial. I remember that none of us said a word, all we could do was just stare and look, and that's really when it hits you, the devastation and the waste, really, of war.

The Mulberry Harbors

Winston Churchill was one of the fathers of the concept of creating artificial harbors that could then be towed to an invasion site to facilitate the landing of more men, supplies, vehicles, and machinery to support the invasion force in the absence of captured port cities. In one of the little known logistical marvels of World War II, two such harbors were fabricated in top secret, towed across the English Channel and assembled in wartime conditions—one at Omaha Beach in the American sector and one at Gold Beach in the British sector. Prefabricated concrete caissons, in some instances three stories tall, were towed and maneuvered into place and sunk in position with old vessels that had their bottoms carefully blown out to create a breakwater. Floating piers were then assembled, and pontoon bridge roadways were then built to connect the piers to the beaches. Two hundred thousand British workers labored for eight months in southern England, most not having any idea of what they were working on. The first convoy arrived in the Omaha beach sector in the early afternoon on June 7, and the sinking of the breakwater components was immediately underway; cargo was being unloaded even before the Mulberry harbors were fully completed.

Soon after, we got caught up in the action because we had to bring in ammunition barges and we were towing supplies in. That is when we also got involved with the artificial harbors called Mulberry harbors; our job was to position the mulberries and get the different ships onto the harbor.

The idea of towing a [man-made] harbor across the English Channel [was dreamed up] years before the invasion. When they were planning it, some thought that it was absolutely ridiculous. They said, 'How could you tow a harbor across an English Channel, especially at wartime, put it together, and get troops ashore?' Well, they went ahead with the idea, but they never had a chance to test it before the war. It came right off the drawing boards and unbelievably, I guess it worked. Those huge caissons, which are like huge [floating three-story] cement boxes, were towed across the channel.

I was surprised to find out later that those Mulberry harbors were one of the top secrets of the war at that time. It took 45,000 workers back in England and Scotland to build [the parts for the] artificial harbors, and there was no way we could hide them from the Germans during construction. German planes flew over and photographed them but had no idea what they were; the idea was formed about two or three years earlier, but the idea of towing an artificial harbor in sections across the English Channel and assembling it on an enemy shore was unheard of—many top officials thought the plan was absolutely crazy! But they went ahead with that because they would become vital once the men got ashore; they had to have ammunition, food, and supplies and so the mulberries became a very important part of the invasion.

As soon as it was light [on June 7], they began bringing in these huge concrete caissons that were part of the Mulberry harbor [off Omaha Beach]. We wondered, 'What the heck are these?' They were several stories high, these huge concrete boxes, and we didn't know what they were for. We found out that they were to be partially sunk to become part of the breakwater. Then they brought in what they called 'blockships,' old freighters and other ships that had outlived their seagoing days. In the tugs we pushed them into position to form a breakwater; they would place charges in the holds and blow out the bottoms, causing them to sink and form the breakwater. Then, there was another unit that had four steel columns on each corner. They served as a dock or unloading platform—those four corners were driven down into the seabed, designed to rise and fall with the tide. They were connected to the beach by pontoon bridges called 'whales,' everything had a code name. The partially sunken ships were called 'gooseberries' and it was all part of this artificial harbor. Of course, the whole harbor operation was the 'Mulberry' harbor.

They were manned by anti-aircraft guns, and in fact, during the day the Allies had air superiority, but the Germans would come over just about every night for the next week or two after the invasion.[30] That was really quite a little nerve-wrecking and scary to me because it was pitch black, then all of a sudden down at the British beach, I think the first one was Gold, a Canadian-British beach, you could see when the Germans started coming over, all the tracers would be going up in the sky. We would first see the tracers shooting up from the British guns and knew they would soon be over us. It was like a huge fireworks display; you knew they were going to be over Omaha pretty soon. When those anti-aircraft guns started going off, I was on the small tug; the famous war correspondent Ernie Pyle said that it was the greatest concentration of anti-aircraft fire ever in an equivalent space; I can believe that because you had to figure all of the Army anti-aircraft units on shore and all the Navy ships in the harbor, plus the blockships had anti-aircraft guns. When all of those were firing at once, the noise was terrific!

In the one hundred days that followed D-Day, two and a half million men, half a million vehicles, and four million tons of supplies landed at the British Mulberry alone.[15]

The artificial harbors did really prove their worth because it gave us time until the major ports were captured. I saw an unbelievable amount of equipment—the tanks, the men, supplies—that went ashore because I was there on Omaha Beach a couple weeks or so. When we had a few minutes of spare time, a lot of us would hitch a ride on a couple of small LCVPs or Higgins boats that were going back and forth; we were curious to see what was on the blockships.

---

[30] According to economic historian Adam Tooze, "On D-Day the entire Luftwaffe in the West managed only 275 sorties, as compared with 14,000 flown by Allied aircraft." Tooze, Adam, *The Wages of Destruction: The Making and Breaking of the Nazi Economy.* New York: Penguin Books, 2007. (Location 11,563)

A few of us got on one of the blockships and looked it over, of course it was a rusted hulk, and while we were there we were shelled, we were kind of caught out there. We couldn't get back and there was some shellfire coming from the shore, you could hear the shells going over, that 'whoosh' sound, and fortunately they were overshooting us, but this is when I realized how much damage shrapnel can do. You don't have to be hit by a shell, all you have to be is anywhere near it when it explodes because we could hear the little bits of bolt-sized pieces of shrapnel hitting against the side of the boat, it sounded just like hail on a tin roof—it was quite an experience.

The Great Storm

Another thing too, after D-Day, one of the worst storms along the Channel on the French coast in years caused more destruction than any of the night-bombing attacks. I was on that small army tug that probably wasn't much more than half the width of this room and maybe half a bit further long; it was just a small army tug. But when that storm blew, we were bouncing around! A lot of ships, supply barges and ammunition barges, were breaking loose from their moorings because of the storm, so our job was to try to get those back into position and to assist any of the larger ships that were in distress. It had gale-force winds and waves, and it lasted three days. A lot of the ships and small craft were breaking loose from their moorings. Our tug was out there trying to aid some of the ships and barges that were in distress. It did more damage than any of the bombing raids did. It virtually destroyed the Mulberry harbor at Omaha Beach. The one at the British beach survived pretty well; I think they salvaged some parts from us to reinforce the British harbor. But the harbors really did a job because it gave us time until the port of Cherbourg was captured. That was one; in fact, there were two major ports. At one end there was Le Havre and the other was Cherbourg.

After the storm we went to Cherbourg; I think Cherbourg was captured on June 26, and a few days after that I was assigned to the signal station. I went by truck and we went through some of the villages. We were right off a place called Vierville. I remember, a few days after the beach was secured and a couple young boys came down. I tried to ask them where we were, using my high school French. They got a kick out of that and said, 'Vierville! Vierville!' We walked along the beach sometimes; there were mine warning signs everywhere in German. Driving through the villages from Omaha Beach to Cherbourg, we saw a lot of destruction. It was really a mess. When we got to Cherbourg, we were assigned to the signal station at Fort du Homet, an old fort, dated 1857 or so. We were at a Navy signal station up at the top of the fort; the rest of the fort was Army. Our job was to position and contact ships in the harbor. We weren't bothered too much by air raids then, because most of the fighting had moved inland. But it was interesting.

The End of the War

I was at Cherbourg until January or February of 1945. Then we were sent back to an advance naval base at Plymouth, England. I was in Plymouth when Germany surrendered. It was really wild with the VE Day celebrations.

My grandmother was living in Southampton, England, during the war. She refused to leave her home and Southampton was a large seaport that was heavily bombed earlier in the war. A lot of those English people were pretty spunky.

Yes, I was able to get leave and see her and other relatives sometime in May I believe. That was when I got to appreciate what they went through. They had very strict rationing and that lasted until well after the war ended. Yet, they offered what they had. I felt guilty imposing on them.

I was in Plymouth when I heard about the death of President Roosevelt. I was quite shocked, as we all were; we didn't know how much his health had deteriorated during the war. And to me, being a teenager at the time, he was a sort of father figure to me. I was brought up during the Depression in the 1930s, [listening to] the 'Fireside Chats' on the radio. He encouraged people during the Depression and early stages of the war. So, we felt pretty badly at the time.

I came home sometime in July of 1945. We went by train from Plymouth back up to Scotland. The *Queen Mary* was waiting there in the Firth of Clyde. She was loading up with a lot of soldiers that had seen combat in Europe. That was quite a sight, as we had been overseas for about 18 months. We came back to New York City and saw the Statue of Liberty and the city skyline. It was a great feeling. You knew you were back home after seeing how the people in Europe had suffered. They had been in the war a lot longer than we had.

Yes, World War II was quite an experience, coming right out of high school and meeting people from all over the country.

Mr. Harris passed away in 2008 at the age of 83.

PART FOUR

BREAKOUT

"Once you were up front, they keep you there until you get killed."

—Private First Class [by choice] Joe Dominelli, Normandy

CHAPTER SEVENTEEN

Fighting Inland

By early July the city of Cherbourg had fallen, but the Germans had utterly scuttled, sabotaged, and boobytrapped the vital port. One million Allied soldiers were now afield in Normandy, but the crucial cities of Saint-Lô and Caen remained beyond Allied control despite heavy bombardment and attacks; the German defenders were by no means prepared to roll over, but at a cost thus far of 100,000 dead and wounded, replacement soldiers now numbered just 10,000.[16] When Saint-Lô finally fell into American hands later in July, 40,000 American soldiers had already become casualties; seven weeks after D-Day, Allied divisions had penetrated just to a maximum depth of 30 miles at a cost of over 120,000 killed, wounded, or missing.[17] Part of the problem stemmed from the unfamiliar 'bocage country' terrain, a network of ancient hedgerows of bushes and small trees growing out of piles of stones picked out of the fields, spring after spring, serving to divide farmers' fields and doing dual duty over the centuries marking boundaries and penning in cattle. Well-worn sunken roads weaved between them; breaks in the hedgerows were meticulously cross registered for enemy machine gunners' field of fire. Tanks could not even break through these earthen, organic barriers that in some sections towered twenty feet high; attempting to roll over them exposed the Achilles' heel underbelly to German panzerfaust blasts. It was slow going and deadly, the perfect hunting country for hidden snipers in the bush and treetops. And no one in the high command had seemed to know anything about it. It would be up to the GIs to figure their way through them, slogging it out and enduring costly lessons.

CHAPTER EIGHTEEN

Hedgerow Country

I became acquainted with Frank Towers in 2007 when he read a newspaper story in the Associated Press about my work organizing a reunion of Holocaust survivors with the tankers of the 743rd Tank Battalion who liberated them hours before execution. They had come across a death train filled with Jewish men, women and children on their way to fight their last major battle in the closing days of World War II. As it turned out, it was Frank who was tasked with transporting the victims to safer quarters and medical attention. We commenced a long and fruitful relationship tracking down survivors worldwide and planning nearly a dozen reunions on three continents, with the help of an Israeli friend; you can learn much more in my 2016 book, A Train Near Magdeburg.

Frank remembered his reception in Normandy as a member of the 30th Infantry Division well. It was his 27th birthday.

Frank W. Towers

I was born in Boston in June of 1917 so I'm an old Yankee, but I wound up in the Old Hickory Division, a former National Guard division based in the South. To make a long story short, my family moved to Vermont and I grew up in St. Johnsbury and went to school there. After I got out of school, I joined the Vermont National Guard, which is the 43rd Infantry Division. The rumblings of war were just beginning then, and the National Guard was to be federalized and come to Florida at Camp Blanding for one year of training, and then go back home and hopefully the war would be settled. But while we were at Camp Blanding, Pearl Harbor was bombed.

It was a Sunday afternoon, and I was just kind of loafing around with some of the other guys and talking, and when we heard it on the radio, we were kind of dumbfounded, and we realized, after reading the newspaper the next day, that we were going to be involved in the war, and that we were going to be in for the duration.

The 43rd was scheduled to go to the Pacific immediately, and in preparing to ship to the Pacific, I was picked out to go to Fort Benning to go to Officer Candidate School. When I finished Officer Candidate School I was supposed to have gone back to the 43rd, but they had already shipped out to California, so I got transferred over to Camp Wheeler in Georgia and I spent 14 months there as the training instructor and then I was re-assigned to the 30th Infantry Division, which at that time was in Tennessee completing the summer maneuvers at Camp Atterbury, Indiana. The 30th, incidentally, was in Tennessee, North Carolina, South Carolina, another National Guard organization.

We left for overseas out of Camp Miles Standish in Boston, and we sailed out of there on the 12th of February, and landed in Glasgow on the 22nd of February 1944, at the time the largest convoy that had ever crossed the ocean. Many of the ships were cargo ships carrying equipment and supplies, and there was nothing but ships in every direction, just getting ready for the invasion, I guess, even though it was still five months off, though no one knew that, obviously. We were there 'til June, and of course we were doing very intensive training getting ready for the invasion during that period of time, some sand table training, showing us what the beach would look like, what the cliffs would look like, but we didn't know exactly where that was going to be.

Just prior to D-Day, the 30th Infantry Division was located in various towns scattered along the south coast of England. I was with Company M of the 3rd Battalion, and we were billeted in several homes in the adjacent suburb of Felpham.

Then came D-Day, June 6. We knew that this was the day and the real thing, after many false alerts, because of the roar of the planes overhead from midnight onwards. Fortunately, we were not in the first wave of the invasion. This task was assigned to the 1st, 29th, and 4th Infantry Divisions; later this was followed by the 2nd, 9th, and the 30th Infantry Divisions. The 82nd and the 101st Airborne Divisions were the very first troops—paratroopers—to land in Normandy, in the early hours of the morning of June 6. These are the ones that we heard roaring overhead on the night of June 5-6.

It soon became our turn to go to the marshalling area, where we were quarantined and 'locked in' for a few days while waiting for our scheduled time of embarkment. This was in an area just outside of Southampton. Here we were out of touch with the outside world. No one in or no one out, no letters could be mailed, just marking time, and checking equipment, reading, sleeping, playing card games, whiling away the time, thinking of family back home and lots of time for worrying.

Finally, our call came, and we were trucked from our marshalling area to the docks where our transports lay awaiting us. On our particular Landing Craft Infantry (LCI) was loaded the 3rd Battalion of the 120th Regiment, and the service company and cannon company of the 120th.

After being loaded aboard the assigned vessel, in which we were packed like sardines, just prior to midnight of the 12th of June, we pulled out into the English Channel to a point just south of the Isle of Wight. This point was called 'Piccadilly Circus' and was the point at which all the vessels rendezvoused and formed into packets, depending on the order in which they were to go, and their destination.

Somehow, by error, the LCI that we were on was a U.S. vessel, commanded by Canadians and under the control of the British dispatchers, and it became a part of the wrong convoy in leaving 'Piccadilly Circus' and crossing the Channel.

On our somewhat rough trip across the English Channel, and being dedicated landlubbers, each man was issued a 'sanitary bag,' so as to keep the floor of the vessel neat and tidy. Needless to say, more than a few 'sanitary bags' broke or overflowed, and the steel deck was a slippery and slimy mess. Being packed in like sardines, movement was limited, and most of those in need could not make it to the railing in time. One poor guy, being very sick, could not make it to the side of the vessel to throw up overboard. Being a 'neat person,' and not wanting to mess up the deck any more than it already was, he dutifully threw up in his helmet. Along with the vomit came his false teeth. What to do? It didn't take him long to figure it out. Why, quite naturally, he reached into his helmet and retrieved his false teeth—and stuck them back into his mouth. Needless to say, despite being very hungry, we did not eat much breakfast that morning.

So, the 3rd Battalion, the cannon company and the service company of the 120th Regiment, landing on the 13th of June, did not take the brunt of the initial assault, but it was there early on, and evidence of the terrific carnage that befell our predecessors was a horrible and frightening sight. Only upon reaching and landing on Utah Beach did we realize that something was wrong. We had been told and oriented on sand table models that Omaha Beach, our targeted landing area, was all cleared and out of range of mortar and artillery, and that we would land on a very narrow beach and would be facing substantial cliffs, and then we were to march up through a draw, or ravine, between two of these impressive cliffs. Not so. Our approach was to a wide beach with no cliffs, and sporadic mortar and artillery shells were landing on the beach. This was Utah Beach, not the Omaha Beach for which we had been oriented.

When the error was discovered—we were notified by the beachmaster—after disembarking the entire battalion and the service company, we had to immediately re-embark and get out of there. With the tide going out rapidly, the service company was not able to get its vehicles back on the LCI, so they were left to fend for themselves.

In the meantime, with the tide going out, and as we boarded the LCI, it became grounded on a sand bar. During this time, a few enemy mortar and artillery shells fell in the area, but only one was a direct hit on our LCI, [but thankfully] there were very few minor personnel casualties. Another nearby LCI came to our rescue, and with ropes thrown to our vessel, was able to drag us off the sand bar, and we proceeded to Omaha Beach, where we should have been landed several hours earlier.

I well remember this incident on this day, as it was my 27th birthday, and this was the biggest reception, although not very friendly, that I had ever received—even to date. My company had the dubious honor of landing on Utah Beach and Omaha Beach on the same day, June 13, 1944.

Prior to disembarking from our LCI at Omaha Beach, we were sternly warned that when we went over the side and down the rope ladder/netting, to be extremely cautious that we had our weapons under control and well secured, and to hold them high above our heads as we waded ashore. This was your protection of your life, and there would be no immediate replacements. 'Hang on to it—keep it dry.' Over the side we went, and who was the first one to drop and lose his rifle? Our company commander, Capt. Phil

Chandler, the very one who had been so emphatic on the warning to us to hang on to your weapon. He did not hear the end of that episode for a long time, and he was very embarrassed about it.

As we landed on Omaha Beach in the late afternoon, it was still littered with many vehicles that had been knocked out during the first few days of the invasion, and much equipment that had been damaged was scattered all about on the beach. Dozens of wounded soldiers were lined up on the beach, awaiting transportation back to England, where they would be cared for in hospitals located there; most of the men had received all of the medical treatment that was available to them at the time, and further procedures and treatment were only available back in England. Most were heavily sedated, and many were moaning and groaning from the pain of their wounds, and this was not a very encouraging sight for us who had not yet received our baptism of fire from the enemy.

By the time that we got there, the beaches were cleared of mines and that sort of thing, but we were still well within artillery range. You know, artillery fire is good for three to five miles, and the Germans had equipment that was still capable of firing on the beach.

We went inland about four or five miles to set up our initial camp and to get organized and prepared for going into combat. The 29th Division and the 101st Airborne were already established, and we sort of broke in on their line in between the two divisions and took over a part of their area. That was our first combat front, which was about maybe two miles wide.

There were many military policemen around the area directing traffic, and to prevent looting of abandoned vehicles and supplies. They directed us off of the beach to a narrow lane that had been cleared of enemy mines earlier by the engineers, which had the warning signs, 'Mines,' and white tape on each side of the path. This was called a draw, and was actually a narrow ravine leading up the hill to the top of the cliffs overlooking the beach. This road was about one kilometer up to the village of Vierville-sur-Mer. All of the men of our Company M were struggling up this long hill carrying all of their equipment in the loose sand, making it very difficult walking.

Here I was very fortunate. Our battalion commander, being landed late, and with all of the rest of the regiment having moved on forward and into an assembly area, we were not sure as to where to go. I was delegated to go forward by jeep and find out where the regiment was located in the general assembly area, then report back and lead the battalion to that location. Of course, I had a map of the area where we were supposed to go, so I followed my instinct as to where the regiment might be. After much searching and making inquiries along the way, I finally found the regiment's location, and was shown the specific area where our 3rd Battalion was to bivouac for the night. I was quite content to lead the way, riding in a jeep rather than walking.

We drove westward and then southward along some narrow farm roads bordered by hedgerows. This was our first introduction to the famous Normandy hedgerows, which we would see much of. We never trained for hedgerow fighting while we were in England, so this was a new experience for us, and we had to improvise our tactics and defense as we went along.

*

The hedgerows were the local version of fences between the fields. They had been created by the farmers over the centuries of farming in this area. As the farmers were plowing their fields and came upon rocks, they would pile them along the circumference of the field that they wished to lay out to separate their cattle from their crop fields. As the years went by, the piles became higher. Soil accumulated among the rocks. Seed from trees, shrubs, and weeds in the adjoining areas settled among the rocks and sprouted in the soil. More rocks were piled up through the continuing years, until this time when the hedgerows reached a height of 8 to 10 feet in places, but more normally, 6 to 8 feet in height and about 10 to 12 feet through at the base. They would leave a 10 to 12-foot opening from a road into each of these fields for access for cattle or farm wagons.

These hedgerows were formidable barriers when trying to go cross country with tanks or other vehicles. Entry to each field could only be made through the one entrance to each field, purposely left. The enemy knew exactly where these entry points were, and they had them zeroed in with their artillery, thus denying us access to any of the fields in our route of march. Since they were too high for tanks to go over, the only alternative was to go through them. With these solid barriers of rocks and tree roots, it was impossible to dig one's way through, so we had to make a very small hole and fill it with dynamite and blow our way through. Eventually the tanks were equipped with long spikes on the front of their dozer tanks, and they would punch them into the hedgerow, and lift them, as a forklift does today, and this would create a narrow passage through the hedgerow.

On the 15th of June 1944, the 120th Regiment of the 30th Division made its first contact with the enemy, and we were to remain in nearly continual contact with the enemy until 8 May 1945.

Bill Gast

The hedgerow fighting began. Being inside the tank protected us from machine-gun and rifle fire, as well as fragments from artillery and mortar explosions. Being under constant fire, we would be buttoned up in our tanks sometimes for three or four days and nights at a time. Our steel helmets served many purposes. We would place them on a Bunsen burner to heat some soup or coffee or whatever we had to eat. We used the same helmets for our elimination, then opened the hatch and quickly emptied it out over the side. Sometimes at night halts we would be able to get out of our tanks and dig a hole or trench large enough so we could lie down, make a dirt pile in front of the trench, then drive the tank over it. This would give some of us a chance to get some very much needed sleep. Of course, at least one would always stand guard in the tank; we alternated our turns. This was also the time our supplies tried to catch up to us, primarily ammunition, rations, and fuel. Our gasoline was transported by 6 x 6 trucks in five-gallon jerry cans. With artillery shells coming in, the driver would abandon his truck for a much safer place; you can imagine what would happen if a shell hit the truck. The driver often did not return to his truck until it was emptied, so in order to get gas, we would have to sometimes walk half a mile or more and hand-carry two five-gallon cans at a time back to our tank, lift them up onto the deck, and the driver would pour it into the tank, which held about 250 gallons. Then, if we were still alive, we could try to get some sleep.

We continued fighting through hedgerow after hedgerow, liberating town after town. The 743rd, being a separate battalion, was called upon to clean up little so-called 'pockets of resistance.' One of these pockets was Mortain, France, August 6–12, 1944, when Hitler with his 1st SS Panzer Division threw his punch to cut off General Patton's Third Army from the US First Army and the beachhead supply base.

The soldiers of the 30th Infantry Division and the 743rd Tank Battalion would face new trials in the coming weeks—a surprise Hitler-ordered panzer counterattack in a sleepy French town, and before that, a rain of ruin from the heavens-from their own air force, not once, but two days in a row.

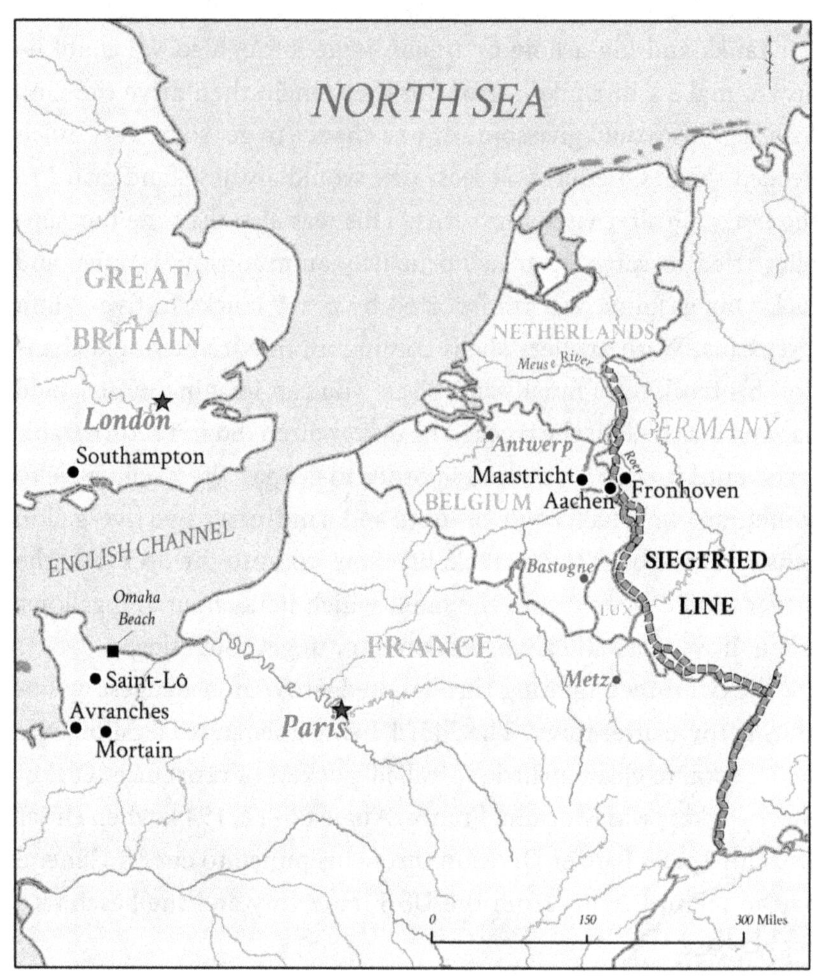

Mortain, France, in relation to the Normandy beaches and Paris. Map by Susan Winchell.

CHAPTER NINETEEN

Cobra/Mortain

Bill Gast's 743rd Tank Battalion was now attached to Frank Tower's 30th Infantry Division. The 30th Division, later christened the 'Workhorse of the Western Front,' had a history that dated back to the trenches of France in an earlier fight against the Germans, and it was now fully committed again in the ancient Norman hedgerows.[31] With centuries-old sunken lanes and earthen embankments, this terrain was a nightmare of ambush, attack, and counterattack at the hands of a determined enemy well-concealed behind the screen of foliage. The maze of hedgerows was dubbed 'Green Death' for the way it divided the battlefront into innumerable 'small boxes, with each box a separate battle, a lone tactical problem on a checkerboard of fields, each in itself a single objective to be fought for, gained, or lost.'[18] But push on, they did. Casualties were high as they fought towards the west bank of the Vire River, and more replacements were needed.

By July 20 Saint-Lô had finally given way, and the men of the 30th Infantry Division, the 743rd Tank Battalion, and the attached 823rd Tank Destroyer Battalion were gearing up for the vaunted breakthrough just to the west. It would be rough, so the high

---

[31] The 30th Infantry Division was also nicknamed the 'Old Hickory' division, being from the South and in honor of President Andrew Jackson.

command decided to coordinate the largest air assault in support of ground troops ever, waves of medium and heavy bombers winging their way from England over the target area five miles wide. At the jump-off point on July 24, soldiers and tankers looked up as hundreds of planes droned overhead and began to release their deadly payloads in response to the red smoke that rose to mark the target area. Tankers started their engines, and the infantry began to deploy. H-hour was here, but so was the south wind which carried the red smoke directly over their positions 1,200 yards behind the target area. Twenty-four men of the 30th Infantry Division were killed and more than five times that number were wounded, but the men of the 743rd were relatively unscathed, though badly shaken. The attack was called off and postponed for 24 hours.

July 25 brought another clear day, and three miles up the bombers appeared again in their stately formations to rip their holes in the German lines. The men on the ground readied themselves and breathed a little easier as the first bombs hit their marks. Soon thereafter the second wave appeared, and the earth quaked as those bombers hit their marks. A sergeant of the 743rd looked up, watching the next wave of medium bombers, and saw that when the bombers were directly over their heads, their bomb bays dropped open, and, to his horror, the bombs began tumbling out like peanuts coming straight down at the tankers. He dived under a bulldozer as the ground shook and the sky grew dark; dense smoke now covered the target area, and the red smoke was no longer distinguishable. As the day turned to night and the bombing intensified, men were buried alive or blown apart, including Lieutenant General Lesley McNair, the commander of all ground forces who was visiting from Washington, D.C.—the highest-ranking American officer to be killed in the European Theater of World War II. The 30th Infantry Division lost another 64 killed, with 324 wounded and 60 more missing, probably blown to bits.[32] An additional 164 men were classified with 'combat fatigue'; nevertheless, the 30th was ordered to jump off as planned through the opening in the German lines.

Dazed men staggered forward and tanks rode over the dead. Infuriation at the airmen diffused into unmitigated fury for the enemy. Utter destruction was the norm as the bombardment also buried German tanks, knocked out enemy communications and strongpoints, and cratered the fields and roadways. For the next two days, 100,000 men poured forward as the Allied forces smashed out of Normandy and the hedgerow country. After 49 days of combat, the men of the 30th Infantry Division and the 743rd Tank Battalion were finally pulled off the line, with the opportunity to take their first showers, replace more equipment and men, and maybe even catch a USO show or a few hours of much needed shuteye. Soon enough, they would be back in the thick of it.

Showdown at Mortain

Summertime in France. At four o'clock, the birds began to sing, and the morning glow intensified as the tankers stirred from their half-sleep. Eighteen hours later, dusk would give way to dark, but the men on many of these days would still be on alert and on the go. German planes and artillery would take advantage of less than six hours of darkness to harass the weary men. Everyone was on edge but there was little time for settling in; they were on their way to relieve the 1st Division holding the line at a sleepy little town called

---

[32] *60 more missing, probably blown to bits*- Veteran Frank Towers recalls, 'Those who were missing were later recovered with bulldozers... and many of them are still buried in the American Military Cemetery overlooking Omaha Beach, where they first landed only a month earlier.' Towers, Frank W. *Operation Cobra*, http://www.30thinfantry.org.

Mortain. On the 45-mile trek to Mortain, the roads were lined with the young and old, welcoming the soldiers and tankers as their liberators, 'cheering and throwing bouquets, and offering drinks at every halt. One could easily feel that the Germans would not stop [retreating] short of the Rhine River,' one officer remembered.[19] It was a much needed boost to their morale, but little did the men know that Mortain was the very place that the Germans would launch a major counterattack with four panzer divisions, conceived by the Führer himself.[33]

The breakthrough in Normandy had telegraphed to the German High Command the unwelcome possibility that the Germans might have to withdraw from France or risk being encircled and trapped. Neither option was acceptable, so Hitler himself drew up the plans with the expectation of punching through the American lines and driving to the coast at Avranches, forcing a wedge into the advancing armies and stopping the hemorrhaging, perhaps even pushing the invader back all the way to the sea. Having survived the July 20 assassination attempt, he was in no mood to listen to objections; and so it was that the 30th Infantry Division, 743rd Tank Battalion, and the 823rd Tank Destroyer Battalion came to one of the crossroads of the entire Normandy campaign.

The soldiers and tankers took their positions in and around the small town of 1,300 but had had little time to reconnoiter the surrounding territory. Roadblocks were set up, and on the high ground of Hill 314, with its commanding views of the countryside, 700 men tried to settle in. Control of the hill meant control of the roads. Five days later, only half were able to stagger off the hill under their own power.[20]

Shortly after midnight on August 7, 26,000 Germans and the first of 400 tanks, including the lead elements of the black-

---

[33] *panzer*-German armor, generally tanks.

uniformed crews of the 1st SS Panzer Division *Leibstandarte SS Adolf Hitler*, began to attack. With a barrage of rockets, artillery fire, and mortar rounds, they enveloped most of the American positions on the roads surrounding the town in short order. The afternoon would bring counterattacks by the rockets of RAF Typhoon fighter bombers targeting the panzers, but also taking out some of the 743rd's Sherman tanks. As dark fell on the evening of the 7th, the men on Hill 314 were surrounded by the 2nd SS Panzer Division.[34] The 743rd's assault gun platoons fired shells packed with morphine and medical supplies, which burst on impact.

As the Germans repeatedly tried to scale the hill, an artillery spotter called down round after round through his fading radio set, delivering death on his doorstep from five miles distant.[21] The hill held. Watching the battle closely, Hitler called for a renewed effort to take Mortain and this troublesome obstacle. Under a white flag of truce, the SS officer expressed his admiration for the stand and demanded surrender. The senior officer refused, releasing a pent-up, colorful reply and calling in an artillery barrage on his own position as the Germans attacked it.[22] The hill held, and on August 11 the Germans began their withdrawal amid constant shelling and harassment from the air. While the 30th had lost over 2,000 men, the Germans had had their attack blunted and nearly 100 tanks knocked out or abandoned.[23] It was the start of the German movement to the Siegfried Line and their westward defenses on the

---

[34] *2nd SS Panzer Division* – The 'Das Reich' SS Division had already distinguished itself in keeping with the standards of barbarity the SS has been noted for. In a reprisal raid on June 10 in the quaint Norman town of Oradour-sur-Glane, members systematically murdered 642 French civilians and razed the town. Men were herded into garages and barns and shot; women and children were forced into a stone church and burned to death. The town was never rebuilt and stands today as a silent memorial to wartime atrocity. See Atkinson, Rick. *The Guns at Last Light: The War in Western Europe, 1944-1945.* New York: Henry Holt & Co., 2013. 94.

border of the Reich itself; by the end of August, some 10,000 Germans had been killed in the pocket and 50,000 captured. The German commander, relieved of his command and summoned back to Germany by Hitler, chose to commit suicide by cyanide instead.

Bill Gast, one of the surviving tankers who made it through the Omaha Beach landing on D-Day, received the Silver Star for his actions at Mortain.

Bill Gast

Casualties were heavy. Many were killed, many were wounded, and again, we lost a lot of equipment. We had our tanks parked in the middle of a field, camouflaged with tree branches and leaves. I lost three tank commanders in this battle, so at the same time I was driver and tank commander. An order came over the radio to deliver a message to the infantry CP. Another soldier and I got out of our tanks and on foot went to the designated CP area, equipped with a .45-caliber pistol and a .45-caliber Thompson sub-machine gun with a 30-round clip; we found the CP was all blown away, nothing there. We raced back to our tanks under machine-gun and rifle fire, with artillery and mortar shells exploding all around us, to find one of our tanks knocked out. After helping these men and receiving orders to retreat—this was the only time, during the entire war, that we were ordered to retreat—I started to remove the camouflage from my tank, when an incoming artillery shell exploded beside my tank and a piece of the shrapnel hit me in the back. I was taken to a field hospital for surgery and recovery. [At the field hospital], German bombs intended for Patton's convoy nearby missed their target and landed on the hospital and we had more casualties, there seemed to be no end. I quickly discharged myself from the hospital and started my journey back to the 743rd, wherever it was, and in no time, I joined up with them again.

Omaha Beach, France, Netherlands, Belgium, Germany; the hedgerows, Saint-Lô, Mortain, the Battle of the Bulge—the bitter bleakness of the frozen Ardennes, Malmédy, Aachen. And then, [the final battle at] Magdeburg, where we fired our last shell. I was thankful to be alive.

Bill Gast passed away in his hometown of Lancaster, Pennsylvania, on December 6, 2018.

CHAPTER TWENTY

Assault on Brest

Allied planners had estimated that by the fall of 1944, Allied divisions in France pushing into the Nazi frontier would need over 25,000 tons of supplies each day. To break the back of the Nazi beast, ports had to be secured. The Mulberry harbors were designed to be temporary. Cherbourg was vital but had been spiked by the Germans to the point of being of limited capacity for weeks. Brest, on the tip of the Brittany peninsula, had been selected as another point to be taken. Here too, the Germans were of no mind to let it slip away. Heavily fortified and defended, it took a major diversion of George S. Patton's Third Army to crack that nut between August 7 and September 19, 1944; during that time, and probably because of this operation and others, Paris was liberated earlier than expected, on August 25, 1944. Joseph Dominelli of the 29th Division continues:

Joseph S. Dominelli

We were supposed to occupy the village of Saint-Lô, day one. Well, that was June the sixth. We didn't get into Saint-Lô until the first part of July. And then I was wounded outside of Saint-Lô, the first time. It was a heavy artillery barrage; I ducked down in a hole and I got hit in the leg with a piece of shrapnel. It was a pretty good wound, you know. I said, 'Maybe I'm safe now to go back.' They sent me back to the first aid station, took the wound, cleaned it all up, wrapped it up, and sent me back in.

I said, 'I can't believe this.' That was the first time I was wounded.

Our division, I forget the exact date in July, we took Saint-Lô, finally. And once we took Saint-Lô, that was a major, major victory, as I recall ...

*

General Patton's Third Army was released behind us. We went all the way to Brest, France. Patton circled it, then they put us on trucks and brought us to Brest, France.

We took the outskirts of Brest, France. Patton, he left; he went to Paris. You know, [that's] how fast he went. But we were left there in Brest, France, and they told us, 'Nothing to it.' You know what was there? The Germans had paratroopers, regular army, all kind of soldiers were there that we didn't know about, and it was one hell of a fight!

Seventy thousand Americans were committed to the fight; one in seven were wounded, including Mr. Dominelli.

It was a real big city, and the first time I went into a big city like that overseas. We were walking into a five-and-dime store, just like State Street in Schenectady, walk in, look around, nothing there. Walk into a bank, no money in it. Strange feeling, going to a bank, looking all around the bank, opening all the vaults. Didn't find a penny, right? But that's what you did. [And we didn't have much contact with the people of France] in the combat area, because when you were coming, they were gone. They hopefully got out of there, you know what I mean? They couldn't live in a combat zone, they'd be killed. They evacuated themselves, truthfully. If they got away from the Germans, they'd go behind our lines. They suffered something terrible, they really did. The Germans committed an act there that we found out about later. That's what we were up against.

Prisoners

We had a lot of guys who joined us later on who were from the South. Uneducated, from the farms, and never been anywhere, but tremendous soldiers, lot of guts, could shoot like hell. Liked to kill people, you know, they really did. If you caught prisoners and you told three of these crackers to take the prisoners back to a holding area, they'd be gone ten minutes, and they'd shoot them and come back. They wouldn't take them back; they'd kill them. Terrible, isn't it? You got to feed them; they shot them instead. I never saw it, but we knew what happened. And that's the way it went; nobody ever said anything about it. Who cared?

*

Hell, I was in combat from June 1944 [to the end]. I carried a carbine and I finally got myself into what they call a mortar squad. My job was to carry two bags of mortar shells. And I was a private first class, that's all. I could've been a sergeant in two minutes if I wanted, but who the hell wanted it? Could've been a lieutenant right in the field if I wanted it—they couldn't get anybody to take them! There were no sergeants. They were rare, because everybody got killed.

I got wounded a second time there in Brest. In fact, I got shot with what they call a phosphorus grenade, which throws off shrapnel plus a burning power. It burned all my leg, burned my pants, my arms. But they sent me back to combat, again!

*

'Keep You There Until You Get Killed'

Brest fell in, had to be sometime in September, maybe, because then they put us on troop trains and sent us to Germany. Put us on boxcars, and that's what transported us all the way across from one end of France, all the way across France to [the border with] Germany. That took a few days, I'll tell you, terrible, packed us in them cars like rats. Every so often they would stop, and they'd come by with trucks and throw food in there. Boxed rations, that's what it was. They wouldn't hand it, they'd throw it right into the car, and you'd scrabble for it, you know, like animals! They didn't let us off the car, get in line and eat like a gentleman, no. You're going [straight] to Germany, [because] when we got to Paris, a lot of guys left. They took off, they just deserted—they didn't give a goddamn. If I hadn't had a wife and kid, I might've done it, I might've thought about it. But if you didn't show up again, they'd send a telegram home that your husband is 'Missing In Action.' I didn't want that to happen. So many guys left, they really did. Then they put us under armed guard. Every time they stopped the train, they'd have armed guards to keep you on the train; you can't blame them. You're in a combat unit. Guys in the back, they had it made; I would've loved to have been assigned in the back. But you don't get them jobs. Once you were up front, they keep you there until you get killed.

We were right on the border of Holland and Germany, that's where we went. It's called Maastricht, [in the Netherlands]; that's where our division occupied the line, only 25 miles from Aachen, the biggest city in Germany that we had to take, and that was going to be a terrible battle.

They used to do these things, it's traditional-like with the army. They'd send patrols out, scouting patrols, to pick up intelligence. We were alongside a huge hedgerow, lying there. And I turn around, I see what looked like forty people marching, maybe 300 yards away. And I never forgot the words I said, even to this day. I said, 'That can't be our people. Our people are coming from the other way!' And all at once, I hear a voice.

'Komm, komrade!' Know what that means? 'Come here, brother.' Like, Jesus Christ, they're German!

As soon as they said that, a couple of our stupid fools who were lying down and keeping their mouth shut, started shooting at them with submachine guns, spraying that whole area.

Now, I was in good shape, I was six-foot, must've weighed about 140, 150 at the time. Believe me when I tell you, I got over that hedgerow in one leap. Right over it! And I got into the other side, said, 'Where am I going? Where the hell am I going to go?' I had a lot of guys with me, [we moved out fast]. When you're in the service, the first thing they tell you when you got into a city, you always set up a machine gun at the head of the street, so you can spray the street. I forgot all about that, because the anxiety and the fear. So, we all ran. All the streets are all cobblestone. We were running down this street. And all at once, the guys set up a machine gun, and the bullets were bouncing off the cobblestones. I said, 'Get out of this goddamned street!'

I ran and down to [a set of tall double doors]. We went into one of them. And when we pushed the door open, little did I know, there was a German soldier on the other end of it, and he sprayed us with machine gun fire. It hit me in the arm, and legs; down I went, but somebody else who was with me killed him. Two guys grabbed me and we ran out the other end of the building, the garage. And they said, 'We got to go back this way because our line is back there!' So they grabbed me, one on each side, and what do you think we run through? A cabbage patch! Now, did you ever run through a cabbage patch? You know what noise that makes? But we couldn't help it. Now, we hear bullets; they're starting to spray the whole cabbage field! But none of us got hit.

Finally, we got back to where we thought our line was, and we didn't have the password—you get a different password every day. We didn't know what the password was, we didn't even know if the guys in front of us were German or American. They sprayed a couple of shots ... the Americans!

Guy said, 'Got to holler out! [Who does] Joe DiMaggio [play for]?'

[Someone replied], 'New York Yankees!' Honest to God!

'Americans! Come on, come on!'

It was only a matter of maybe a hundred yards, we got back to our line. I was lucky.

So that was the end of me. That's when I went back to the hospital. And that's when I stayed.

Joseph was awarded three Purple Hearts and three Bronze Stars for his combat in Europe.

I had been wounded three times. But sheesh, I'll tell you the truth. I never [received any medals] until I got in the hospital. They gave me one for D-Day. They gave me one for Brest, and they gave me one for what happened when I got wounded in Germany.

I got out of the hospital in Paris. Beautiful hospital, really. I was there for about maybe ten days, but they couldn't do nothing for me. So, they said, 'We're going to send you back to England.' Oh, was I so happy! I went back thinking I'm safe, you know?

But in Paris, they treated us great, really, they did. Good food, you know. And after about a week and a half, a guy comes by. 'Look,' he said, 'you got to go back to England.'

I said, 'Oh, really?'

'Yeah.' And they sent us to England. They loaded us in a plane, they flew us back to England. Landed in Wales; I'll never forget that jerk town. Terrible place! We spent two nights there.

And from there, I went to a big hospital for quite a while, until they sent me back to the United States.

When they told me I was being sent back to the United States, wow! These doctors walked our ward every day, and we used to watch them. If you saw them go near the guy and whisper in his ear, you knew that guy was going home. But if he walked right by your bed, forget it, [*waves hand dismissively*] you're going to be there a while, you know. He walked by my bed for weeks on end. I'd think, 'That son of a gun. Never whispers in my ear.' [*Laughs*]

In France, they had said, 'We can't do this here. You got to go back to England,' which was great with me. And I stayed in England for quite a while. Beautiful hospital, too, near Taunton. I was there quite a while, and finally I said, 'What am I doing here? Why don't you send me home? What am I staying here for?'

'We're trying to get a doctor that can operate on you.' They couldn't find a doctor that could do it, because what you can see here, these scars [*points to inside of left forearm*], your nerves in your arm are thinner than your hair. Are you aware of that? In them days, this was all new to the medical profession, they never had surgeons that could do this kind of work. Didn't have them. And so, in effect, they were experimenting, they were learning. The war trained them all. So, they sent me back to the United States.

I went back on a hospital ship, big ship. Shot craps, played poker all the way home; I made about $2,000 shooting craps. I lost the one night out of New York. We stopped, the hospital ship, right near the Statue of Liberty. And we laid there for a day and a half; what are we laying here for? I was shooting craps, poker, you know. But then you go through a line, the doctors look at your wounds. They want to figure out where to send you. They had a big hospital up in Utica, used to be all crazy houses, all them buildings. They would send soldiers there.

I said, 'Well, Jesus, I'd like to go to Utica. It's not too far from Schenectady.'

'No, no, no, no, no, no. We have nobody up there [who can help you]. You're going to go to Atlantic City.'

Now I was pissed off they're sending me to Atlantic City! Once I got there, oh, my God, beautiful hotel. Beautiful. The Army took over the whole of Atlantic City, every hotel on that boardwalk, the Army took over, for soldiers. They made hospitals out of them. But they kept all civilian personnel in the kitchen, so all food they cooked was like if you were a guest, the food was excellent.

I was there quite a few months. A long time, long time; nine, ten months I was there. Jeez. Couldn't get a doctor to do this [operation]! They just didn't have them.

I walked around for months like this [*carries left arm as if it is in a sling*]. Crippled! Couldn't straighten my arm out, couldn't straighten my hand out. I said, 'I'm going to live like this the rest of my life?' [*Makes a grimace, pauses*] Christ, if I got out of the Army, I didn't give a goddamn [*laughs*], because at that point in my life, I knew I was safe, because I was back in this country. They couldn't use me like this, right [*folds left arm in again*]?

Finally, they found someone to operate on me, it was a young guy, very young guy. He had apprenticed with one of the few that could do it, and then he operated on me.

Many years later, I went to a surgeon in Schenectady for some other operation, and when he was looking me over, he looks at the scar. He said, 'Where'd you get that done?'

'I got it done in Atlantic City, New Jersey.'

He called his staff in. He said, 'Look at that operation. That's the first one that was ever done like that in the United States, in Atlantic City. That's the only place they could do it, because they had the surgeons there.' And he knew every one of them surgeons, this doctor did. I'll never forget it. He had been there himself, but I'd never seen him.

Again, they wouldn't let me out. I said, 'Won't you let me go home, for Chrissake? What am I doing here?'

'Well, aren't you having a good time?'

'Yeah, but I mean, I've got a wife and a kid. I'm making $25 a month, are you kidding me?'

Twenty-five dollars a month. People don't know what us guys went through, they really don't. But like I say, I was just one of sixteen million. What the hell, you know? [*Shrugs shoulders*] I had a lot of company. A lot of guys got good jobs, and a lot of guys suffered.

They kept me in that hospital a long time in Atlantic City. I couldn't believe it. And I couldn't get the guy to send me home! Even after they operated on it, they wouldn't let me go. They wanted to watch it. That's what it was. I knew what they were doing, which is fine. I think it was '46 I got out.

'Got No Job Here For You'

No, never had any trouble, but I don't have any feeling. I got to be careful in the wintertime. I could freeze them [*traces left hand fingers with left index finger*]; still no feeling, though. But I can move them. I never thought I would. I was really lucky. My legs, no problem. I was a very fortunate guy, really. Was a hell of an experience.

I didn't go back to work for a year [after I got home]. Then when I went back to work, I'll tell you how patriotic that GE was, which let me go when I got drafted, right?

Under the law, it was mandatory that you go back to your job. Mandatory. One year, they had to give you the job back. That was the law. I went back maybe three weeks before the year was up, and I walked into the shop I worked in, and walked into the office. I said, 'I want to go back to work.' I had my job over there, it was on a machine. The general foreman—made even worse, he was a goddamned East German, and I hated the son of a bitch—now, he said, 'Got no job here for you.'

I said, 'You got no job here for me? Because you don't read English? You don't read the paper? You don't know what the law is?'

'No job for you.'

'I'll be back.'

I walked from there down to the general superintendent's office, another no-good son of a bitch. I walked over there, and I sat [outside of his office] there for an hour. Finally, I walk in, he's sitting in his chair like this [*leans back, imitates relaxed pose*]. Big American flag on the back wall—he's the guy, when I went to ask for a deferment, he said to me, 'Don't you want to serve your country?' He told me that! Now I go back for my job, he's sitting there like that, right?

I said, 'Mr. Collins, I got a little bit of a problem.'

He said, 'What's your problem?'

I said, 'That punk boss of yours you got down there, that German, he won't give me my job back.'

'Well,' he said, 'I don't think there's a job here for you.'

'Oh. Well, you leaned back in the chair the last time I was here, you wanted to know why I didn't want to go in the Army. Now you don't want to give me my job back.' I said, 'I served in the Army for you.'

I said, 'Let me tell you something, pal. Not only am I going to get my job back, I'm going to probably have you locked up by the time I'm done.' And I turned around and I walked right out.

Them days, the union was powerful. I went down to Union Hall, and my business agent was a man named Jandreau. Powerful guy. I knew him, but I didn't know him that well. So, I walked in and sat down, I say, 'I want to see this business agent.' Walked in his office, shook hands with him, gave him the story. Told him I was wounded and everything, you know.

He said, 'What happened?'

I said, 'They won't give me my job back.'

Then I told him who the boss was, who the superintendent was, and the whole story, right? He said, 'Sit right there.' Picks up the phone.

He said, 'We're going to call this Mr. So-and-so, the superintendent of the division.'

Gets him on the phone. I think his name was Harry, and the business agent said, 'This is Leo Jandreau. I got a man in here who your people won't rehire, just come out of the Army wounded. Three medals. And you won't give him his job back.' And he told him my name.

'Well, no,' the superintendent said. 'We don't have to give him his job.'

Jandreau said, 'Well,' he said, 'I'll tell you what. Be ready for the front page of the *Union Star* tonight, because before I hang up, I'm going to call a cameraman in. I'm going to call an editor over. And we're going to take pictures of this fella, and I'm going to put on the front page 'General Electric Company Refuses to Hire Wounded Veteran with Three Medals!"

Told him that right on the phone. Well, this guy probably crapped, right? 'And furthermore,' Jandreau said, 'when I'm through talking to you, I'm going to talk to the general superintendent of the whole plant, the general manager!'

That's when the guy got frightened. He said, 'Send him back, send him back.' Me, I went back, got in my car, drove back to the parking lot. Walked into the plant, walked into the building, walked over to this German. I said, 'That's my machine right over there.' I said, 'But before I do that, I want a card to punch.' He wrote out a card, and handed it to me.

He said, 'Go ahead, punch it.' Boom, just like that.

I walked down. I said to the guy on my machine, 'Look, I'm sorry, fella. This is my job. You're going to have to get a job somewhere else.' And I started to work.

That German didn't come near me for a week, that foreman. Never come near me for a week.

Finally, I don't know how it came about, but he did come over and start engaging me in a little bit of a conversation. Because then I got very active in the union, I became the union representative. And I broke his balls like they've never been broke before. [*Laughs*]

*

We started a veterans' organization down on Union Street, right across from the old public library, there's a big building, big, red brick building. It's still there. This veteran McGee was a very wealthy man, and we were meeting in Union Hall, us veterans as an organization. He called us up. We met him in his office downtown.

'I want to give you that building free. You make a veterans' post, but all I want is my name on the front of the building.' Why not? 'Now, as you go back there, all you fellas, whatever has to be done, you call the people up that's got to do it, and let them send the bill to me.'

Gave us this beautiful building. I'll bet you within three weeks, I had 5,000 members. Couldn't get them in the building, naturally. Then shortly thereafter, you won't remember this, of course, the General Electric Company went on strike, and I was the [union] chairman of the veterans' committee. We marched down Erie Boulevard on strike; I had about 9,000 veterans behind me. Blocked off the street right to the Union Hall. And I was right out in the front. Yeah. So, I had some good experiences.

*

How did [the war] affect my life? Well, you know, it was pretty hard, as a person, to think what you would've done if you didn't get involved in what I got involved in. What would I have done?

Maybe I would've went to college; I was a great basketball player—and I had a full scholarship to Syracuse! But I couldn't go; I had to go to work. Full scholarship! That might've happened. I don't know. Probably would have happened; I always wanted to be a lawyer. That certainly didn't happen.

But all in all, when I look back at it, in retrospect, I had a good life. I did a lot of things that I wouldn't have done if I went the other way, really. If I became a lawyer, what would I have been? Just another lawyer. I wouldn't have done what I've done. Don't forget, I've been all over the world. I was president of the state chiefs of police; I was president of every police organization in the world! I was the president! From New York State, me, from Schenectady! I'm talking about Los Angeles, Chicago, big city chiefs, little me. I went all through them years, six years it took me to get to be president.

Ronald Reagan sent me all over the world. He became president and he sent me with three guys from the Drug Enforcement Administration to England, France, Germany, Italy. Came home, stayed a month, they sent me out to the Far East, all over. Hawaii, oh, Philippine Islands, China, Thailand. One of the most beautiful countries I've ever seen in my life was Thailand. People were great, treated you wonderfully, beautiful women. They were glad to see us there. But in them days, of course, Great Britain controlled most of the Far East, you know? Hong Kong, I went to Hong Kong. The British owned it. Boy, did they live there. Beautiful.

Joseph S. Dominelli passed away at the age of 93 on June 29, 2011. His mark on his community can be seen today; the Rotterdam, New York Police Department's headquarters is named the Joseph S. Dominelli Public Safety Building in his honor.

CHAPTER TWENTY-ONE

The Armored Sergeant

Bill Butz served in the 6th Armored Division under General Patton. A recipient of the Silver and Bronze Star, he met the general in combat on one colorful occasion. He participated in the Brest Campaign and the Battle of the Bulge and was present at the liberation of Buchenwald concentration camp in Germany. In this selection, he discusses how he got into the Army, meeting General Patton in combat in the Brest campaign, and the circumstances that led to his being awarded the Silver Star for actions there.

William C. Butz

I was born in Lockport, New York, September 15, 1919. My father was born in Germany, and my mother was born in Scotland. My father came over in 1911. At that time, they moved to Buffalo, and that area. And when the Depression came, we moved back this way, to Cohoes, New York. I had to quit work to help support our family. My mother and father had five children, and that was in 1936. I was going into my senior year in school at Troy High, so I had to leave there, but I did go back to night school [later].

[I found out about Pearl Harbor] when I lived on Harrison Avenue in Glens Falls, and my wife came over to where I was working, I was running the hot houses there, that was my trade back then. And she said, 'They just bombed Pearl Harbor.' My youngest brother enlisted right away in the Marines. And then my second brother followed within two weeks, and then my oldest brother, he went in the Army about a year later, so this was gnawing away at me for a long time. See, we had one daughter; I was [classified] 3-A, and it bothered me. Half the nights I couldn't sleep, I said, 'Those three boys are gone, my brothers.' And I felt a little guilty, I should be in there [with them]. So I went to see the sergeant down at the post office in Glens Falls.

A soldier said, 'Let me see your card, your draft card.' I was 3-A. He said, 'No, you can't join.'

And I said, 'Well I don't understand.'

He said, 'Well you'd mess up everything anyway, but you're 3-A, you're going to have to wait. I can't tell you, it might be a year or more.'

And you see I was upset, and as I started out the door, I said, 'That's pretty good, the country's at war and I can't go.'

So he said, 'Come back in here a moment.' He said, 'How bad do you want to go?'

I said, 'I want to go, that's why I'm here.'

He said, 'There is a way.' That's what the sergeant said, he said, 'You take this card back, get your wife to sign it. You're going to be put in 1-A.'

Ten days later I was off and gone; it went that quick. I was already in combat when I got an envelope from the draft service that showed that I had voluntarily enlisted, early in '43. Very cold. I went down to Camp Upton, we said goodbye and everything at Glens Falls with the family, and when I get there at Camp Upton, they said, 'Well, now that you got your papers and you're all set and you've got your uniforms,' he said, 'you go home.'

I say, 'What do you mean I go home?'

'Well, you're going to get a week.'

'Oh.'

'Then you're to report back.'

'No,' I said. 'I don't want to do that. I said goodbye, and listen, I don't want to go through that again.'

'Well,' he said. 'That's all right. We'll put you in the group that's going to ship off to Fort Sheridan.' That's how I got to Fort Sheridan. It was a big camp, and [the men there] were awful good, once you got to know them. They didn't like the Yankees, for some reason, but I suppose that goes way back. The academy was off in Louisiana, of course, and boy, they spoke that funny language. They were good boys, but they pulled a fast one on me at Camp Upton, when they stripped us to give us the shots, and then we're lined up to get our clothes.

We got to the clothes part, and he said, 'What size shoes you wear?'

I said, 'Eight, wide.'

He said, 'Pair of nine, wides.'

'No,' I said, 'eight.'

'Jeez, I'm sorry,' he said. 'Make that ten, then.'

I didn't dare say any more. Here came the shoes, and then we move down, and they have them long OD [olive drab] coats.

'Do you know your size?'

I said, 'Yeah.' And I told him, and he made it a size larger. I didn't say nothing. Got all the clothes. Put them on, line them up and here comes the major. He stopped right in front of me, and he said, 'Soldier, don't you know your size?'

Well, boy. Before I said a word, he was on his way. But these guys at Fort Sheridan, they took care of me. One said, 'Boy, I feel sorry for you in a way. Tomorrow we're going on a 20-mile hike. I'll tell you what to do. I'll give you a couple extra pairs of socks and try to get them on. Take [those shoes] tonight and put them in soapy water and soak them a while and then put them out in a sunny part of the barracks; the sun will be out tomorrow.' And he said, 'I think maybe by tomorrow night we might be able to do something with them shoes.' [Later he] jumped up and down and they split across the toes; he said, 'They're no good. Bring them down and make sure you get the right size.' For the coat, they put six guys on the big part of the coat and six on the sleeve, and boy, there was a tug-of-war, they had an awful job ripping the sleeves on that coat. But I got a new coat. And that's too bad that stuff happened, that's just the way it happened.

At Fort Sheridan, while I was there, my brother stopped in once, the oldest brother. He wound up stationed in England. I never saw my two younger brothers. They went in the 1st and 3rd Marines, but they met in Bougainville; I got a letter that they had a chance to meet once in Bougainville.

After Fort Sheridan, we went to Camp Davis, North Carolina, and they threw us in half-tracks with automatic weapons. The first half-track had four .50s and they came two to a section. And we had eight sections in our company, but anyway that's 16 half-tracks. But anyway, the second [section] had a 37mm cannon with twin .50s, .50 on each side.[35] They were operated by two men and the gunner. The man on the right, he could only crank the guns to the right. The man on the left could only crank it to the left. The gunner, he called the shots and elevated the gun. I was a sergeant, so I ordered

---

[35]*twin .50s, .50 on each side*- Browning M-2 .50-caliber heavy machine gun, classically a belt-fed, air-cooled, recoil-operated machine gun nearly six-feet long and weighing 84 pounds, capable of firing up to 550 rounds per minute. Utilized by all the American armed forces in World War II, it had an effective range of 6,000 feet, but its maximum range is four miles. 'A wounded Audie Murphy, America's most highly decorated soldier, fired one atop a burning tank destroyer and held off six Panzer tanks and 250 German soldiers for more than an hour during a battle in Eastern France, an act of bravery that won him the Medal of Honor.' Source: Huard, Paul. *Call it 'Ma Deuce' or 50-cal, the Browning M-2 machine gun is one bad mother of a weapon.* We Are The Mighty, Jan. 12, 2016.

the track with the radio at that time until I got staff sergeant and then I was given the jeep.

The Foxhole

We went to Camp Campbell, Kentucky, for equipment, and then we went into Tennessee Maneuvers and anyway, they came to me one day and told me we were going to have a big inspection with a brigadier general. They said, 'This guy is sharp.'

[I told the men], 'We're going to dig these foxholes deep, and I want five of them right around the back of the half-track, and I want you to take all the dirt and get rid of it.' Jeez, they hollered.

I said, 'No, I want it out of here. I don't want no mound. Carry it to the swamp and dump it there.' So they worked in there all night, sweating and cursing. And then we put fine twigs across the holes and there was a lot of nice, short ferns there. We got just enough twigs to hold that fern and it looked pretty good; it wouldn't in two or three days, it'd be wilting bad, but it looked good. Pretty soon I had a guy way out by the dirt road and he came running, he said, 'I think they're coming.' So I was up on the half-track and I looked and the general stepped out, and the captain was with him. The general had an orderly and he followed the general, and the captain was behind him, and the general was heading right for one of the holes. My first thought was 'Hey, whoa.' And then next thing you know, he let out a holler and down he went in the hole. [*Chuckles*]

I kind of turned, I didn't want them to see me smiling. The orderly pulled [the general] out and he's dusting dirt off. 'Who's in charge here?'

Our captain said, 'I'll take care of him.'

The general said, 'You keep out of this,' to the captain. He said, 'I want to shake his hand.' I'm walking towards him then to give him a salute and he said, 'Congratulations, sergeant, this is a hell of a good job.' He turned around to our captain and he said, 'Look, I've seen enough, let's go back in.' And the next day we got a report that we had, I think, a 98% rating.

We went back to camp and we loaded up and went to Camp Kilmer, New Jersey, ready for overseas. And the guys are kidding me all the way across the sea. 'Hey Butz, there's a general in your foxhole.' I never forgot that; they never let go of that one. [*Laughs*]

Overseas

We went on the New Amsterdam, one of the biggest ships except the *Queen Mary*. We were backing up and I looked over the side and them tugs down there looked like little toys and they were bucking and pushing on that big New Amsterdam. You had to turn it just right, and there was a big foghorn blast. Boy, I looked back, and here comes the *Queen Mary*, pulled in there. We got turned around and they started us out and then we took off slowly, but anyway seven days later we pulled into Glasgow. We made it across in seven days.

[On that ship], they put my men at the head of a three-inch gun, and they dropped a smoke pot when we got two or three days out on the trip. You would fire at that to see how close you'd come. We never hit it, but we came close. Boy, I couldn't believe it; I can't tell you how many decks there were. We heard we could go anywhere on the ship and so I said to the corporal of mine, 'Hey, what do you say? We're off duty, let's go down and look the ship over.' And we kept going down and down and it got noisier and noisier. We must be getting near the engine room, and at the lowest deck, it was straight down, like a fire escape. When I first looked in there, I couldn't believe it. I said, 'Corporal, take a look there.' And the guys had their shirts off, and it was all black soldiers and they were playing cards and dice, and boy, it must've been hot. Sweat was running off them, and of course we were near the engines and you couldn't hear anything.

There was a submarine [scare] off of Ireland. We never saw it, but boy could you see the wake for a mile back of the ship if you were looking at the sea, but nothing ever came of it. I don't even know if it was a foreign or American sub, but we landed in Glasgow and that was a long hike from the docks to the train station.

We had to hike, load up our packs, and then go to the train station. We went from there to near Southampton, put up pup tents in the field and we were next to a pretty good-sized airfield, and every day we'd count the bombers as they went out in groups. There was [36] in a group and we would all count as they came in; [there was only] one day where [36] came back—[sometimes] [only half] the group came back, so I know what they were going through. There were holes that big in them [*gestures with arms*]. Now I've seen them come with only two [engines running], skimming low and just making the cliffs, and taking out wounded after wounded in the planes. That was the 8th Air Force and they supported us too.

Two or three times they had us down for a kind of mock run [of the invasion] and then we'd get down there and it was all for nothing, but all our mail was censored anyway.

We weren't attached to the 6th Armored yet. We joined really the 6th and the 3rd in France.

The first bombing where we really got bombed hard was at Arromanches. It was a funny thing. There was one tank in front of me and a tank right behind my half-track and it was June, the last of June, hot and dry. The [troops ahead of us] wouldn't cross the bridge, they said they're waiting for engineers to check and see if it's ready to blow. It looked pretty good to me, but to the right of us there was a railroad bridge. Now I say to the right, probably 100 yards to the right. But anyway, the troops kept coming in behind us. There was no incoming artillery at the time and that's kind of spooky; if somebody's shooting at you at least you'll know where they are. So I didn't like that, but I could hear planes and I look way up there. I took a picture, of course they look like specks in the sky. But anyway, I called our captain and with field glasses you could see the iron crosses.

I said, 'Hey, you see those German planes circling?'

'Yeah, they ain't doing nothing, they ain't hurting us.'

I said, 'I don't like it. They ain't up there for nothing.'

That was an hour before dark. In the ditches there were some logs laying, and in front of that bridge they must've jack hammered the road around. About that wide, right across [*gestures with arms*]. And then I put two and two together.

I said, 'Look at these logs in the ditch, they are just as smooth as glass.' I didn't know what kind of wood it was, [what it was for]. 'I bet we came up here on them too fast, I bet you they were going to stick them right in front of that bridge, to barricade the bridge.'

So just after dark, they caught a couple Germans wading across to the stream, infiltrating and watching. One guy with baggy camouflage was carrying the grenades. I was kind of alerted to that. All of a sudden, I hear this engine, and it was right above me, overhead. And I don't know why to this day I said, 'Here it comes!' I never had that experience before in my life, but I knew there was a bomb coming. That plane had powered up and pulled out of there and kaboom! Heads rolling, dust, and boy, I flew high up in the air. Then a flare went up, the Germans fired a flare and it drifted and drifted and I watched, and it lit up that railroad bridge... plastered that railroad bridge and it was getting pretty hot around there. One guy had a tank, he kept braking and spun it around, he pulled over on the side... this left a clear shot for me [to move out]. We had a big camouflage net on the front of that half-track—that was my headquarters track with the radio and stuff, but with all the bombing, it was covered with white dust. I heard the rustle in this hedgerow alongside the ditch. It was one of the boys from the Red Ball Express who would come up [to the front] with the gas, to gas us up.[36] I looked down. 'Don't shoot,' he said, 'I'm an American soldier!'

I said to the driver, 'Let's get out of here!'

He said, 'I can't see behind us, I can't move!'

I said, 'That's all open, let's go.' The black fellow jumped on the camouflage net after he came out of the ditch. He must've saw the other tank go back, and he hollers something, sounded like 'wrong way' or something, and he got off and ran, but we went across and I said to my driver, 'When we get across this area, don't stay the direction we're going, go either right or left. The first change, whatever looks the best.'

Now the Germans had gotten hit there probably from our air corps because their trucks had been all blown up and there were several bodies in the road, bloated, and they must have pulled out quite a while before but we didn't know that. The half-track driver pulled and twisted that thing around, but he hit one. I'm in the turret looking around, and boy, I thought I was going to die. That's an awful thing, the juice of a bloated body.

We did see an opening to the left. I said, 'Pull in there.' There was only a little bit of a town, but we never went through it; we pulled to the left and went out in this open field. I called on the radio and told the captain.

He said something like, 'Do you got company over there?'

I said, 'No, we don't [see anything now].'

I put guys out down the road, set up an outpost, and one of them came running to me.

He said, 'Hey Sarge, there's tanks coming!'

---

[36] *Red Ball Express*- the truck convoy system from the ports supplying Allied armies after the breakout. Most of its drivers were African-American.

I said to myself, 'Oh boy, goodnight.' We're over here with a half-track, nothing else. So I said, 'Take the bazooka—we had two bazookas—and grenades and run down and get in the bushes along the ditch there!'

And here they came. And boy, it was the 4th Armored, and when I saw those guys, boy, I'll tell you! Yeah, the 4th Armored. And they were saying, 'What are you doing here?'

They were tough, the 4th Armored, and that was Patton's favorite division next to the 6th. And we fought side by side in a lot of battles, the 4th and the 6th. But anyways, I think they were put out to see what was there, really. A couple civilians came out and my gunner, he was a Frenchman, he could talk French pretty good, because he was French Canadian out of Maine, and they told him the Germans had just pulled out, they were no longer in the town.

After Saint-Lô they brought Patton in and he gave a talk there and boy, I'll tell you, he was to my estimation the greatest general that ever lived, but his vocabulary, his language was something else.

Brest

But anyway, we turned right and that put us heading towards the Brest peninsula. Now on that peninsula, they figured 100,000 Germans were on there, and if we could cut across and cut it off, that was the main supply route to the Brest submarine pens; cut that road and everything would be cut off. Now there were a lot of miles involved. I was not on the point at the start of that. I was in Combat Command A, I had two sections out of half-tracks, that's four of them. And I had them mix them in with so many tanks, armor, and the 44th was with us.

Our objective was cut right straight across. Command B was going to go down to the right and then across, but anyway it was tough going. And it looked like Patton, he always figured if you can keep moving there'll be less casualties and I felt sorry some days for the infantry; the 35th Division followed us. And some days you could hear like a regular, full-scale battle going on behind us, and they let us know about it more than once. Usually at night, the 35th would pull up, go out around all our armor, and dig in. And we could get a little bit of shut-eye, not too long, but we could get some.

But they would say, 'Jeez, don't you guys ever knock out anything? We're running into anti-tank guns!'

'Yeah, if there's a moving vehicle we'll run them down, but Patton told us not to hold up...' He didn't want a foot by foot operation, he wanted us to go around and go around, but keep going.

The first time I saw Patton was when we ran out of gas on the second day on the drive. Our casualties weren't too bad at that point. On the second day, that night before, we were supposed to stop and dig in like we usually did at night, and then they would come up with the supplies; the Red Ball Express would bring up the gas, and ammunition trucks would come up. But Patton changed the plan. He said, 'We got these guys on the run. Full speed ahead!'

Well I don't know whether he knew that one of our gas trucks had already been picked off with a Tiger tank; we had two 6x6 gas trucks, five-gallon cans stacked right to the rack, and one of them got hit by a tank, so we lost that one shortly after we started the drive. [My half-track] had two 30-gallon tanks and I asked the driver, 'How are we standing?'

He said, 'I'm already on the second tank.'

Oh boy, this was in the night, and I said, 'I'll tell you what. Keep a good eye on that second tank, and when it's low, you take it right to the side of the road.' I gave the next section the same orders. 'You take the left, the next one, take the right. And spread out whenever we can.' And just before daylight was about as far as we were going to go. We were scattered, spread out as much as we could, and the artillery started coming in. [The Germans] knew where we were, they had spotted us, a lot of 88s, coming from way back, but luckily no mortars. We radioed back, 'They're not too close or we'd be getting the mortar fire, but we're getting a lot of 88 fire.' They replied that there'll be gas dropped to us. Well I knew those para-bundles were from England, they're about as long as this table [*gestures to table before him*] and a little wider, and had ten 5-gallon cans. When the canvas was tied shut, they put two canvas straps completely around with buckles, buckled them tight.

We carried a boot knife, sharp as a razor [and ready to cut the gas tanks loose], and when the first C-47 dropped the gas, they went right to the Germans, although we were waving from our armor. The second bundles dropped a little shorter; two landed about I'd say 150 feet away at the most.

The 'Sunday School Picnic'

I said, 'Boy, two bundles, that'll take care of both the tank and our half-track.' I said to the corporal, 'You follow me...' and here came this armored car that had I'd say like a siren, and it was Patton. He jumped out and ran up and down that ditch—everybody's in the ditch because there are 88 shells coming in, and we're waiting on the gas—and he let out a bellow.

He said, 'What in the hell do you think this is, a Sunday school picnic? Get after that, get that gas!' And boy, he bellowed it out, and so I then said to the corporal, 'You follow me, but I'm not setting out there with all this shrapnel [flying around and taking the time to] unbuckle the straps!' I really went full run and I came right down [with that knife] and when I hit into the first strap, I went too deep and the gas was spurting out! The corporal was yanking out the cans. And I came back and grabbed the next ones. I said to him, 'You start getting the gas in, I'll go back and get two more.'

Well the guys in the tank already got a couple, and they were pouring it in, and then the Germans started dropping in some mortars. I said, 'Oh brother, they're getting close to us.' I hit the ground with the two cans of gas, and I happened to look up, and the guy on the tank who was pouring the gas, he flew over backwards and over the tank, so I said, 'Oh boy, he's hit.'

Another tanker, he jumped down and grabbed the gas quick. We were losing gas, and my first impression was, 'Look at that, that gas is more important than that soldier.' Then I thought, 'Ah, he's got to be killed instantly.' And I didn't know until I talked to that tanker about a day and a half later; he said, 'Yeah, he was hit by his ear, you could put your fist in. He never knew what hit him, nothing you can do.' I always remember that.

Now [we were getting] a lot of machine gun fire and mortar fire. We got gassed up but didn't move ahead too fast until it quieted down. They asked how far it was to the next half-track where I had the four .50s; they wanted that brought right out. You could put four .50s in there, and you can do a lot of damage with a .50 caliber, it's quite a gun and you've got four of these on that armored half-track.

There's one bad [thing], though, with that half-track, and Patton found that out and I lost a lot of men because of it, because the four .50s guns were in an armored turret. The gunner was protected, and the man on each side sat in the forward track when we had the chests with different amounts of ammunition, so the four guns didn't run out at once. A man on one side would take care of two chests, one for each gun on that side, and the one on the other took care of the other two chests. Now when we wanted to shoot at a plane coming at us, there were no problems, but if you wanted to get lower [over the cab] the guns would automatically stop, you couldn't fire them, because you had them over the cab. This was a safety, but you also couldn't fire to shoot into the hedgerows and counter that [threat], you could only get to the side. So I think that day [when we were shot up fetching the gas] he found that out, but later on in the hedgerow country we got into, the orders came that Patton wanted our half-tracks with the four .50s to go back down the sunken roads. But that only lasted about two days, [because] we lost a lot of men; there was no protection with the rifles shot at us and the machine gun fire, because we had no chance in there [on the sunken roads between the hedgerows]. But anyway, he must have remembered that day when I said, 'We can't depress over the cab.'

Silver Star

The second time I was wounded, I was shot through the leg in one of the hedgerows. It went through the boot, clean through, no bone. And it was sore, but it healed up fairly good. And my guy said, 'Well you're going to get a Silver Star...' [He reached for the dog tags, I blocked him]; I went like that [*makes blocking motion with forearm].*

He's like, 'What the hell?'

I said, 'You ain't going to reach for my dog tag.' By the way, they did send that notice home. And my wife got the notice I was involved in an accident. But they had said, 'No, we'll take care of that, we just want to put you down so you get a Silver Star, Purple Heart.' So that's why they took the information, they were going to leave out sending them to my family, but they didn't.

[I did end up with a Silver Star for action] on the Brest peninsula; I didn't get it pinned on me until the war ended, but I was told by our company commander on a three-day rest, 'Boy I bet you've done one hell of a job. Everything fell in line with the report.'

I said, 'What fell in line? What report?'

He said, 'Well, you were awarded a Silver Star. We found the armored car with the dead lieutenant just where you said it was. We found the machine gun and just about the amount of men you figured.' They said it was coming, but then again, you're not a hero when you win a medal. Heroes didn't come home.

As we pulled into that little town with the German cars, everything happened; the Germans heard us coming. Machine gun tracers were flying everywhere, it looked like the 4th of July. That's when a bazooka [round] went by and the next one hit the armored car in front of me and killed the lieutenant.

That driver came back and said, 'Are you in charge?'

'What do you mean, I'm just a sergeant.'

He said, 'Well is there anybody higher than a sergeant here?'

Well, there wasn't. I didn't know anything more than we took the wrong road miles back, because that lieutenant had called me up to him in the dark and said, 'Get down on the ground and feel this.'

I said, 'What are they?'

'They're tank tracks, they went this way.'

If we walked thirty feet more, there wasn't any track. The whole column of [enemy] tanks was in front of us; they turned to the right. They left a tank for guard, but we were too [far] behind, they thought we were gone; they didn't notice anybody. If we would have walked down that road [to the right] we'd have known shortly, but we kept going, went right through a town full of Germans. They must have heard us, but they never fired a shot or anything; they must have thought it was their men headed for Brest. We were on the road heading right to Brest, and of course, they were headed out. We were seven miles from the front; little by little, we put wounded in the truck and had a time going in and backing up, to get turned and get the wounded out of there.... That machine gun opened up before we got everything done, and this corporal fellow was talking here, the driver for that lieutenant and one of my men was to the side of him. And that machine gun opened up right through us, right through the hedgerow. He went down, and I stood there.

Here I am, he's gone, but I don't even know, I don't feel anything. Then I looked up the column and I see the tracers coming back. I dove right in the ditch and [the rounds] went right over my head. I had to go about 30 feet back to our half-track and get the other ones back. The guns on that track, we couldn't fire that direction. And I said, 'Don't fire ahead.' I figured a mile of our men are in front; they weren't, but I didn't know. I was so scared that that machine gun was just after me, nobody else, and that's the only reason [I think I'm here] today, to tell you the truth. I figured that guy's going to get me or I'm going to get him—and it just fed a rage where I threw two grenades and the gun stopped. There were Germans there and [later] they found them.

[Another thing happened]; we had stopped in front of the first house in town. It was about 6:00 AM and just getting light. A woman ran out of the house towards our half-track, and she yelled something in French. Louie LeVesque, my machine gunner, could understand French. He yelled to me that she said a German officer was upstairs in her house. I sent Corporal Stanford around the side of the house and almost immediately I heard his M1 rifle fire. He no more than said, 'I got him!' when the French woman appeared again and said we had shot her husband.

Sure enough, the husband had been shot in the head. We felt bad, but that's war. What in the world did he move that curtain for? Boy, that hurt; that gunner of mine, he sat on the steps there and he cried, he felt so bad. The woman, I do remember slightly, she went over to the porch—I was standing beside the porch and he was sitting on the steps crying. She put her arm around him; I never forgot that.

Later, [my incident] was verified, but I didn't get that pinned on me until the end of the war. And when they pinned them on—three medals at once [Silver Star, Bronze Star, and Purple Heart]—you know what went through my mind? Points! The war was over then. You had to have eighty-seven points or more [to be the first] to get home. When they got done counting [with me, I had] 128 points. Every major battle was at five points; every medal was five points. If you had two children, that's ten points. And boy, they added up.

The fight for Brest had been costly. The old city was razed to the ground and when the German garrison surrendered on September 19, the port facilities were rendered useless. When the German general, unimpressed at the stature of U.S. Brigadier General Charles Canham, told him to show his credentials, Canham pointed to his nearby troops and said, 'These are my credentials.' Today his response is the division motto of his former 8th Infantry Division.

The German threat to the Allies' rear in Normandy was gutted, but no war supplies were ever unloaded through Brest—the armies were now moving at a fast clip, beyond Paris, and Brest was 500 miles from the German border. In the Netherlands, Operation Market Garden was underway.

Mr. Butz' story will continue in Part Five.

CHAPTER TWENTY-TWO

The Hürtgen Forest

'Our gains in the forest proper came inch by inch and foot by foot, delivered by men with rifles—bayonets on one end and grim, resolute courage on the other. There was no battle on the continent of Europe that was more devastating, frustrating, or gory.'

—Major General William G. Weaver, 8th Infantry Division[24]

As soon as the guns stopped firing in Brest, the longest single battle the U.S. Army has ever fought began just three miles into Germany on September 19, 1944. It was a stop-and-start horror show in the worst conditions in Europe—ice, mud, fog, rain, sleet; damp, cold, and wet—and it did not let up until February 1945. Pushed off the front pages by the opening salvos of the Battle of the Bulge that unfolded back across the border that December, it remains relatively unknown today, given the high costs. Thirty-three thousand Americans were killed or wounded for very little gain. Foxholes filled with water, shells bursting in treetops terrorized and maimed countless GIs. Many rifle companies turned over 100 percent—out of one company of 160 men of the 28th Division, one recalled, 'By the time I left the forest, I had the instincts of an animal,' being only one of the twenty lucky enough to walk out.[25]

John Webster was wounded in a major action midway through the Hurtgen Forest assault.

John O. Webster

The Battle of Schmidt

Our outfit, the 20th Combat Engineers, was attached to the 112th Infantry Regiment of the 28th Infantry Division. In Germany, we just got through the Siegfried Line, the Hürtgen Forest. From November 2 to November 9, my company went from about 150 men down to about 14. The official historian for the Army that wrote up the story of the Battle of Schmidt, Germany, summarizes the battle as one of the costliest division actions in the whole Hürtgen Forest, just before the Battle of the Bulge. They figure that in just the division alone, that one division action, there were over 6,000 casualties in those seven days! The German casualties were only about half that.

When we were relieved, that particular front sort of quieted down because the German troops were getting ready [for what would become the Battle of the Bulge]; within one month they had started the Ardennes Offensive just south of us and we were back in action again, trying to contain that situation. But I mean, the only reason I mention this is that we didn't have television then; the only thing people back home in America knew what was going on was what they read in the papers. The Battle over Schmidt where we lost over 6,000 men probably wasn't much more than a squiggle in the paper like, 'American forces continue to make limited gains south of Aachen' or some little thing like that. [*Gets emotional*] There were as many people killed in those weeks fighting as were lost in the enormous tragedy of the World Trade Center, for example, though certainly, that terrible tragedy haunts us all, I'm sure. But here we have a World War II we are talking about, and things almost of that magnitude were going on every week, and nobody ever knew it was happening, but we did.

Now I went in to help with my platoon of mine detectors. There was a time when our outfit was in a defensive position in the woods on a hill and there were a whole bunch of tanks behind us, and the Germans were trying to shell the tanks with artillery fire. They weren't trying to hit us, we were dug in the woods, they were trying to hit the tanks, but their shells were falling short, they didn't have them elevated high enough to hit the tanks. So instead of the shells hitting where the tanks were, they were hitting where we were. I was dug into the ground pretty nicely at that particular time; it was a nice trench, I could actually squat down in it and I had some dirt and twigs and branches over me so I actually had some cover over my foxhole; I felt pretty secure that nothing could get me unless it was a direct hit. And one of these heavy shells hit right beside my foxhole and the dirt from the explosion crater absolutely covered me up completely; I was just like a woodchuck in the ground, but I had some air because it was a big enough hole, so I wasn't out of air right away. I stayed that way for as long as I thought I'd ought to, and then until it started to die down. Then I dug my way out with my hands until I got air. Didn't get a scratch then, just scared, that's all. But I was later wounded in that battle—I got hit in the face with shrapnel. Yes, it knocked out my upper teeth and I still have a piece of shrapnel left in the side of my face that they didn't take out. It moves around a little bit, but it doesn't go very far. But when I shave every morning I can tell where it is.

'People Cannot Make the Same Mistakes Again'

The battle for Schmidt was such a rough battle that the Army put a crew of historians on it, interviewing hundreds of soldiers after it was over with. They interviewed not just generals, colonels and lieutenant colonels, but everybody that they could get their hands on—privates, corporals, T5s, sergeants, and lieutenants, and they wrote a history that detailed each day of this event, of this action, what each of the engineers did, what the tankers did, what the infantry did, what the enemy did, and made a whole thick book on it, to try to analyze what the American Army did wrong because at the end of this one division action there were so many casualties, and we only ended up with the line between the Americans and the Germans at almost where we started. We didn't gain any ground really; all we did was lose all these men! It was sort of a valiant effort, but it didn't accomplish very much, but maybe that particular battle of the war would be studied by the war colleges, so people cannot make the same mistakes again.

John Webster served four consecutive terms as town supervisor of Queensbury, New York, shepherding it through explosive growth with the opening of the new Interstate 87, the Adirondack Northway. In retirement he tended to his gardens and operated a roadside stand for many years. He died on July 22, 2015, at the age of 95.

CHAPTER TWENTY-THREE

The Forward Observer

John Holden 'Jack' Vier served in the 44th Field Artillery attached to the 22nd Infantry Regiment. He was assigned to the 4th Infantry Division and stationed in Newton Abbott, England, where he received special training by the British commandos prior to D-Day. On June 6, 1944, Corporal Vier landed on Utah Beach serving as an artillery forward observer. He also fought in the Battle at the Hürtgen Forest, the Battle of the Bulge, and several other major battles. Mr. Vier received a battlefield commission and later was promoted to first lieutenant, receiving three Purple Hearts, a Silver Star, a Bronze Star, and the Conspicuous Service Medal for his actions during the war. In this 2001 interview, he gives an animated account of growing up in a rough and tumble 1930s neighborhood, his wartime experiences and frustrations, and dealing with combat-related stress and trauma long after the war.

John Holden 'Jack' Vier

I was born on March 7, 1918, in White Plains, New York. I had just graduated from Georgetown, June of 1941, and I [felt that we would be in the war], and I knew darn well that after World War I a lot of the GIs who came home didn't have their same job. So, I took up the first job offering [out of college], which was that of a Federal Reserve bank examiner down on 33 Liberty Street, New York City. I didn't like it, but it was a job. I was out hunting when the Japs struck Pearl Harbor, on December the 7th of '41; that got my Irish up, and so I decided, 'I'm going to quit my job Monday morning,' and then join up with the Marines or the Army or somebody.

So, I went 9:00 to the Federal Reserve and I told my boss I was quitting. And he said, 'Good.' And I went over to the Marines, and I was wearing glasses even then, so they refused me. I went over to Whitehall Street, where the Army induction center was, and they felt I was still a warm body, still a little bit alive, and so they signed me up. And then I went home for about two days.

Tough Guys

And then about two days later, they sent me up to Camp Upton, out at Yaphank, Long Island, and so darn many of us had volunteered in that little short period of time that they ran out of uniforms. And for the next few days, I was walking around in civilian clothes—some of us were in uniforms, and some were not. I tell you what, we were overcrowded something terrible. These boys are mostly from New York City, a lot of them were from around Third Avenue, and a lot of these guys were damn tough. Like, personally, I was in my bunk down below. Head to toe, sleeping in these cots, and oh, God, if you took a cigarette out of somebody's footlocker, bam, boy, there'd be a fight. These were tough cookies.

I learned to mind my Ps and Qs, and after about not quite a full week, I think, I told them I wanted to be in the artillery. I thought I could kill more Japs—oh, was I out to kill Japs!—[I thought I could do it better] with artillery shells than I could with bullets. So, they sent me down to Fort Bragg, Fayetteville, North Carolina, for my basic training, and that was one big damn camp, I think, oh, at least 80,000 troops and all that stuff. That's where I got my basic training, and at the end of an eight-week stint, or whatever the heck it was,

I had palled around with a guy by the name of Johnny Adamkowicz, and he was a tough Polack. So many of these guys in this generation [who were] a little bit older than I was, and I was about 23, 24, at that time, to impress somebody, they'd say, 'Oh, yeah, I used to be a bootlegger.' We were so gung-ho, and we wanted action. We wanted to be with a line outfit, and all that stuff.

They said to Adamkowicz and myself, 'Now look, your group is moving out, and we're going to keep you here, and when the next group comes in, we're going to make a cadre out of you.' So Adamkowicz and I thought, 'Well, we're pretty smart guys. What we'll do is raise all kinds of hell, and they won't want us.' Well, I got a pass to go home for one weekend. I came back with a bunch of booze, and he had gotten some booze, and so the next several days, maybe almost two weeks, oh, God, we managed to get awful damn drunk. And now Adamkowicz was the kind of guy that you didn't fool around with; he'd fight at the drop of a hat. One night we were passed out, and somebody called down from CQ, 'Vier and Adamkowicz, report to CQ immediately.' So, we go down there, with a hangover and still drunk, and they sent both of us down to the train station. Adamkowicz was put on one train, going to some outfit in Virginia, and they put me on another train, and I went down to Augusta, Georgia, and there was a Corporal Friedman waiting for me. I got in there about quarter to five in the morning, and I hadn't gotten much sleep, because all of a sudden, there's such an influx of men coming into the Army, they took these old, old railroad coaches out of mothballs. These coaches, no baloney, had the old original gas light fixtures hanging down, and they just simply strung up electroplate bulbs, and that was it. And now you have electricity in there. And they still had some old steam engines, and these windows were so worn out, you'd open them at the bottom, and the soot sometimes used to come through, and you'd be brushing your uniform off like this [*makes sweeping gesture with hand on opposite forearm*].

So about quarter to five, I got to Georgia, and this Corporal Friedman picked me up with the jeep, brought me up to camp there, and I was assigned to Battery C of the 44th Field Artillery Battalion, 4th Infantry Division. This outfit was reactivated in Mississippi, Louisiana, and Alabama about eight months before I joined up. So, all the non-com positions were taken up, and these were real Southern boys. They were hillbillies, and tougher than hell. And these guys too, like I told you about the Third Avenue boys, oh, they'd fight at the drop of a hat. As I again learned quickly, as I mentioned before, you stayed the hell away from some other guy's footlocker. Otherwise, Jesus, cots would go rolling, and it would be flesh on flesh!

I was a Yankee in this group. At my first dinner, in this mess hall, one of these Southern crackers came up alongside of me—he was from North Carolina—and he was a hard-shell Baptist. And he said, 'Vier. Vier, where the hell are you from?'

I said, 'I'm from White Plains, New York.'

He said, 'Jesus Christ,' out loud for everyone's benefit, 'did you hear that? He's a goddamn blankety-blank Yankee.'

Then he said to me, 'What's your religion, Vier?'

I said, 'I'm a Roman Catholic.'

'Goddamn, fellows, did you hear that?' You couldn't be any lower in those Baptists' eyes than if you were a Yankee, and a Catholic, and from New York. Oh, you couldn't be any lower. I finally won their confidence, but it took months and months. And another thing I learned, if some guy's a big fat guy, don't underestimate his strength. Because I was brand-new, and a Yankee, and a Catholic to boot, can't get any lower, I was put on KP for one week. I mean, you got your ass out of bed at 4:30. You were in the goddamn kitchen working at 5:00. And they didn't let you out of there until about damn near 12 o'clock. I learned to lose weight that way. About the second or third day, an Army supply truck pulled in, dropped off all these bags of sugar, and this big fat boy I was with, Reedy was his name, and he was from Richmond, Virginia, and this guy was a thug, no other word to describe him. So, we went down these five steps from the kitchen, and all the stuff was out on the ground. And this son of a gun took one hand, big hand, and he put it down on a 100-pound bag of sugar, and with the other hand, grabbed onto another 100-pound bag of sugar, and that bastard picked both of them up, put them on his shoulder, and walked up those five steps into the goddamn mess hall like he was carrying a piece of paper or something like that.

We had a sergeant. We called him Bulldog, I forget his real name now. He, too, was a Southern boy, and again, as I mentioned before, guys who were a little bit older than me, if they wanted to make an impression, they'd say, 'Yeah, during Prohibition, I was a bootlegger.' And so, this guy claimed the same thing. He had a build on him like crazy. God, he had shoulders, and a massive chest, probably no waist to him at all. And he was in the Army for several years. He was a real old-time regular Army first sergeant. And, oh, he could do a close-order drill like crazy. He was good.

So, to get on with it, this guy, John—I guess his first name was John—Reedy, he was always getting goddamn drunk, and so you had to be back at 12 o'clock. During the winter months, even down there, it would be inky black when you had to be out on the drill field at 2:00 AM for roll call and all that. The first sergeant would call out, 'Vier,' and I'd say, 'here,' you know. So he called out, 'Reedy,' and there was no goddamn Reedy to be seen in the ranks. And then across the drill field, all of a sudden in the inky black, we could make out here comes old Reedy, drunker than the lord, staggering around! And the first sergeant, oh, he chewed his ass out something terrible. And then the two of them damn near squared off; it would have been the battle of the century. Some of the other sergeants broke it up, and they put him back into our ranks. And of course it was all short order drill, left flank, right flank, and about face. This guy, Reedy, because of his size, he was knocking down other GIs because he was always going the wrong way!

Convoy

We were supposed to go over to North Africa with the 1st and 9th, and at the last minute we were canceled out. We went up to Fort Sill, because we were in the artillery, went out there for more training. And then up to Fort Dix in New Jersey, where we finally shipped out on a big convoy, and they decided to put me on a turret gun, out in the goddamn open. It was just a little bit of a platform in the side of the ship, they put some pipe around you, and either you got a 20-millimeter or a 40-millimeter gun. We'd practice those things in the daylight, you fired one shot up and poof—we'd put smoke up there, then aim for the smoke. That's how we got our practice in.

One night, I had the graveyard shift on this one particular so-called turret. I think I was on a 40-millimeter that night, oh God, it was a big goddamn convoy. I looked over to my left, and Jesus, there was something coming through the water that night on the water, the ocean. When you ruffle up that water, you ruffle up phosphorous. I thought, Jesus Christ, that's a goddamn U-boat there with his periscope up! And I took aim, but I had been given orders that before you open fire, there's a telephone next to you, call down to the officer at the other end of that wire. So I called down, I said, 'I'm about to open fire, there's a goddamn U-boat periscope, I got my sights right on him, and I'm going to fire.'

Oh, this guy got excited like crazy and oh, British accent and all that stuff, and he told me to hold my fire, chewed my ass out about it at the same time. See, what they do on a convoy like that is they'll take a long rope, I guess it's called a lanyard, and they'll tie a log behind it, and at the stern of the boat, they'll throw it out in the water. That thing will be towed behind that boat maybe a hundred yards, whatever the hell they want, and that is to keep boats behind you in the convoy from coming up to you. Inky, inky black of night, floating out there at the end of your stern. So that was what it was!

They packed us in like flies. It was a passenger ship originally, but oh jeez, there'd be one bunk right here, and about this high above it would be another, another, so on [*raises hand just above head*]. If you ever raised your head too fast at night, you'd rap your head against some steel above you. And if you had to bathe sometime, fresh water was precious on these troop ships. Your helmet had an insert; if you popped the insert up and out, what you had was just the steel helmet, so you'd get just a little bit of water, you'd strip down bare ass, and then you'd bathe yourself starting from the head right down to your toes. You'd squeeze it out, a sponge or a rag or whatever, and oh Jesus, that water was inky black by the time you got down to your goddamn feet!

We landed in Southampton, England, the 31st of January of '44, and then we were sent over to [the town of] Newton Abbott, right on the Channel. We got settled down there. And my best buddy was a guy named Dresspat from Ohio. We got a pass after we were there two or three days to go on into Newton Abbott and go to the pubs. Back in those days, it was funny telling your buddies, 'Hey, let's go to town tonight and get good and goddamn drunk,' and Jesus, you would do exactly that. We got into this one pub, and everything's all inky black around you, the whole town's blacked out. There were a couple of little Scottish soldiers, kilts and all that stuff; they were small men. But of course, they were already in the pub, so they were already drunk. And the English and the Australian marines, they were big bastards. They had to be a minimum of six feet tall, and boy, they knew how to wear their uniforms. They'd click their heels, and you could hear that sharp crack. They were good soldiers.

These two Scots were drunker than hell. They knew that we were Yanks, and they said to us, 'Yanks, you know who we hate, would rather fight more than the goddamn Jerries? These goddamn Blimeys; they're no goddamn good.' The Scots and the Welsh and the Irish, all three, they're Celts, and boy, their memories go back generations, they don't forget easily. I said to myself, 'Oh jeez, there is going to be bloodshed.' These big Englishmen, six feet and more, they could have wiped the floor with these guys. But I've heard they have a lot of patience, more so than the Americans... And nothing happened at all!

British Commandos

We were there till, oh, the end of May. And then we're sent to a big marshalling area, to get on the LCTs and the LSTs. One day, some British commandos came into the camp, and they were to teach us hand-to-hand combat. Let me tell you one thing—they were a tough bunch of bastards. They were no bigger than we are, but one of them seemed to be the leader. I don't know why he picked on me, but he said, 'Hi there, Yank,' and he came toward me with his hand extended, I thought in friendship. I grabbed his hand. He grabbed my hand, gave me a pull, he gave me his hip, I went ass over teakettle, skipping down the hard dirt. They proceeded to teach us what comes down to dirty tricks. Because they went on to Dieppe and those kinds of places, they had to contend with German guards, and had to come up behind them and [neutralize them]. And if you want to hear, I'll tell you some dirty tricks they taught me. They said, 'First thing, you never keep your strap from your steel helmet clipped underneath your chin.' If you came up behind a German, a guard, you just reach over the front of his head and snap the helmet back, and you've broken his goddamn neck. Not just hurt him, you break his goddamn neck.

Then they showed us when somebody comes up and gives you the bear hug, and you can't break out of it, there's several ways of breaking out. The first one that comes to mind, of course, is you bring your knee up and hit them in the balls, but then if you take the side of your foot, and rake him down the shin like that [*demonstrates for interviewer*], you go right down on his foot too. That is awfully goddamn painful. Then if you get your hands just free enough to get them around his ears, you clap his ears—you don't just hurt him, you break his goddamn eardrums! Or if you can get your two fingers under the nostrils of his nose, you can literally lift his nostrils right off his goddamn nose!

And they taught us, 'Yanks, go on, when you're walking along, do this,' you hold the left hand out, and you take the right hand, and you want to build this muscle up right here [*repeatedly pounds the outside edge of left hand into right palm in chopping motion*]. And just keep doing this all day long, and they did have muscle right in there [*runs fingers over edge of left hand*]. That's so you can give a guy a chop across his Adam's apple [*demonstrates outward chopping motion, neck level*], so that's another trick.

Now let me just jump ahead, I'll get back to the war in a minute. Those things were instilled in my mind. So I got discharged in October of '45. Went home, and this one particular evening, I was all by myself. I came into this bar and grill, and I saw a couple old acquaintances. So we said hi, there are two of them, and I sat down with them in this booth; I sat on one side with one of them, the other guy was opposite us. And so we're just talking to each other what outfits we were in, whether we're in the Pacific or the ETO, and all that kind of crap.

Then another guy came in, a little bigger than myself, he came up to the booth that we're in, and I assumed he was buddy-buddy with these other two guys—he just slid himself in, nobody invited him, he slid in. And so they said, 'Vier, where the hell were you?' So I told them, just gave it to them the way it was. And this guy said to me, 'You're full of shit.'

I said, 'Look, buddy, those are fighting words. Don't you talk like that to me.' I was wearing glasses then, I said, 'Don't let my goddamn glasses stop you.' I put my glasses down [*removes his eyeglasses, puts them on table*], I said, 'You take the first goddamn crack, you see what the goddamn hell happens to you.'

And I had my glasses, he didn't do a goddamn thing until I reached back for my glasses, went like this [*makes motion to retrieve glasses*]. Oh, he popped me one across the top of the eye, he really opened up my eyebrow, no question about that [*points to eyebrow*]. So I threw the whole goddamn table on him with these other guys, and to make this very short, went out on the street—we were pushed out on the street by the waiters, and I whipped his ass. You know what's funny? You get into a fight like that with somebody, and Jesus, it's kill or be killed, that's the first thing we're taught in the Army, kill or be killed. And after I got the upper hand, 'Well, shit. Should I keep beating him, or what the hell do I do next?' So I foolishly said to him, 'Let that be a goddamn lesson to you, you watch your goddamn tongue.' I fought him three times that night. The second time that we had the fight, he went back inside, and he said, 'That son of a bitch is just plain lucky. I could whip his ass.'

I said, 'You get your goddamn ass out in the street.' And of course, what I was doing to him and he didn't realize, I was pulling the same goddamn dirty tricks that the British commandos taught me. I'd kick him in the stomach, he'd double up, and then knock the shit out of his face. I think he was better than I was at fighting, at boxing, but even though I grew up as a skinny kid, I could always wrestle. I hadn't had my ass beaten yet in wrestling; I never went to college or high school where they had real, true wrestling, I'm just talking street fights.

Jesus, I had this fellow down again, and I had his head, and I started to rap his head on the goddamn concrete pavement. All of a sudden, two goddamn headlights come right up, right up to me. It was a car, of course, and two cops jumped out. One cop grabbed me from one side, the other cop from the other side, and they pulled me off. They didn't make any arrests, they just chewed our asses out and all that. By the time I got home, this goddamn cut on my eye, it was really a cut, it was bleeding, bleeding, bleeding. And I had just bought a brand-new suit; I'm talking 1946, I think. It was Memorial Day, I remember that, the holiday. So Jesus, I had a brand-new thirty-five dollar Robert Hall suit on, it was all bloody and torn, the knees were out. My father was a surgeon, he was chief of staff at St. Ives Hospital, White Plains, for about 20 years or so; he led a respectable life. So I get my ass in bed, and I have my goddamn bloody clothes all tucked away under the bed, and I'm lying on my back and bleeding, bleeding, bleeding. Now I know goddamn well it needs stitches. I got up, I get these torn-up bloody clothes on, and I go over to St. Ives Hospital, five in the morning. And of course, the first thing they want to know, 'What's your name and where do you live?'

And of course, 'Jack Vier.'

'Oh, Doctor Vier's son!'

'Yeah.'

So I got patched up, and what a big goddamn bandage I had over my eye. My older brother, he was ordained, he was a priest at the time. He had another priest friend with him, this other priest stayed over that night. I come down for the breakfast table, oh Jesus, beat up, bruised, bandaged, all that stuff. The nutcase of the family. But of course, what I'm telling this story for is about how those dirty tricks that the British commandos taught me came in good stead.

Landing in Normandy

But getting back to combat, we went over to Dartmouth, England. That's where we loaded up on the boats, very early in the morning before sunrise. God, once we got out into the channel, it was tremendously impressive to see the size of it. And then to see the fleets of thousands of airplanes, aircrafts, going over to the shore. As we got closer to the shore, I'm talking battleships themselves, not cruisers but battleships, they were behind us. Oh, Jesus Christ, the noise, and you see the flare [from the big guns]; when those 16-inch shells went over you, it sounded to me like a goddamn freight train going over. They used delayed action fuses on them, and of course the delayed action fuse will not detonate the very second it hits something hard. It'll detonate maybe just two seconds later. But those two seconds, that burrows into rock, ground, or anything, and then goes off. The craters those goddamn things left were so big that later, when the guys went ashore with trucks and everything like that, they could get out of the small arms fire range by going down there, and some even set up temporary command posts down in there. That's how big they were.

I thought, 'This is pretty serious stuff now.' And it was, but I tell you what. I wasn't as afraid right then—and anyone that says they wasn't afraid in combat is a goddamn freaking liar—then when I got onshore, that's when fear hit me.

We landed at Utah Beach at Sainte-Mère-Église. We were sort of married off that day to the 82nd Airborne; they had been dropped in behind us. And as you probably know, there are a rough lot of mistakes made when they dropped off those poor bastards on the 82nd. So we went to meet our team ashore, actually, about 11:00.

They already had secured the beachhead. Omaha was worse, but Utah was no Sunday picnic either.

*

One of the first things that impressed me were [the bodies I saw]; I realized I was in trouble. Several, not one, but several in a group of these 82nd Airborne troops were deader than hell. They had parachuted in, and their parachutes got caught up in the tops of some of these trees—the Germans just simply machine-gunned them to death, and these poor bastards, they had their heads down; you got the feeling they're looking at you, their bodies were just swaying back and forth with the breeze. One of the next things I remember very clearly, I could hear a machine gun, one of our own machine guns, going off close to me. I didn't see it, but I knew where the sound was coming from. What happened was another one of these poor paratroopers had landed way in, and he came upon a German staff car with a key still in the ignition. So this poor bastard thought it would be quite a lark to get in that command car, and come back into our lines and show it off. Of course, as soon as these guys, Americans, in the little bit of the nest they had created, saw a staff car coming up, German markings across and all, they opened up on him. This poor bastard, he only got as far as his hand on the doorknob to open the door, and he had gotten it open, and he went flying out ass over teacup up against it. Oh, God [*shakes head*]. He was riddled, the car was riddled.

German Tanks

Then the Germans put a few 88s close to us. That was the meanest, goddamn... for me, most feared weapon of the whole goddamn war. It had a tremendous speed to it, way above the speed of sound. That goddamn gun was invented by the Germans right after Hitler took over. When they went down, Hitler volunteered the troops in the Spanish Civil War, 1936 and '37. Germans were smart. They quickly realized that goddamn gun, though it had been invented for anti-aircraft, they could use it against [ground troops]. They could pick a trench apart with it, and they realized that was a mean goddamn weapon to put at the front of their tanks. So when we came ashore with Sherman tanks, oh Jesus—there was no contest [*throws hands upward and forward, as if in exasperation*]. The only thing the Sherman tanks were good for, was they were produced by mass production. We could make them fast. We need them fast, so okay, and also they had hydraulically driven turrets. They could turn around with hydraulics, whereas the German tanks, they had to crank them. But the German tanks had much more armor on the front of them. I've seen these puny goddamn tank shells, solid projectile, hit the front of a German tank, and just ricochet right the hell off, but not so with a goddamn 88. That son of a bitch went through a goddamn Sherman turret, making a very clean hole in and a clean hole going out. I think anybody inside the Sherman tank was destined to be killed, because the steel that was taken out by that hole would shatter all through the interior of the tank, and you'd look down the side and see all these dead GIs, there are about five in the tank, I think. Their uniforms were all puffed up like this [*pulls sweater out*]. One time, when we were either married off to the 2nd Armored or the 4th Armored, one of those outfits ... Again, you get on the back of them, like 4:30 in the morning, before it got daylight. Because I was an artillery forward observer, I was always at about the third, maybe the fourth tank. I had heard the worst about the first tank, because that first tank was almost always destined to be knocked out. The Germans were goddamn masters at camouflage, and they knew that the road coming up to them was only a single lane, and they'd be beautifully camouflaged around a bend. That first poor goddamn tank of ours would be sure to be knocked out, and probably the second one too. So it was my position with my two men to get our ass off when that happens, and then to adjust artillery fire. You knew about where that German tank was, and you'd try to get artillery fire out at that point.

I think of this day, it was just before we got out of the hedgerow country, we had a battalion of the tanks and tank destroyers behind us as support. And see, because I was a forward observer, I only had to take care of three different rifle companies, which was the 22nd Infantry Regiment, 4th Infantry Division. And I could go from Company K to M to I at my own will. I didn't take any orders from the rifle company commanders; I took orders from my captain back at my battery. So this one day, I knew we had tanks behind us. I got up to this position with K Company, Captain Whaley, 'Look over there. We know goddamn well there's a crowd of tanks over that next bridge, behind there. Cover us with artillery fire.'

I said, 'What I'll do is I'll fire white phosphorous shells.' Now, white phosphorus will burn the goddamn hide off you, burn the clothes off you, but also, it'll serve as a smoke screen, give you some protection. I could make out just about where they were, so I called my commands down through the radio. The procedure is, when you're in a position like mine, you'll only ask for one round, because what you are doing is finding the coordinates on your map... and you knew that was a hillside, so all right. I had a good idea of where our battery was located, because you had to figure angles coming across. Then you start to [fine tune] with left and right, and over and short. You ask for one round, then pick up the air for that. You always gave the area. You didn't give the corrections. I'd say, '100 yards left. 50 yards short.' They'd do the arithmetic back at the battery, and then another round, and then when you figured you were on target, I'd just say, 'Fire for effect.'

But I wasn't getting any goddamn response at all! No shells coming over, nothing at all. So then I started to curse and raise hell to the radio—and this went on and on. So finally, this Captain Whaley came through, he said, 'Vier, we can't wait any longer. We got to jump off.' And I said, 'Well Jesus Christ, I don't know what the hell else to do.'

So they jumped off, and then the tanks behind us came over this crest, and they started to come down. That's when the German tanks opened up on us. We actually were still advancing, and you always crouched down to make less of a target, this was still hedgerow country. The back of my helmet hit something hard; I heard a loud bonk, and I looked up and Jesus, there was a goddamn German tank, had just been knocked out, and the barrel was beautifully camouflaged with a vine wrapped around it, and I couldn't see it until I was right on top of the goddamn thing!

Well here's what happened, the tragic note of all of this story was this. They knocked the shit out of our tanks—we lost 17 tanks, and we lost 55 tankers, tankers being the men in the tanks. So, oh, I was [very angry]. Captain Higgins was my commanding officer, he and I were buddies. So I went and pulled my gun out, I had a .45, and I said, 'Goddamn it, Higgins, I'm going to kill these son of a bitches, these goddamn bastards who didn't give me firepower! Why didn't I get firepower?' I was livid.

He said, 'Take it easy, Vier. Take it easy.'

I always had quite a temper. What it all came down to, it had come to a point where the 28th Infantry Division was on our left flank, and some of the 28th rang over to our outfit that they had troops at this one point where I wanted to fire my artillery, which was bullshit. They told me that story, so I said, 'Goddamn it, if I can find the bastards over there, I'm going to kill them.' Because they killed 55 of our boys, and we lost 17 goddamn tanks.

The Hedgerows

I guess for centuries in Normandy there were first walls, and a lot of vegetation would grow into them to support them, hold them up. There was no one set distance apart, but it made a beautiful goddamn defense for the enemy. Because Jesus, a few goddamn troops behind that could take care of a hell of a lot more guys coming at them, and they were hard as hell to see. We were never told anything about the goddamn hedgerows. But speaking of the hedgerows now, there was this one guy, a rifleman, who I thought was crazy. To get from this point to that point, he'd go right along the hedgerow, and then go fast across [the open field]. This one GI, he did it more than once. He'd walk right through the middle of the hedgerow, into the field between the hedgerows.

Right in that period of time, we took a small barn and we were living in a small, very small, annex on one side of it. See, I had gone from corporal to second lieutenant—I never was a sergeant. I was working underneath a guy named Shaward. He was an Alabama boy, tall, lanky fellow, and a real Southern accent. We knew that there were SS troops right in front of us, and it was the first time we ever heard the creaking and the groaning of a German tank right close by to us. Suddenly we realized this one tree right in front of us was loaded with German snipers. They had their camouflage capes on, but they were hard to make out. They had a fake tree with leaves on it, it was hard as hell to find them. Lieutenant Shaward went up into this very small little attic, and he had this little small aperture, this little window up there. And there's an open front door here in the front, and another door right behind me. So Jesus, if you got in the front doorway, you were silhouetted perfectly for a sniper. I ran and I grabbed that wall, and got tight against the wall, but I didn't have the radio. But the other enlisted man was up behind the rear door with a radio. So Shaward called down to me to give the coordinates, and I would relay them out to the guy in the back, and getting back to this one guy that I thought was taking unnecessary chances. He was out there on the other side of the door. I'm looking forward, on my left, hugging right along that open front door. The other guy was a big burly first lieutenant from Missouri, I got to know him just a little bit. He was right in front of me, so he was on my side of the door. We put phosphorus shells out there, the whole area—Jesus, that got effect; those goddamn Krauts came scampering down as fast as they could. Anyhow, these two guys took their M1s, and pop, pop, pop, pop, pop! Of course, these M1s held a clip of eight. This big husky first lieutenant, he ran out of ammo first, and he called over to the other guy, who had a bandolier on of all these clips. The first lieutenant said, 'Give me more ammo!', and don't ever ask me why, because if I live to be 150 years old, I'll never know why. This poor bastard [who had always crossed the fields between the hedgerows] stepped out from where he was, into the open doorway, to hand the lieutenant the goddamn clip. [*Shouts, claps hands together suddenly*] BAM! Just like that, this Kraut shot him between the eyes, his helmet went flying [*points between his eyes*]! He was physically picked up off his feet, and his back came slamming up against a barrel I could reach over and put my hand on, and that barrel supported him upright like this [*hunches shoulders up, back against the wall, then slowly drops head and upper body to the right*]. And he just slumped his head over, of course, dead as hell. His goddamn helmet just continued to spin around on the floor, like a child's top...

And I looked down into his head. The whole goddamn top of his head was removed, and I was always a sissy, particularly somebody else's blood. My blood didn't bother me as much as yours, so I looked down there and [*imitates a dripping sound, looks down for a long interval*]. I had blood, pieces of brain I guess, and everything else on my shoes and the bottom of my trousers.

I said, 'Oh, shit, I'm going to faint now.' I managed to get a swig of water into me, and I was still very, very shaky. I got my ass out of there, I got my ass out of there fast as hell, through that goddamn door.

You mentioned hedgerows before, these goddamn radios we carried operated on great, big, heavy, clumsy old batteries, and they were 70 pounds. They'd make them in two halves, one weighs about 40 pounds, the other weighs about 30, close to that; when you got to your destination and want to use them, you'd take a male and a female coupling, and give it a quarter turn, and then you would have it set up.

This one particular day, it was the 12th of July, I was not an officer yet, and we ran up against SS troops. And what the Krauts did in both World War I and World War II, when the German navy was bottled up, was take the big goddamn guns off these battleships, they'd take the guns off, mount them up on flatcars, I'm talking freight trains, flatcars on rails. Then an engine would take them up to wherever they wanted to be, and they had 20-mile, 22-mile ranges—and goddamn accurate, too.

This one day, boy, we knew that this was big stuff coming in on us. And again, see, not an 88 that's ahead of the sound, but these big, slower, large shells. You could hear them coming, and my ear became very much attuned to how far away they were. One shell came over, and hit the tree almost, not quite, but almost over my head. I ran for the hedgerow, and I caught my left forearm in a [branch] on one of these scrub trees growing out of the hedgerow. I felt down here [*rubs left forearm*], and it was warm, and I see blood, so I went back to the first aid station not far back. They put a few stitches in it and wrapped it up, so I came back to where I was located, and there was a very nice, clean-looking second lieutenant—to see somebody clean shaven, that was very unusual, because we couldn't get near a razor. So this nice-looking second lieutenant said to me, 'Hey, soldier,' he said, 'Are you all right?'

I said, 'Yeah.'

He said, 'Tell me, what happened?'

Oh Jesus, I was using the English language like you can't believe. F-ing this, and f-ing that... oh, I was really going to a great length.

His smile got bigger and bigger, and he finally said to me, 'Soldier, would you like to go to a confession?'

I said, 'Yeah, but where the goddamn blankety-blank, blank, blank, blank is there a place to go to confession around here?'

He said, 'Right here.'

I said, 'Oh, are you the chaplain?'

He said, 'Yeah.'

I said, 'Father, I think you've heard it all. Not much more I can tell you than what you've already heard there.'

The funny part was, I got back to my radio, and I could not receive anything. I was barking orders, and screaming, and yelling, going crazy into the speaker, it was handheld. Come to find out, that same shell that went off, one fragment went through part, just part of that radio. I could be heard, I could transmit, but I couldn't receive. So a day or two later, my battery gave out, and I went back to the jeep to get another battery. All the guys in my outfit, back at the battery see, they were laughing like hell when I came in. They said, 'Vier, you sure know the King's English. Wow, did we learn a few words from you!'

It was my frustration coming out, and they had been talking back to me, like, 'What are your coordinates,' and all that stuff. I couldn't hear them.

The Hürtgen Forest

Well, I'll tell you the dirtiest place that we were at, the 28th Infantry, the 1st was there, the 9th was there, was taking the Hürtgen Forest in Germany. That was just across Luxembourg, and it was dense as hell. What you worried about the most, because it created by far the greatest casualties, were shell bursts going up in the trees above you. Because Jesus, when a goddamn shell goes up over you, it just showers the goddamn ground. If you're in a slit trench, you can still get it. So that was the biggest worry.

Getting back to Lieutenant Shaward, who was up in that little attic of that barn I just got through telling you about. He had one outfit ... By this time, I wasn't sworn in, but I was now considered a second lieutenant, and I had two men under me. One day, we took our objective very far. I got a radio message up to me, saying that Lieutenant Shaward was killed.

I said, 'Whoa there,' and I was to take over his team of two men. I got over there, and what had happened was the Germans had thrown a few goddamn mortars over, not very many; they always did that, just while you're digging in. This poor bastard Shaward, he was digging the slit trench, because it was so cold, and rainy, and crappy; you'd get two, maybe three into a slit trench, getting the body warmth of another guy. These two enlisted men were a little bit teed off at [Shaward] because he said to them, 'Go out and get some goddamn boughs.' See, because of these tree bursts, branches of these pine trees were always coming down, so what you would do, you'd lay these boughs [crisscross] across the slit trench, and then the dirt that you had dug up, you'd put it on top of the boughs, and squeeze into the trench, and just hope to God that would be enough to stop any shell fragmentation from coming down on you. What happened was these two guys are out, and they're getting boughs, and they knew the mortar came in pretty close to them.

This one goddamn mortar came into the slit trench, hit Lieutenant Shaward, and blew him to smithereens. I was told to pick up whatever little effects there were, and I guess the graveyard crew would pick up the remains.

I found my way over to this slit trench, and I asked these two GIs, I said, 'Where in the hell is Shaward? Where's his body?'

They said, 'Under the raincoat.'

I pulled the raincoat back. I swear to God, all that was left of this guy, and this is on my mother's grave, was a stump of a head, two bare hands, and two bare feet! That meant the concussion took his combat boots that go up to about here on you [*points to mid-calf*], blew them and his socks off, two bare feet. That's all that was left of that poor bastard.

Now I'm going to jump ahead. The last time I got hit was March 2nd, and after being patched up at an evacuation hospital in Luxembourg, I was flown over to Bristol where I had another operation. I literally am half-assed [*laughs*], because I had my left buttocks shot off. Nobody remembers I had two shots in the shoulder and one in the head! My head's so hard, nothing could ever penetrate that. So I was sent over to Bristol, I had another operation. I was sent up to a convalescent hospital. And my younger brother was a lieutenant in the infantry, and he had been banged up. He was down in Salisbury. Salisbury in England was like our West Point, a very permanent post, big post.

So now I'm a bigshot, I'm still second louie. I'm down there, so he says, 'Let's go off to the bar and have a drink.' I go off to the bar and have a drink with him. All of a sudden, I swear to God, I had the most eerie feeling I've ever had in my life. One guy was talking, and I could swear to God that was Lieutenant Shaward's voice. I went over to him, I tapped him on the shoulder, I don't know if he's a first louie or a captain, whatever the hell he was.

I tapped him on the shoulder and I said, 'I beg your pardon, sir, to intrude,' I said, 'but any goddamn crazy ass chance could you be a Shaward?'

He said, 'Yes sir, I sure am. Why do you ask that question?'

Now, this guy was built differently, he had a very husky build and all, and I told him what had happened to his brother.

He said [*imitates boisterous Southern accent*], 'Well, I'll be god-damned!' He said, 'Thank you for telling me. He was Daddy's boy, and I'll be sure to tell Daddy how he died. Thank you very much!'

Now, suppose I had gone to Jimmy the Greek, the gambler, and said, 'What are the odds that I could ever find his brother just out of the clear blue sky in thousands and thousands of troops still in England itself?'

Hürtgen Forest was rainy, it was snowy, and oh Jesus, you could-n't send out patrols to see what was out ahead of you because you'd get lost. And of course, what happened is you'd go into an attack and, oh shit, there'd be these rolls of wire, barbed wire and all this kind of concertina wire.

[I had gotten] a battlefield commission. [Remember], I went in on D-Day; the first week, I was a survey corporal. There was a hell of a nice guy, built like crazy, Lieutenant Ward, another Southern boy, and another guy with another Irish name.[37] So one day, we had lost this lieutenant, who's over me, in the Hürtgen Forest. And my captain called up and said, 'Vier, you're going to be an acting

---

[37] *another Southern boy, and another guy with another Irish name*-Mr. Vier explained: *'It's a funny thing [with some of these Irish] down south, I'm not talking religion now, but I'm just talking the facts. See, the railroads were built going down south. A lot of Irish immigrants came in, they were Catho-lics, but they got ahead of the priests. They got down to some of those Southern towns, where there was only one church, maybe a Baptist church, and boy if you wanted to socialize or be accepted, you had to be one of them. So there are a lot of names of these Southern boys in my outfit that would be Irish as hell, but not Catholics.'*

[commander].' That meant I had all the authority of a second lieutenant, but I was actually not sworn in until, I think it was the 8th day of January '45, but I had my own outfit, my own little group of two guys. I got a Bronze star, a battlefield commission. And would you believe after all these stories, I got a Good Conduct Medal?

The Germans gave us a counterattack in the Hürtgen Forest, but I never saw the actual [advance]. The goddamn forest was so thick, you couldn't see 25 yards down the goddamn road. They had put a wedge between our lines, and our lines were very thinly held. The Germans counterattacked, and were getting closer, and I knew the only thing to do was give coordinates [right on my own] position. I gave the coordinates, and [we were fired on], but we had dug in enough, and we got enough Krauts to where we broke up that counterattack.

I got the Bronze Star [later], the second time I got hit—I got hit twice, just outside of Prague, early in the 2nd of February, '45. I was with a Captain Lee, a hell of a nice guy out of Ogden, Utah. He was a rifle company commander, so there was this crest of a hill. Two things happened that day. To get good observation, I went up the hill. This house was still very much intact, it was a tall house right on top of the hill. I went up to the attic, and I guess if I thought twice, I would not have done it, because it's a pretty conspicuous observation post, is what it comes down to. Now at the same time, I was told that I had corps artillery behind me. Oh, that was a thrill! It gave me a sense of power that I've never had before or since, because now I had 240s. Oh Jesus, they made peanuts out of a 105. A 105 was designed for anti-personnel; 240 was to take a building down! So I got up there, there's another house down in this valley right ahead of me, and there was a German tank there. So I thought, 'Oh, that's a nice target. I got 240s, great.' First shot, again, is always sent to see where that first shell lands, and then you make your corrections from that.

So I missed them, and the krauts in the tank first got out of the tank, then when I got that one shell close to them, they probably were smart enough to know that some observer knew where they were and was homing in on them. So they came out, and they pointed at this goddamn house I was in, and that's when I should've gotten my goddamn ass out of there, fast.

Before I could get another round off, they just pointed that goddamn tank 88 up there. Wham, next thing I knew, it was red as hell all over this goddamn attic, so thick that you couldn't see anything in there! All I could see was in the rear, some of the back wall of this attic was shot out, so I thought, 'That's where I'm going to get my ass out, through there.'

So I got down on my hands and knees [to crawl in that direction], and just then a second shell hit right where I had just been. At that point, I was knocked out with a concussion, and I banged up my knee. [I was out of combat for] only about two or three days. My knee was swollen black and blue, but after that I was able to walk, so I came right the hell back. I was in the hospital, just cut a little bit. But oh yeah, the last time I was hit, they didn't have any clusters, so they said, 'Oh, hell. Three times. Here.' So I wound up with two Purple Hearts, and one cluster, so leave it at that.

But it [also happened that friendly] artillery fire came in on you, we had two or three cases. This wasn't at all unusual in combat, what with friendly fire coming in from behind us. The biggest problem was to tell those goddamn gunners back at the battery that they're mistaken, and the rounds are coming in on us—'It's not me, it's not me,' they're all defending themselves. Bullshit! Well okay, we survived that.

The last time I got hit, it was early in the morning, March 2. I had a replacement for one of my two enlisted men. Something happened to one guy, and I got a raw ass recruit up there, and I looked him over, and I said, 'Where in the goddamn living hell is your trench shovel?' He said, 'Well,' he's another cracker, [giving me excuses]. I said, 'Oh, bullshit. You goddamn idiot.'

There was a German observer—you always gave the enemy credit for being just as smart, maybe smarter than you, because they were smart. We started our takeoff, and this [German observer started] another show. I knew this guy was zeroing in on us, because one or two rounds were getting closer and closer. So I dug as fast as I could, I was pooped out, so I flipped the shovel over to [the new replacement soldier].

I said, 'Now, you bastard, you dig your ass off. Come on, dig!' And he was digging, and all of a sudden I knew this goddamn shell [coming in] was too close to us, just from the sound of the trajectory. He was in a slit trench, so he flattened himself out, and I got on top of him. I was right at ground level. All of a sudden, the earth and everything flew up around me, and it was like somebody hitting my ass with a baseball bat.

See, when a shell breaks up, it's red hot. This is steel breaking up, and I know once or twice before when I was brand new in combat, I picked up a piece of fragmentation, [and dropped it right away], saying, 'Man, hot!' Well I had [taken] two pieces that crisscrossed, that's why I'm half-assed, I don't have a left buttock. It burned like hell! Two pieces that cut my shoulder, and one piece—I wish to hell I still had it, it went through my helmet and creased my head, though that was just a superficial cut; a few stitches took care of that.

I got hit, so my battery commander came up and picked me up in a jeep with a stretcher on it. Goddamn it, I was on the stretcher, and we went around a hairpin turn, my goddamn helmet [with the hole in it] came off, went down this embankment. He stopped, started to go after it. I said, 'That's it, let's get back,' and now I wake up at night saying, 'Jeez, that'd be a nice goddamn thing to give my grandchildren and all that,' but it's long gone.

The Germans were mixed up in the Hürtgen Forest. They had a hell of a lot of artillery, an awful lot of artillery, and mortars too. But the composure of the men themselves was also real mixed up. You might get a real veteran, I'm talking about when we took prisoners, then you might pick up a kid, 16 years old, something like that.

There was a Jewish boy in our outfit. Of course, at that time in combat, we knew that Hitler had concentration camps, and that he didn't like the Jews. We knew that much, but we didn't know to the extent, six million Jews exterminated and all that. Anyways, this guy named Green, he and I dug foxholes pretty close to each other, and we woke up the following morning. We didn't sleep much that night. I thought, 'Something's going on here,' and this Jewish boy, Green, was sitting outside of his foxhole, and he was going like this with one hand [*imitates the 'come forward' motion*] and holding his M1 like this [*arm out, as if peering down the gunsight*]. And out of all this fog came this [German kid], just a kid, maybe he was sixteen. But see, what was happening then, the Germans were scraping the bottom of the barrel. They'd had a mixture of seasoned troops with raw ass troops.

Flashbacks and Nightmares

But oh, jeez, that Hürtgen Forest, I can't say enough bad things about it because the casualty rate was terribly high. There was one guy from Northern New Jersey. When I was in college, we had a pretty good football team, and that was our common bond. He knew some of the guys who were on that team and all that, so he was a first lieutenant in the infantry. One of these goddamn shells went off, and they picked him up on the stretcher right behind me. That poor bastard had his shoulder off, and actually also the arm below it was gone. I think he was already dead, but he had that stare; I felt like he was looking at me, but apparently, he was dead already by then.

Those kinds of things stick in your mind, and where I have most of my trouble now. These flashbacks will come to me at night, and they'll be realistic as all goddamn hell. The funny thing is, my wife and I raised six kids. When we had a houseful of six children, there's always action going on, something's always happening. And that took my mind off the combat [I had been in] to a certain extent, to where I was at least not having nightmares. After the kids got a little bit older and left, then [the trauma] started to come back to me. One thing that accentuated this, and I spoke to one of these support group leaders [about it]. Well, [my daughter] was 23 years old back in '86, and she was the apple of my eye. Oh God, she was National Honor Society student, good-looking as hell. She and I were buddy-buddies and all that kind of stuff... She took off for our house up in Vermont at 6:30 in the morning, and she wanted to go up there the night before with her fiancé, and I said, 'Oh Jesus, it's raining down in Rye; up around Poughkeepsie, it's going to be colder, it's going to be ice up there.'

And so about 8:30 or so, I was painting in my playroom, and looking down the window going down the drive, and up comes a New York state trooper and a local cop. I thought, 'This is strange, what the hell are those two guys doing?' So they came up to the door, and they asked me to identify myself. So I said, 'Jack Vier or Johnny Vier.'

Then they asked me, 'Now, what year was your daughter Marilyn born?'

I knew goddamn well something was very wrong. So I said, 'She was born in June of 1962.' [*Speaks in a quieter tone*] Then they announced that they had bad news, and that she was killed at 6:30.

So anyhow, I spoke to this one [counselor], a wonderful guy. I go to two different support groups with other guys, they've all got their own problems—air corps, tankers, whatever. Just the group of us, we talk as we damn well please; I went to one of them this morning. I said to this one guy who was making up this application for another interview [*gets a bit emotional, speaking about applying for an increase in his VA disability benefits*]. I said, 'Should I put this down?'

He said, 'Goddamn right, Jack, because that probably accelerated your deterioration, and brought more vividly back to mind these nightmares, these flashbacks.' So that accelerated it.

[I came home] about the second week of June 1945. I was checked out of this convalescent hospital in England about the fourth or fifth day of June. Then I was flown back to where my outfit was; now the war's over [in Europe], of course, by a month. And I met up with all of them, and so Captain Higgins, who had given me the battlefield commission, he and I were buddies right up to the day he died—I came back and I said, 'Well where is this guy? Where is that guy? Where is somebody else?'

And they said to me, 'Well, Vier, he had enough points. He was discharged.' I said, 'In a pig's ass, goddamn it. I had 100 more points than anybody else in the outfit!'

They said, 'But Vier, you took a battlefield commission, so your points don't mean anything.'

And goddamn it, they told me that my original outfit was going to go over to Japan! The strange thing was, they said they're taking away the Sherman tanks with a 105 Howitzer on the front, and then where the turret had been mounted, they now had an outdoor 50 caliber machine gun. And of course, these were self-propelled, so they could move down the roads fast, and they were going to give us the old-fashioned towed 105s!

One-oh-fives, Jesus Christ! [*Slaps forehead, showing exasperation*] Tell me I got shot up three times, now I'm going to fight the goddamn Japs in Japan! And then the last day of my rehabilitation leave, they dropped the second atomic bomb on [Nagasaki], and then the war was over. I was at Camp Butner, North Carolina.

The Common Bond

So, I'll tell you what [about World War II]. I learned comradeship, and made good friends, but then at the same time, I didn't like dealing with the infantry. The artillery didn't have casualties at all like the infantry, naturally. You're almost afraid after a while, after you lose a few good buddies, of becoming too close to anyone, because you figure, 'It's going to be tough when this guy gets knocked off.' You always figured somehow or another, you would get through. [Maybe] not the other guy, though sometimes you have doubts about yourself getting through.

These two different support groups that I go to now, they're in White Plains. There's a common bond we all have. Three of these guys were prisoners of war, one in Japan and two over in Germany, and another guy is ... What a small world it is. There are two guys in our group on Wednesday mornings in White Plains who grew up together in the same neighborhood, New Rochelle, and then they went into different outfits. One of them went into the Air Corps, the other went to the infantry. One was shot down over Germany, he was shot down the same goddamn day his buddy was captured in Italy; a guy had gotten too far out from the rest of his outfit. They were both in prison camps and all that, and you know when you sit down with those guys, there's just a common bond that makes you very close to them.

Mr. Vier was a highly regarded speaker at numerous schools, sharing his World War II experiences. In June 2004, he returned to Normandy for the 60th anniversary of D-Day. He passed away on August 14, 2008, at the age of 90.

PART FIVE

THE BULGE BREAKS

"About midnight I was sleeping—my buddy was on duty—and somehow or other, the Germans got within 20 yards of our position. Gordon got ripped by a machine gun from roughly the left thigh through the right waist. Well, when you're that far from your home base and it's snowing and the temperature's zero, you don't have a chance. We were cut off. The Germans had overrun our position and we were in the foxhole by ourselves, so basically, we both knew he was going to die.

He slowly froze to death, bled to death. The next morning, as we looked at our gear, it looked as if I'd have spent a day in a butcher shop. My clothes were all covered with blood; his clothes were all covered with blood and the territory we were in was all covered... he just... it was a butcher shop."

—Bob Conroy, Private, 75th Infantry: 1944[26]

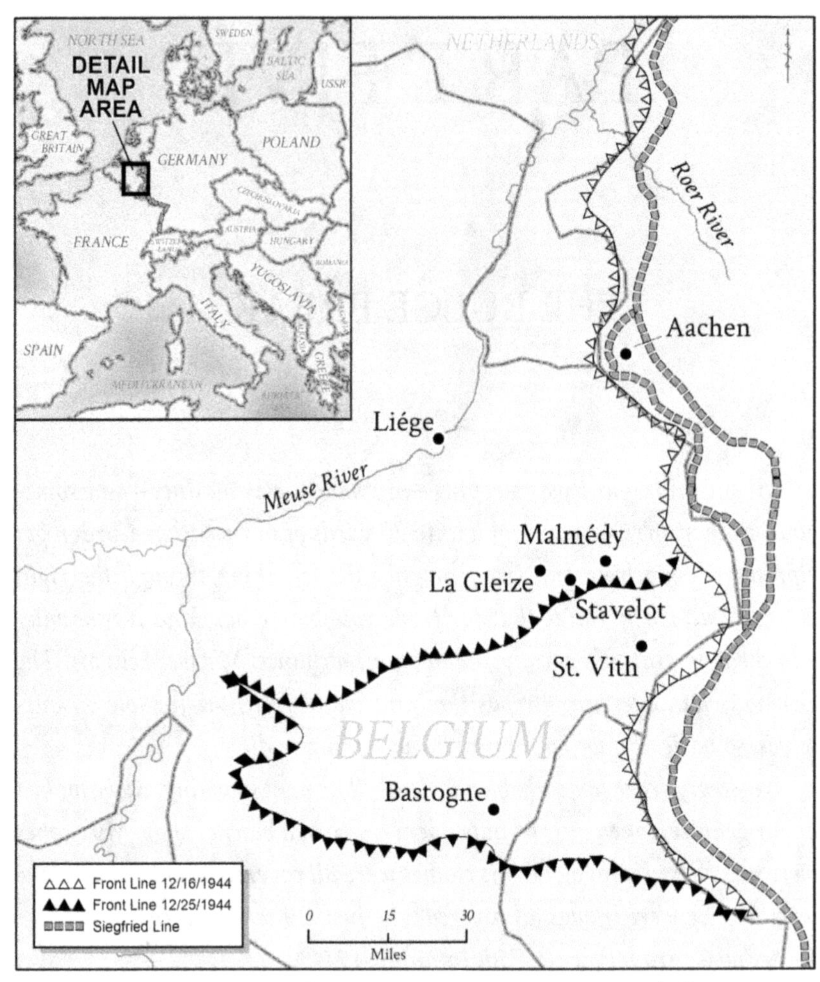

The Battle of the Bulge. Map by Susan Winchell.

CHAPTER TWENTY-FOUR

The Battle of the Bulge

Five months after the landings at Normandy, the Germans launched an all-out surprise counterattack against scantily defended American lines in the Ardennes Forest. Hitler's last gamble to counterattack between the advancing American and British forces in northern France and the Low Countries had been in the planning stages since around the time the Allies paraded down the Champs-Élysées in Paris, foreshadowing the German Army's final collapse in France. The incredible magnitude of American industrial capacity dictated to Hitler that somehow the supply lines had to be cut, and he chose the Ardennes Forest for the avenue of attack in the hopes of reaching the port of Antwerp. By combining the elements of surprise, hostile terrain, and bad weather with a massive quarter-million man offensive, the ultimate goal was to have the Germans encircle and split Allied forces and thereby push the Western Allies to the conference table to accept a favorable peace agreement with Germany to end the war in the west.

In the early morning frozen hours of December 16, 1944, six hundred German tanks broke through the thinly manned American lines after a tremendous artillery barrage, creating a 'bulge' or pocket they hoped to exploit to the sea, sowing desperation, panic, and confusion in the blitzkrieg's wake. Allied soldiers, including those of the hapless 28th Infantry Division, recently pulled from the Hurtgen Forest, found themselves in a desperate struggle for survival as temperatures plunged to the coldest in European memory during the winter of 1944–45. Many had little experience, having replaced those killed and wounded in the Normandy campaign thus far. The average American replacement was 19 years old, and in this battle, the second bloodiest in United States military history, just over 19,000 were killed.[38] More than 700,000 Americans would eventually be engaged in yet another death match that would herald the outcome of World War II in Europe, many just a year or two beyond lazily daydreaming in a high school or college classroom.

---

[38] *the second bloodiest in United States military history*- 19,276 Americans were killed between December 16, 1944 and January 25, 1945.The bloodiest campaign/battle was World War I's Meuse-Argonne Offensive from September 26 to November 11, 1918, with 26,277 Americans killed. Source: List of battles with most United States military fatalities, en.wikipedia.org/wiki/List_of_battles_with_most_United_States_military_fatalities#Campaigns

CHAPTER TWENTY-FIVE

The Military Policeman

Jacob Cutler was a military policeman serving with the 1st Army. He continues his narrative with his experiences at the Battle of the Bulge, moving into Germany, encounters with Russian soldiers, and the liberation of the concentration camp at Buchenwald.

Jacob N. Cutler

The Bulge Breaks

I was on duty one night on a post outside the camp, outside the headquarters building. There was a walkway. It was on a street, a little sentry booth there that had been used by the Free Belgian forces. When we came in, we took over from them.

One night, this was late December, one of our army medics came running up to me with a little Belgian kid in tow. He says, 'This kid says he saw a German paratrooper come down all in white.' It was snow on the ground then. It was winter. It was snow. I sent out an alarm. A couple of jeeploads of men went out, rode around the highway, the roads there in the area, and came back and said, 'It must have been his imagination. We didn't find anything.'

I was relieved at about 2:00 in the morning from my post. I went in. Eupen was the main headquarters; it was about five miles from the German border, about that much back of us. I was getting ready to go to sleep. All of a sudden, whistles blowing. Everybody out. All the jeeps went down the road with the machine guns. One of our men driving there had a paratrooper land on the road in front of him and he captured him. He took him into headquarters. He insisted they wake up the general, I believe it was either General Gerow or General Hodges. He says, 'I got this guy and I want to see the general.' Well, the general, they woke him. He came out and thanked the guy. I think he got a medal, too.

They interrogated this prisoner and they found out that he was a stray. These guys had strayed, their parachutes had drifted or whatever. They were landing in a big attack in an area north of us, which became the Bulge. The target was Liège in Belgium, which was a big communication center, railroad center, communications. It was a big city. The Germans were trying to attack that. Of course, they had, at this time, surrounded Bastogne; the surrender demand by the German general [was given to General McAuliffe] and his response [to the Germans] was, 'Nuts.' He became a big hero to us after that, he was wonderful, and everybody loved him. Of course, they finally broke the siege, they broke the Bulge. It was a last-ditch stand.

Into Germany

Then, we crossed into Germany, we just marched across Germany. Crossing into the Rhineland, the Rhine River, that was the big thrill, 'Hey! Here's the Rhine. We're crossing it.' Of course, it was not a very impressive river. I think the Hudson River is bigger or nicer, but it's a famous river. Now we were in the heart of

Germany, now we went through and we saw the destructions that our planes did, all the bombed-out facilities and whatnot.

There were some really remarkable things, though, there were some things that were impressive. There were churches that had been blown up and yet some of the things that remained were the statues of the Virgin Mary and the crosses seemed to be unharmed, maybe it was because they were solid stone or whatever, we don't know why. Divine intervention? Nobody knows, but they were just like miraculous things. It was more than one occasion. It happened in several places that we saw this.

Buchenwald

We went across Germany. I entered the Buchenwald concentration camp. I was a bodyguard for the Jewish chaplain, I was Jewish like him. It was only a few days after it had been freed. We saw many of these victims. [*Gets emotional, pauses, composes himself*] Got to excuse me. It's a bad memory. These people were being fed by the soldiers. They couldn't feed themselves. The dead bodies were stacked like cordwood because the Germans had been routed and couldn't clear the area. They always tried to make sure that the evidence was never found but we found it. The remains were still in the furnaces. We saw the gas chambers. Of course, we saw the bodies. We saw the bunks where they had been forced to live, bunks about as big as this floor and wide. They just were stacked one above the other where they had to lay there and try to survive. Some did survive; maybe they were late arrivals or whatever, in better health. Some of the healthy prisoners killed some of the German guards. They showed the soldiers around as to what atrocities the Nazis had done. [I guess it] made me happy when I saw the destruction in Germany. We had no use for any Germans. These first civilians were brought in and we forced them to see... they said they didn't believe it, they didn't know. They had the crocodile tears and whatnot; maybe some didn't know, [but] I don't see how they could not know because the camp was there. It was surrounded by barbed wire and trees and the smoke coming out of the chimneys. There was no way they couldn't know something terrible was going on, or what was actually going on. I don't know how close civilians had been allowed to get there.

But anyway, the Germans were routed. We then went through and continued up until I think it was May 7, we entered Pilsen, Czechoslovakia. That's when the war ended. Germany surrendered, and the Cold War started. In August, when they dropped the atom bomb in Japan, we were just excited and thrilled. Nobody thought about the horrors it created later, but as far as we're concerned, we wouldn't have to go to Japan and fight again. It was over. After the second one, they surrendered. It was all over. We just waited to go home.

The Russians

Eisenhower ordered the troops to stop at Pilsen, and the Russians entered Prague. I think we were 30 miles apart, and about 15 miles in the middle was now a barbed wire dividing line. The Cold War was on. Some of them with special passes were allowed [to move around], but we weren't allowed to go there. They weren't allowed to come here but the civilians made a great exodus. See, every weekend all the Pilseners went to Prague and all the Praguers went to Pilsen, I guess they had relatives and whatnot. Now, they were free of the Germans and could do whatever they liked.

The Russians were crazy for watches. They bought any kind of watch. I mean, the guys started sending home for watches. That time, a wristwatch was $2, $3; the Russians would pay the equivalent of $50 or $100 for them, they'd wear them on their arms; I don't know what they did with them. A lot of the Russians made their own vodka, which killed them or blinded them. They were crazy; I don't know how they made this vodka, what they made it from, I guess they took alcohol from the car engines or something and drank it. Of course, our guys were warned, 'Don't take any vodka or liquor from the Russians. It's dangerous.'

In Pilsen, we had an easy life because now we lived in what had been an army barracks. Our duties were in town. I did traffic control and I did guard duty at the Grand Hotel, which became headquarters for V Corps. All the bigwigs, army generals and whatnot came there for conferences. I had a lot of free time, went to the beaches and watched the Pilseners. I stayed there until October when I was told I was going home.

We were shipped into France to wait for ships to take us home, and we were there a long time. Finally, November, we boarded ships to take us home. I was in another tub, *Athos II*. The first *Athos* sank. *Athos II* broke down in the ocean. They were radioing for the Coast Guard to come and get us but they finally got things going again. We got into the harbor; with everybody greeting us there, it was great, a wonderful sight.

That was it. Everybody rushed to the PX, drank chocolate malts, and got sick as heck, got diarrhea because they hadn't had real milk for two years.

World War II probably changed what I would have been, not that I have any complaints. I wanted to go to college and become a dentist, but after the war I just couldn't concentrate on studying. I thought of my year [in school], the war was already on, and already my mind was elsewhere; I had great difficulty concentrating or studying. When I got out, I just felt I couldn't really go back to school.

Since I had been interested so much in electronics, I went to a radio school on the G.I. Bill but there was really nothing [for me].

Yeah, everything I looked at, you had to have experience. There weren't really any good jobs available unless you were also very experienced, which you can only get by working. So, it was a vicious cycle. I didn't have any in that. So, then I went to dental mechanic school. I worked for a while at that and didn't care for it much.

So, eventually I got into the camera business, I was a camera salesman. I was very interested in photography, so I became a camera salesman, then I became the buyer for a very big business. I worked there for 33 years. I married my best friend's younger sister. I had arrived in New York on Thanksgiving Day, 1945; I was discharged November 27, 1945. I started going with this girl a year later. We were married November 28, 1948. We've been happily married since then. I never joined any veterans' organizations.... I wasn't a joiner. I was kind of a shy-type person and I wasn't a joiner, so I never joined anything. I never went to a reunion; I would have liked to have gone to the D-Day reunion they had at the 50th anniversary, but the cost was much too much—it would have cost us probably about $10,000 or something, which was way beyond my means. We like to travel across the United States; we've been to about half the states so far. We enjoy that, so that's what we do.

[I never really contacted anyone who I served with]; I remember a few of the people but I don't know. After I had transferred to the military police, one buddy I knew was still in the Signal Corps. We had been shelled, but the brunt of the shelling hit the Signal Corps battalion. I know he was very badly wounded and sent home, but I lost track after that. The unfortunate thing is he had been a teacher and he had a throat injury; I think he couldn't talk. It was really [tragic]... but I never really kept in touch. I remember some other people and I think, 'I wonder where these guys are.' I know there was one guy named John Aletto from Oneonta, New York, a couple of years older than me. I sometimes think about him. I said, 'I wonder if I could ever contact him or reach him,' but somehow, I just never got around to it, but who knows if he stayed there? He also had been a teacher. I don't know if he went back and remained there or moved to a bigger city or whatever. He could be anywhere.

Mr. Cutler passed away in 2018 at the age of 95.

CHAPTER TWENTY-SIX

The Armored Sergeant

Bill Butz served in the 6th Armored Division and received the Silver Star for his actions in the Brest Campaign. At the Battle of the Bulge, he and his undersupplied men took winter gear off of the bodies of dead Germans before winter supplies caught up with them. He survived that ordeal to be present at the liberation of Buchenwald concentration camp in Germany; like many of our GIs, he was a witness to the greatest crime in the history of the world.

William C. Butz

Battle of the Bulge

[We were in] Nancy, and they had a rumor out that the war was going to be over by Christmas. Everybody was pretty happy, and we got our Thanksgiving turkey they promised. They rolled up through that mud to where we were dug in for a week. Rain, rain, rain. Tanks couldn't do anything. We had a foxhole; I said to those guys, 'I'll tell you what we'll do. We'll start down about two feet on one end. And then go out about two feet, then go down four feet. Later, we go deeper; with all this water, when you sit down to maybe take a nap and get water up to your knees, well then you'd better start paddling,' and that's just the way it turned out.

One day there came an armored car, six-wheel drive, and it came across through the mud.

'Here's your Thanksgiving turkey,' and they [tossed it to us] all rolled up just like you would buy it today in a plastic bag, frozen solid. And it's a good thing there was plastic because we just bailed some water from the hole and just splashed the mud off it.

We had a stove there and were trying to heat that. I hacked off the frozen legs and put them in a canteen cup, you know how big they are, and tried to heat it up, and finally a guy said, 'Oh boy, I think it's ready.' So I said, 'Here, you try it first.' He chewed and handed it right around and when it got to me, geez, I looked and it was all bloody. They ate the outside where it was cooked enough to eat, so it went back in the can [to cook some more]. The next day they said, 'We're going to pull out,' and we never got any hot meal.

They sent us down to the Colmar Pocket. There was a lot of coal mines and the Germans were putting up an awful battle to hold those mines. It got to be December, I think it was the 17th. The word was that the 35th Division's coming in to relieve us, take us off the line,[but] we already heard the rumor, but nothing official, that the Germans had broken through our lines up north, a big breakthrough and yet they didn't call it the Bulge right then when we heard about it, but we knew there was something big going on.

They pulled us back and we loaded up, gassed up, we drove all night and half the next day. We pushed the engines in our half-tracks so they were red-hot. They had so much anti-freeze in there that you could take it, you know, but they were hot and overheating, but Combat Command A of the division got in the Metz; I think it was the 23rd of December. We were gassed up again and got our ammunition to form a feeler, just to see... the whole 6th

Armored Division was coming behind us, heading for Metz, so our objective was to go up and see what to expect.

We got into it, we got in pretty deep. We went through the outfits that had dug in on the south end of the Bulge. Artillery was already coming in, 88s. And it's a good thing they were there because after about a six or eight-hour battle, we were getting low on supplies, ammunition, and evidently the Germans had decided maybe to get to Bastogne better, they could come down deeper and go around. They already had Bastogne encircled. From where we were at that position, on the 23rd, we could hear them pounding Bastogne pretty heavy.

That would have been to my left and north a little. I don't know the name of this town we was in, but anyway it was a good thing what happened—even though we got hit pretty bad—because our big radios called back to the division. By now, they had reached Metz. The weather was quickly changing; we had rubber tread, so we tipped them off that with the snow and ice we couldn't get anywhere. By the way, there had been no snow in Metz and we walked right into the heavy snow and freezing weather. When it went down below zero, I froze my feet.

[We had no winter gear], nothing. We had made a mistake down in southern France when our feet were sweating, we got an idea if we cut a slit on each side of our boots, we'd let a little air in there. And it worked, but little did we know, in a few weeks we're going to be wading through two or three feet of snow, and that was the worst thing, it just pushed in those cracks, and then the trench foot was running rampant; lots of our men were sent to England with trench foot. And I was scared to death; 'Where does it come from?' This was even after my frozen feet. And they said, 'Well it comes from not keeping your feet clean enough.' Jeez, you can forget showers, that's unheard of. How are you going to wash your feet and you only had two pairs of socks? My feet were soaked anyway, but I found out something that seemed to work. I packed the snow in a sock and squeezed it, shook it out. Then I turned the sock inside out and filled it up with snow again and I squeezed it some more and then shook it out. Then I'd open my shirt and went around with the tank pants on and I would slide one sock in there, and boy it was cold, but the next day, boy, I had a nice, dry, warm pair of socks. So all through that [winter], that's what I did. Everybody else had other ideas and some guys had extra socks, they must've bought them, but we also would ruin one pair because we had no mittens, so we took a sock and put it over our hand and made a hole for your fingers.

My first snow cape was off a dead German, he didn't need it anyway. The Bulge was starting to go pretty fast when the first shipment came in, capes made for our army in the States. And then we got the big [tanker] gloves, and had mittens, then gloves and the trigger finger, but they came late. Many of our men took boots off dead Germans, too.

Wounded

I was wounded [again]. We were in a situation where we had already lost three vehicles through mines. My orders were dig in where we were and hold, until we got replacements. Just dig in. And I dug maybe three or four [spadefuls], it was tough, hard, three or four chunks out of there, and boy, [what I thought was] a bullet hit the tree and it knocked me right down but I didn't feel anything, you know? I got up, I got the shovel again, and something ain't right. I reached around, I had tank pants on, and then ODs underneath, and I felt a rip there. And now I worked my hand through there [and pulled it out], and there was a little blood. I said, 'Jeez, I guess I'm hit.' And just as I realized I was hit, I looked down and here come the replacements. All shiny uniforms and it makes you sick. I said, 'Look at 'em.' They couldn't hear us with all the stuff going on, it's too far in the back, but they didn't want to come up to us in a sense, and they were too bunched up. Well then a mortar hit and it didn't look to me like I could see any movement at all after another batch of mortars came in.

When the medics got to me, they said, 'Well you're not going to get any replacements.'

I said, 'I guess not.'

One of the medics, he ripped the pants around, and I wish I had kept that wallet where the shrapnel went right through the wallet, went through everything.

He said, 'I can see it.' And geez, they pulled it out, and that hurt after he pulled it. And it was a point of a mortar with a swastika on it. I got that home yet; he put that in my pocket as a souvenir. The other medic pulled out my dog tags.

I said, 'What are you doing?'

'Well, you see, we got to get your information to send to your family.'

I said, 'Don't you do that.'

He said, 'Why?'

I said, 'My wife's due to have a baby.'

The baby was born the 10th, a few days before, but I didn't know it. I didn't find out until that girl was six weeks old when I got the word, that's how bad the mail was. But anyway, he thought he got it all out. He said, 'You'll have to ride the jeep to the field hospital.' I got set up on the jeep, they helped me up, and I said, 'Jeez, I'm all right. I can walk.' And the jeep had two men on the hood on two stretchers and two stretchers on the back, so I grabbed and hung on the side. We got to this field hospital and boy, those two doctors, they were just nothing but blood. I looked around; I could see a few arms and legs lying around inside the tent, where they figured [amputation] was their best bet to save some, I suppose, but anyway, I said, 'You don't need me. I'm all taken care of.'

'Let's take a look.'

He said, 'You know what, you're going to have to be careful with that for infection. It looks like the medics did a good job,' and he said, 'I'll give you some extra sulfur.'

I said, 'Give me some of that [and I'm on my way].'

He said, 'Now wait a minute, you can go back with the next ambulance and ride back or rest. We probably want to keep you here for a few days.'

And I said, 'No. I want to go back on the next jeep. I want to go back with my men. I still got some men out there.'

He said, 'Well that's up to you, but you don't have to.'

I said, 'I'm going back up there.'

Under that [operating] table were cupboards. And one of those docs said, 'Wait a minute. Get your canteen cup off.' And he slid the cupboard open and came out with a bottle of scotch; he poured about half of it and he said, 'You need a drink if you're going back.'

Boy, that was quite a drink, but when I got back up there the new orders came in. They said, 'Listen, we're going to be relieved, we're pulling back, the equipment is in bad shape,' even though it was behind us; the ammunition chests were jammed in and you couldn't get the .50 caliber belts to run. What good are the guns if the ammunition won't load? So we were hit pretty hard there, and I'm thankful we didn't lose any more men; they were dug in while I was getting taken care of. And then to make a long story short on that shrapnel, years and years later I went in the ministry, into the prison ministry, twenty years ago, and [the metal detectors at] Comstock Prison found more shrapnel. The officer said, 'Give me the metal right now.'

I said, 'I don't have any metal.'

He said, 'This machine doesn't lie.'

And I said, 'I'll tell you, I'll take my clothes off.'

He said, 'Were you in the war?'

I said, 'Yeah.'

'Were you hit? Where were you hit?'

I reached around, and he said, 'You still got some in there.'

And so sure enough, now I notice the [airport security] picks it up randomly, when you go on a plane, but at the time they thought that's all there was, was that one piece. But evidently there was a little piece with it.

Buchenwald

The Battle of the Bulge was a far bigger thing than most people realize. And now did you see the news of last night, was it? This guy with my same last name, Butz, [was on television]; he was saying there was no such thing as a concentration camp![39] Well, I could tell him a thing or two. Because I took pictures to prove them all. There certainly were concentration camps. Now, we weren't aware of them, but we went right in by accident. Most of the pictures I took are faded pretty bad now, but they do come out a little bit. But the first thing we did when we were in Buchenwald, I opened a door [to a prisoner barracks] and there was a pile of wooden bowls, and you'd need a hammer and chisel, whatever I saw in them was like hard baked into them bowls; I don't think that they'd been used for a long time, and flies will knock you down. Then I looked at the—well, I call them shelves, they might have called them bunks. They were about four high, I don't think there was enough space between them [*gestures about 18 inches apart, with hands]* for a guy with a good pair of shoulders, he couldn't turn over to go on his belly, so he stayed that way, I guess. But there'd be four or five in the shelf, and

---

[39] *Butz was saying there was no such thing as a concentration camp*-Arthur R. Butz is a well-known Holocaust denier and contributor to anti-Semitic publications that defend Nazi actions.

in lots of cases, sometimes one or two on the shelf are dead! And I said to the fellas, there's a window right here, so we knocked it out, and handed out—we figured might help save some—pulled the dead out before we got the orders to move on. Then the orders come in, they are going to paratroop [drop] doctors in, and don't give them anything to eat or drink, you know. Some were walking around; you could see the ribs and everything...

There were some potatoes buried. They were no good anyway, from what I see. But then some of these guys looked like ants [*makes crouching motion, like hands and knees posture*] and you almost had to hit them or kick them to get through them and see what's going on. Well, they were digging with their [fingers]... and some of them, bloody bones, just trying to dig them potatoes and those that did get one were pushing it into their mouths [*raises fingers to mouth, shakes head*], and oh, boy...

They were in bad shape. We were 10 or 12 miles east of there, when we got the word sent up the line that Eisenhower was going to make that town near Buchenwald march [German] men, women, and kids right through, and they said about half of them fainted. They couldn't believe it; that's what they claimed, they couldn't believe what was going on. But there were furnaces there where they burned the bodies and they run in them. There were three locomotive-type furnaces and they were on a timer, where they could run that iron right back out and dump [the ashes], and it would go on down another trough down into like a paper mill or whatever, two big rollers there, then roll the [cremated] bones down and [crush them] for bone meal fertilizer; they had a system. And in another corner, down the other end from the wooden bowls, there was a big pile in the corner, and there were just glasses. There must have been thousands and thousands of pairs of glasses just thrown in a pile, from how many... But you know, I didn't see any Americans in that camp. We looked too, to see... they were

Polish, there were some Jewish, but I thought mostly Polish, some Russians...

The Hardest Part

Somebody asked me once, what was the hardest part for you in the war? And I thought about a young boy who came in as a replacement; I got him while we were on three-day rest—three-day rest never turns out as three day, it's always one or two; they rush you to get everything in shape and it's over. Anyway, the first thing he said was, 'How long will it be before I'm a veteran?'

I said, 'If I'm talking to you the day after you're in combat, you're a veteran.'

He replaced one of the gunners who had been killed on the back of the half-track. Now, when we had a rest [on the move] where you could actually take a shut-eye for a couple of minutes, he made a little broom out of this stiff grass along the road, tied it on a piece of wood to brush out the bottom of the half-track, empty shells and stuff. He wanted to make sure the guns were in good working order; he was 18 years old, a kid you really like. And all of a sudden, the Germans were pouring this fire in on us. He was working on the track and when he jumped off, he went down. Well, I thought he just kind of tripped and fell. He was a little ways away, and he called my name, so I ran over to him and he was bleeding in the mouth.

From my experience before, [I knew]—[*pauses for a long while, looks down, gets emotional...*] all I could do was hold that kid's hand and tell him it's going to be all right. 'You'll be all right.' I knew he wasn't going to last, and he was gone the minute that he squeezed my hand... [*Pauses again, shakes head*]. The parts like that I just...

Anybody who has been a combat sergeant knows these guys write letters home. You're always mentioned, good or bad, I don't know. So when you lose a man, down the road, maybe it might be two or three months later, you get a letter from a mother. *'So and so, he was under your command and you were his sergeant, he spoke of you all the time. Could you tell me, did he suffer? And just how did he die?'* That's hard, I've started to write those letters, [then had to just] tear it up and wait. Maybe take three or four days, to write some kind of letter back to their parents. That's hard.

'When the Shooting Stops'

And another thing in war [that bothered me] was when the shooting stops, believe it or not. In the morning, when you pull out, you lay your barrage and everything like you usually do, and there ain't nothing there—they're not firing back. They pulled a fast one on us during the night, but they're getting ready, but you don't know where—you might drive two hours, and every minute seems like an hour. Where are they? If they're shooting at you, you're a lot calmer. Everybody was jittery, [wondering], 'When are they going to open up?', 'What's the matter with them?' That's the scary part of war too, I'll tell you... It doesn't sound right, but that was the way I remembered it. That was right and a lot of things. Many a time it was safer behind the enemy than it was in front of them. It's hard to believe that one too. I can't give figures, but the total amount of casualties was no doubt [higher] in front, not when we've cut behind them. Patton was right in a lot of things—many a time it was safer behind the enemy than it was in front of him. What he would do was, Combat Command A, we'd come in here this way, maybe take Schuylerville and then Greenwich [*gestures with right hand, using local towns near interview location for references*]. At the same time, Combat Command B would be headed towards Cambridge, we would get through them and by them, we would swing right [*turns body, makes sweeping motion with his left arm*] and cut off many miles and hopefully take a lot of prisoners, [who would now be trapped]. But once in a while, the deeper you went, it backfired; the Germans might be stronger than we figured, and they were trying to cut off that point and then there would be an awful struggle there to get that straightened out. But most of the time, the man was right. A lot of the men didn't like him; Ol' Blood and Guts was his nickname; they'd say, yeah—our blood and his guts. But I still can't help it; I still like him—I'm glad he was our general.

I saw him [again, one last time]. At the end of the war, he gave a pep talk, just before I came out of Germany, and to talk to us was his last official act for the 6th Armored Division. They had already taken the Third Army away from him, and I'll tell you what, I know he died from that accident, but I'll tell you, that man had aged twenty years, when he came up to speak to us that day.[40] They had to help him up on the wagon, they had a wagon set up where he could see over the troops. I said, 'Boy, he is not in good shape.' That was his last official act in the Third Army; it broke his heart when they took the Third Army away. It all came about with the cursing and swearing about 'now we're going to whip the Russians,' and all that stuff.

'You Don't Owe Me a Thing'

[When I got back to the States], I came into Boston and took a train to New York City. I had to get to Grand Central Station to come to Fort Edward. And I waited [in uniform] for a cab, and

[40] *he died from that accident*- George S. Patton (1885-1945) died on December 21, 1945, in a hospital at Heidelberg, Germany, as a result of a broken neck sustained in a freak automobile accident. He is buried at the Luxembourg American Cemetery in accordance with his wishes to be buried with his men.

waited. [Some women were getting into this cab], but the cab driver calls me over. He said, 'Where are you headed?'

I said, 'Jeez, I got to get to Grand Central.'

He said, 'Ladies, this cab is reserved. Out.' I open the door and the women get out.

He said, 'You come sit in front with me. Grand Central, I'll get you there.' And boy, he zipped through that traffic and we got there to the terminal. He let me right out at the front door.

I said, 'What do I owe you?'

He said, 'You don't owe me a thing.'

He said, 'I lost a son in this war.'

He never asked me for a penny. I thought that was something.

After the war, Mr. Butz rose to become superintendent of a papermill on the Hudson River. He also became active in the ministry and was married for 77 years. He passed away in 2017 at the age of 97.

Last group photo of the 30th Infantry Division Veterans of World War II at their final reunion, 70th anniversary of the end of the war, 2015. Credit: Larry S. Powell

EPILOGUE

The High Price Tag

...For these men are lately drawn from the ways of peace. They fight not for the lust of conquest. They fight to end conquest. They fight to liberate. They fight to let justice arise, and tolerance and goodwill among all Thy people. They yearn but for the end of battle, for their return to the haven of home.

Some will never return. Embrace these, Father, and receive them, Thy heroic servants, into Thy kingdom.

— PRESIDENT FRANKLIN D. ROOSEVELT, ADDRESS TO THE NATION, JUNE 6, 1944

On August 29, 1944, eighty-four days after the first Allied soldiers set foot on the sands of the Normandy beaches, infantrymen of the U.S. 28th Division assembled to parade twenty-four abreast down the Champs-Élysées before hundreds of thousands of adoring Parisians. The German garrison had surrendered the city four days earlier following uprisings and the advance of Free French forces in Sherman tanks, soon followed by the U.S. 4th Division's arrival at the steps of Notre Dame Cathedral. The Battle of Normandy now concluded, the defeat of Germany was foretold by the commander of the Panzer Lehr Division, 'the battle of annihilation in France' laying the 'foundation for the subsequent final and complete annihilation of the greatest military state on earth.'[27] In just those twelve weeks since D-Day, Germany had lost the equivalent of forty divisions—nearly a half million men killed, wounded, or captured. The Allies had sustained over 209,000 killed and wounded, sixty percent of them American youth. Many more would die before the Rhine River was crossed the following spring.

*

A 93-year-old Army veteran arrived in Paris by plane.

As he was fumbling in his bag for a passport, a stern French customs agent asked if he was in France before. He admitted that he had indeed been previously. The lady then said, 'Then you should know to have your passport out and ready, sir.'

The veteran said, 'Well, I didn't have to show it last time.'

'Impossible!' says the customs agent, 'all foreigners have always had to show their passport to enter the country.'

The veteran responded, 'Well, when I came ashore on D-Day in 1944, I couldn't find any [expletive] Frenchmen to show it to!'

The first time I saw this in a chain email, about 15 years ago, the Army veteran was 83. Now it circulates in many incarnations as an Internet meme.

If you've seen it before, like me, on my first read, the tale may have resonated at some level that made you proud.

But then I read comments online like this: *"I have heard about that encounter before and I love to hear it re-told......too bad some of the nations that America has liberated or protected no longer appreciate it, or even seem to remember."*

Oh, there is probably a measure of forgetfulness overseas, and we aren't exactly knocking ourselves out teaching our young people at home, either. And I've encountered rude and intimidating customs officials in many countries.

But maybe our aging D-Day veteran couldn't find a Frenchman to show his passport to because Allied bombing in Normandy killed at least sixty thousand French noncombatants before D-Day, with an additional two thousand in Saint-Lô alone on June 6 and 7, a town that was 95 percent wiped off the map by liberation day on July 18. Stunned soldiers of the 29th Division entered the remains of the crossroads town in silent awe; one GI remarked, 'We sure liberated the hell out of this place.' On the seventy-fifth anniversary, one historian noted, 'I spent my whole life thinking the town of Saint-Lô was destroyed during the battle [for it]. I had no idea it was the Allied bombing [that preceded the battle]. It's not a simple narrative. It's complex and it's hard.'[28] More French civilians were killed in those few months of Allied bombing than in four years of German occupation.

And I'm willing to bet maybe that spectacular encounter highlighting French forgetfulness and ingratitude just didn't happen.

*

As I add the finishing touches to this manuscript this September of 2019, several of the soldier-liberators—and in my mind, all GIs who fought the Axis were liberators, not just those who stumbled across the concentration camps in their paths—have again returned, during this time of the 75th anniversary liberation calendar, to the Low Countries. The graves of their comrades left overseas are cared for, decorated, loved. The old soldiers themselves are receiving ticker-tape parades literally as I write this, welcomed by mayors and feted by dignitaries and ordinary townspeople as the conquering heroes they once were. And as a timely reminder of this Gallic appreciation, yesterday a woman on the 743rd Tank Battalion Facebook page posted:

'Hi! My name is Marie and I've adopted two soldiers of the 743rd TB, who are on the wall of missing in the American Normandy Cemetery, Colleville-sur-Mer, near Omaha Beach. Their names are Thomas H Sweeney (Ohio) and William M Fanning (Kansas). I'm trying to find their families. Thanks for your help!'

And it was one of the soldiers in this book, Frank W. Towers, who helped to set all this in motion. Though we would not meet to combine our efforts to track down Holocaust survivors until 2007, Frank, who would go on to become one of my best World War II veteran friends, returned to Normandy at the same time I was waking up and tuning in as the American president honored the fallen at the cemetery for the fortieth anniversary. Many thankful French families opened their homes and their hearts, creating bonds with returning American GI families over the years. Frank suggested to these French families and public servants that they look at a model in place in the Netherlands where the natives cared for the resting places of American fallen; he set in motion the 'Flowers of Memories' project whereby local families throughout Normandy 'adopted' the graves of American veterans there. Frank passed on July 4, 2016 at the age of 99, but his bi-annual trips sparked a ripple effect so that on this 75th anniversary, over ten thousand American graves have been adopted and are cared for by the French people.[41] On a very

---

[41] *American graves have been adopted and are cared for-* Since the end of World War I, more than 218,000 Americans are buried or memorialized in stately resting places overseas. Since 1923, the American Battle Monuments Commission has been administering and maintaining military cemeteries throughout the world. One might wonder why the families of the deceased would choose not to have the remains of their loved ones repatriated. The reason is two-fold. The obscenely high death and identification rates made it logistically difficult to ship all bodies home in a 'timely' fashion. In fact, by the end of the 1940s, when families were still being notified about the recovery of their loved ones' remains, forty percent opted for the object of

deep and spiritual level, they, and other liberated peoples, have not forgotten American/Allied pain and sacrifice. And what can be deeper than caring for a grave with familial love?

For the living, I get misty-eyed watching the video of my ninety-something-year-old friend from Buffalo, New York, 30th Infantry Division soldier Dick Lacey, riding in the World War II era jeep, overwhelmed at all the attention, who could only choke back five words: 'Wow! Look at all the people!' Our veterans were touched by the crowds, young and old, who came out to wish them well in Mortain and everywhere they went.

*

Bill Gast had no plans to return to Normandy for any anniversary of the D-Day landings. His son said his father did not want to relive that day; 'It's important we don't forget, but you try to hide things somewhere.' But Bill did revisit that day, and the horrors that followed, mustering the spirit to address an auditorium full of hushed high school students when he came with his family to visit my school, and meet the Holocaust survivors that he helped to liberate.

---

their grief to repose in the land where he or she fell. Many families had deemed it more proper for their loved ones to lie with their comrades who had made the ultimate sacrifice beside them. This evolved into a conspicuous expression of the heavy price paid by the United States of America in the far-flung corners of the free world today, though most of the ABMC cemeteries are in Europe. Source: American Battle Monuments Commission. https://www.abmc.gov.

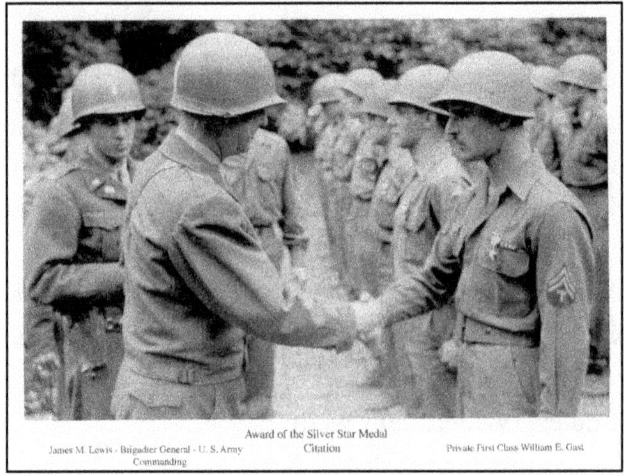

Award of the Silver Star Medal
James M. Lewis - Brigadier General - U. S. Army
Commanding
Citation
Private First Class William E. Gast

Bill Gast is presented with the Silver Star.

He opened with these words:

I'm listed [in the event program] as a liberator—however, I am also a <u>*survivor*</u> *of World War II, having landed on Omaha Beach in Normandy, France, on D-Day and fighting through to the end when the Germans surrendered.*

Pictures.

Video games.

Movies.

Words.

They simply do not convey the feeling of fear, the shock.

The stench, and the noise.

The horror, and the tragedy.

The injured, and the suffering.

The dying, and the dead.

Later, at age 89, Bill was awarded France's Legion d'Honneur at a small ceremony for World War II veterans at the French embassy in Washington; he traveled there and stood up to receive the medal and shook hands with a French diplomat. The Legion of Honor is France's highest distinction and was created by Napoleon to honor extraordinary contributions to the country.[42] Along with Bill, several of my World War II veteran friends, including Frank Towers, have received it in those special ceremonies at French embassies or consulates around the country, and proudly donned it on very special occasions.

On that occasion when Bill spoke to those high school students in 2009, he closed with this remark:

'Freedom is not free; there is a high price tag attached, and many paid that price. They made the supreme sacrifice; they gave their lives. We must ever be thankful, and we must never take freedom for granted.'

And those kids were listening.

*

All the veterans featured in this book are gone now. Bill, along with all of the veterans I met along the way, took something special away from their encounters with young people, and the people from their past who they helped bring life to all those generations ago. And I think it truly helped them to attempt to process what they experienced on the battlefield as young men. Maybe we were able to assure them, after all, that it was all

---

[42] From the French Consulate- 'Upon presentation of their military file as detailed hereunder, US veterans who risked their life during World War II to fight on French territory, may be awarded this distinction. Those selected are appointed to the rank of Knight of the Legion of Honor. The Legion of Honor medal is not awarded posthumously.

worthwhile. And maybe if we say their names, and recall their ordeals, they can live forever.

In the words of Susie Stevens-Harvey, who lost her brother in Vietnam and advocates for all those still missing in action, or prisoners of war:

'Dying for freedom isn't the worst that could happen.
Being forgotten is.'

***

The Things Our Fathers Saw ® Series:

VOICES OF THE PACIFIC THEATER

WAR IN THE AIR: GREAT DEPRESSION TO COMBAT

WAR IN THE AIR: COMBAT, CAPTIVITY, REUNION

UP THE BLOODY BOOT-THE WAR IN ITALY

D-DAY AND BEYOND

THE BULGE AND BEYOND

ACROSS THE RHINE

ON TO TOKYO

HOMEFRONT/WOMEN AT WAR

CHINA, BURMA, INDIA

*

If you liked this book, you'll love hearing more from the World War II generation in my other books. On the following pages you can see some samples, and I can let you know as soon as the new books are out and offer you exclusive discounts on some material. Just sign up at matthewrozellbooks.com

Some of my readers may like to know that all of my books are **directly available from the author, with collector's sets which can be autographed** in paperback and hardcover. They are popular gifts for that 'hard-to-buy-for' guy or gal on your list. Visit my shop at matthewrozellbooks.com for details.

...And if you would like to learn more about our GIs and the Holocaust...

~SOON TO BE A MAJOR FILM~

"What healing this has given to the survivors and military men!"-Reviewer

FROM THE ABC WORLD NEWS 'PERSON OF THE WEEK'

A TRAIN NEAR MAGDEBURG

THE HOLOCAUST, AND THE REUNITING

OF THE SURVIVORS AND SOLDIERS, 70 YEARS ON

–Featuring testimony from 15 American liberators and over 30 Holocaust survivors

–500 pages-extensive notes and bibliographical references

BOOK ONE—THE HOLOCAUST

BOOK TWO—THE AMERICANS

BOOK THREE—LIBERATION

BOOK FOUR—REUNION

THE HOLOCAUST *was a watershed event in history. In this book, Matthew Rozell reconstructs a lost chapter—the liberation of a 'death train' deep in the heart of Nazi Germany in the closing days of World War II. Drawing on never-before published eye-witness accounts, survivor testimony, and wartime reports and letters, Rozell brings to life the incredible true stories behind the iconic 1945 liberation photographs taken by the soldiers who were there. He weaves together a chronology of the Holocaust as it unfolds across Europe, and goes back to literally retrace the steps of the survivors and the American soldiers who freed them. Rozell's work results in joyful reunions on three continents, seven* *decades later. He offers his unique perspective on the lessons of the Holocaust for future generations, and the impact that one person can make.*

A selection of comments left by reviewers:

"**Extraordinary research** into an event which needed to be told. I have read many books about the Holocaust and visited various museums but had not heard reference to this train previously. The fact that people involved were able to connect, support and help heal each other emotionally was amazing."

"**The story of the end of the Holocaust and the Nazi regime** told from a very different and precise angle. First-hand accounts from Jewish survivors and the US soldiers that secured their freedom. Gripping."

"**Mr. Rozell travels 'back to the future'** of people who were not promised a tomorrow; neither the prisoners nor the troops knew what horrors the next moment would bring. He captures the parallel experience of soldiers fighting ruthless Nazism and the ruthless treatment of Jewish prisoners."

"**If you have any trepidation** about reading a book on the Holocaust, this review is for you. [Matthew Rozell] masterfully conveys the individual stories of those featured in the book in a manner that does not leave the reader with a sense of despair, but rather a sense of purpose."

"**Could not put this book down**--I just finished reading *A Train Near Magdeburg*. Tears fell as I read pages and I smiled through others. I wish I could articulate the emotions that accompanied me through the stories of these beautiful people."

"**Everyone should read this book**, detailing the amazing bond that formed between Holocaust survivors likely on their way to death in one last concentration camp as WWII was about to end, and a small number of American soldiers that happened upon the stopped train and liberated the victims. The lifelong friendships that resulted between the survivors and their liberators is a testament to compassion and goodness. It is amazing that the author is not Jewish but a "reluctant" history teacher who ultimately becomes a Holocaust scholar. This is a great book."

ABOUT THE AUTHOR

Photo Credit: Joan K. Lentini; May 2017.

Matthew Rozell is an award-winning history teacher, author, speaker, and blogger on the topic of the most cataclysmic events in the history of mankind—World War II and the Holocaust. Rozell has been featured as the 'ABC World News Person of the Week' and has had his work as a teacher filmed for the CBS Evening News, NBC Learn, the Israeli Broadcast Authority, the United States Holocaust Memorial Museum, and the New York State United Teachers. He writes on the power of teaching and the importance of the study of history at TeachingHistoryMatters.com, and you can 'Like' his Facebook author page at MatthewRozellBooks for updates.

Mr. Rozell is a sought-after speaker on World War II, the Holocaust, and history education, motivating and inspiring his audiences with the lessons of the past. Visit MatthewRozell.com for availability/details.

About this Book/

Acknowledgements

*

A note on historiographical style and convention: to enhance accuracy, consistency, and readability, I corrected punctuation and spelling and sometimes even place names, but only after extensive research. I did take the liberty of occasionally condensing the speaker's voice, eliminating side tangents or incidental information not relevant to the matter at hand. Sometimes two or more interviews with the same person were combined for readability and narrative flow. All of the words of the subjects, however, are essentially their own.

Additionally, I chose to utilize footnotes and endnotes where I deemed them appropriate, directing readers who wish to learn more to my sources, notes, and side commentary. I hope that they do not detract from the flow of the narrative.

First, I wish to acknowledge the hundreds of students who passed through my classes and who forged the bonds with the World War II generation. I promised you these books someday, and now that many of you are yourselves parents, you can tell your children this book is for them. Who says young people are indifferent to the past? Here is evidence to the contrary.

The Hudson Falls Central School District and my former colleagues have my deep appreciation for supporting this endeavor and recognizing its significance throughout the years.

Cara Quinlan's sharp proofing and suggestions helped to clean up the original manuscript.

Naturally this work would not have been possible had it not been for the willingness of the veterans to share their stories for posterity. All of the veterans who were interviewed for this book had the foresight to complete release forms granting access to their stories, and for us to share the information with the New York State Military Museum's Veterans Oral History Project, where copies of the original interviews reside. Wayne Clarke and Mike Russert of the NYSMMVOP were instrumental in cultivating this relationship with my classes over the years and are responsible for some of the interviews in this book as well; Lt. Col. Robert von Hasseln and Michael Aikey also conducted some of these NYSMM interviews. Please see the 'Source Notes.'

I would be remiss if I did not recall the profound influence of my late mother and father, Mary and Tony Rozell, both cutting-edge educators and proud early supporters of my career. To my younger siblings Mary, Ned, Nora, and Drew, all accomplished writers and authors, thank you for your encouragement as well. Final and deepest appreciations go to my wife Laura and our children, Emma, Ned, and Mary. Thank you for indulging the old man as he attempted to bring to life the stories he collected as a young one.

NOTES

[1] Atkinson, Rick. *The Guns at Last Light: The War in Western Europe, 1944-1945*. New York: Henry Holt & Co., 2013. 57.
[2] Snow, Richard. *A Nation at War With Itself.* The Wall Street Journal. April 19, 2016. www.wsj.com/articles/a-nation-at-war-with-itself-1461104812.
[3] *11,000 men were being inducted into the armed forces every day*- Atkinson, Rick. *The Guns at Last Light: The War in Western Europe, 1944-1945*. New York: Henry Holt & Co., 2013, 19; *of the men who landed in Normandy in those coming weeks, less than fifteen percent had seen combat before*- Miller, Donald. *The Story of World War II.* New York: Simon & Schuster, 2001. 283.
[4] *a form of gyroscope used widely on ships*- Source: Soumyajit Dasgupta, *Gyro Compass on Ships: Construction, Working, and Usage*. Marine Insight, July 18, 2011. www.marineinsight.com/marine-navigation/gyro-compass-on-ships-construction-working-and-usage
[5] *Utah Beach was a walk in the park*-veteran Steve Stadlon to NBC News, 2009. *D-Day's Deadly Dress Rehearsal*, History.com. April 27, 2017. www.history.com/news/d-days-deadly-dress-rehearsal
[6] Beevor, Anthony. *D-Day: The Battle for Normandy.* New York: Penguin Books, 2009. 26.
[7] Atkinson, Rick. *The Guns at Last Light: The War in Western Europe, 1944-1945*. New York: Henry Holt & Co., 2013. 50.
[8] Atkinson, Rick. *The Guns at Last Light: The War in Western Europe, 1944-1945*. New York: Henry Holt & Co., 2013. 48.
[9]The U.S. Airborne During WW II: 502nd Parachute Infantry Regiment Unit History. ww2-airborne.us/units/502/502.html

---

[10]*half a million beach obstacles had been installed*-Hargreaves, Richard. The Germans in Normandy. Mechanicsville, PA: Stackpole Books, 2008. 1.
[11] *tides at Normandy*- Atkinson, Rick. *The Guns at Last Light: The War in Western Europe, 1944-1945*. New York: Henry Holt & Co., 2013. 64.
[12] *It still bothers me*- A version of this quote also appears in a local newspaper article: Blow, David. *Never Forgotten: Leone won't let memories of war fade away*, *The Glens Falls Post-Star,* June 6, 2000.
[13] Some of the quotes in the introduction to this chapter were sourced at page 2 of Anthony's mimeographed written account, *Beachhead Journal* (probably 2000, no official publication date or information)
[14] . For more on the V-1, see www.museumofflight.org/Exhibits/fieseler-fi-103-v1.
[15] An informative article on the Mulberry harbors, referenced in this chapter, is Hull, Michael D. *D-Day's Concrete Fleet: Making the Mulberry Harbors.* Warfare History Network, https://warfarehistorynetwork.com. 25 January 2019.
[16] Atkinson, Rick. *The Guns at Last Light: The War in Western Europe, 1944-1945*. New York: Henry Holt & Co., 2013. 129.
[17] Atkinson, Rick. *The Guns at Last Light: The War in Western Europe, 1944-1945*. New York: Henry Holt & Co., 2013. 130.
[18] United States Army; Robinson, Wayne; and Hamilton, Norman E., *Move Out, Verify: The Combat Story of the 743rd Tank Battalion.* 1945. World War Regimental Histories.
[19] Kerley, Ralph A., *Operations of the 2nd Battalion, 120th Infantry*
(30th Infantry Division) at Mortain, France 6–12 August 1944 (Northern France Campaign) Personal Experiences of a Company Commander: An Isolated Infantry Battalion Defending a Key Terrain Feature Monograph written for the Advanced Infantry Officer's Class #1 1949- 1950, Major Ralph A. Kerley. Located at link below.

---

[20] The 30th Infantry Division Veterans of WWII. *Mortain.* www.30thinfantry.org/unit_history_mortain. This website was maintained by Frank W. Towers before his passing.
[21] Weiss, Robert. *Fire Mission!: The Siege at Mortain, Normandy, August 1944.* Shippensburg, Pa.: Burd Street Press, 2002.
[22] Atkinson, Rick. *The Guns at Last Light: The War in Western Europe, 1944-1945*. New York: Henry Holt & Co., 2013. 157.
[23] The 30th Infantry Division Veterans of WWII. *Mortain.*
[24] *no battle…more devastating, frustrating, or gory-* Miller, Donald. *The Story of World War II.* New York: Simon & Schuster, 2001. 333
[25] *rifle companies turned over 100 percent-* Miller, Donald. *The Story of World War II.* New York: Simon & Schuster, 2001. 336.
[26] Lennon, Thomas and Mark Zwonitzer. *The Battle of the Bulge.* American Experience, PBS, 1994.
[27] *complete annihilation of the greatest military state on earth-* General Fritz Bayerlein, quoted in Atkinson, Rick. *The Guns at Last Light: The War in Western Europe, 1944-1945*. New York: Henry Holt & Co., 2013. 181.
[28] Allied bombing in Normandy killed at least sixty thousand French noncombatants before D-Day-Vandiver, John. More than 60,000 civilian deaths are a darker and largely ignored side of the D-Day campaign. Stars and Stripes, 2019. www.stripes.com/news/special-reports/featured/d-day. The figure is probably closer to 70,000 if factoring in those killed post-D-Day by Allied bombing as well.

—THE INTERVIEWS—

Source Notes: **James A. Calascione.** Interviewed by Robert von Hasseln and Michael Aikey, February 27, 2001, Freeport, NY. Deposited at NYS Military Museum.

Source Notes: **Paul F. Hillman.** Interviewed by Matthew Rozell and Ashley Hritz, November 25, 2003, Queensbury, NY. Deposited at NYS Military Museum.

Source Notes: **Frederic G. Sheppard.** Interviewed by Michael Russert and Wayne Clarke, January 29, 2003. Latham, NY. Deposited at NYS Military Museum.

Source Notes: **Ellsworth J. Jones.** Interviewed by Michael Russert and Wayne Clarke, May 14, 2004. Saratoga Springs, NY. Deposited at NYS Military Museum.

Source Notes: **Meyer Sheff.** Interviewed by Robert von Hasseln and Michael Aikey, January 9, 2001. New York, NY. Deposited at NYS Military Museum.

Source Notes: **Harry Rosenthal.** Interviewed by Michael Russert and Wayne Clarke, January 16, 2001. Syracuse, NY. Deposited at NYS Military Museum.

Source Notes: **John O. Webster.** Interviewed by Matthew Rozell, December 2001. Hudson Falls, NY. Deposited at NYS Military Museum.

Source Notes: **James E. Knight.** Interviewed by Michael Russert and Wayne Clarke, August 7, 2002. New York, NY. Deposited at NYS Military Museum.

Source Notes: **William Gast, Jr.** Bill Gast's narrative was constructed using many sources, including his correspondence with me and his testimony at reunions the author and others organized with Holocaust survivors and other veterans in 2008 and 2009.

Source Notes: **Anthony F.J. Leone.** Interviewed by Matthew Rozell, October 11, 2001. Hudson Falls, NY. Deposited at NYS Military Museum.

Source Notes: **Joseph S. Dominelli.** Interviewed by Michael Russert and Wayne Clarke, April 30, 2004. Schenectady, NY. Deposited at NYS Military Museum.

Source Notes: **Jacob N. Cutler.** Interviewed by Michael Russert, August 8, 2002. Queens, NY. Deposited at NYS Military Museum.

Source Notes: **Frederick G. Harris.** Interviewed by Michael Russert and Wayne Clarke, June 17, 2005. Saratoga Springs, NY. Deposited at NYS Military Museum.

Source Notes: **Frank W. Towers.** The author formally interviewed Frank Towers by telephone in November of 2008. His testimony was also recorded at every reunion, and especially useful for this book were those recorded at our school in 2009 and 2011, which can be seen on the author's YouTube channel at http://bit.ly/MRutube. Frank was also interviewed by many others, and he was in the news media quite frequently (a Google search will return many results). Frank and the author also kept up a nearly nine-year email correspondence, most of which is archived by the author.

Source Notes: **William C. Butz.** Interviewed by Wayne Clarke and Eric Stott, February 2, 2006. Saratoga Springs, NY. Deposited at NYS Military Museum.

Source Notes: **John H. Vier.** Interviewed by Michael Aikey. December 14, 2001. Peekskill, NY. Deposited at NYS Military Museum.

Printed in the USA
CPSIA information can be obtained
at www.ICGtesting.com
LVHW020924070124
768343LV00010B/767